Space Policy in the Twenty-First Century

NEW SERIES IN NASA HISTORY

Roger D. Launius, SERIES EDITOR

Space Policy IN THE Twenty-First Century

Edited by W. Henry Lambright

THE JOHNS HOPKINS UNIVERSITY PRESS
BALTIMORE AND LONDON

© 2003 The Johns Hopkins University Press
All rights reserved. Published 2003
Printed in the United States of America on acid-free paper

9 8 7 6 5 4 3 2 1

The Johns Hopkins University Press
2715 North Charles Street
Baltimore, Maryland 21218-4363

www.press.jhu.edu

LIBRARY OF CONGRESS CATALOGING-IN-PUBLICATION DATA

Space policy in the twenty-first century / edited by W. Henry Lambright.
       p.   cm. — (New series in NASA history)
Includes bibliographical references and index.
   ISBN 0-8018-7068-2 (hardcover : alk. paper)
   1. Astronautics—Government policy—United States.   2. Outer space—
Civilian use—Government policy—United States.   3. Outer space—
Exploration—Government policy—United States.   I. Lambright, W. Henry,
1939–   II. Series.
   TL789.8.U5 S588   2002
   629.4'0973—dc21

2001008648

A catalog record for this book is available from the British Library.

To Dan, Nat, Sue, and Kristina

—who will live to see much that is projected in this book.

Contents

Preface

S PACE IS a place. It is also a set of technologies and, as Roger Handberg put it in *Seeking New World Vistas* (Praeger, 2000), a "state of
mind." It is, most critically, an object of policy. All these facets are illu-
minated in the essays that follow. The origin of this book lies in 1997 and
a conference in Washington, D.C., held by the Policy Office of the National Aeronautics and Space Administration (NASA). After the meeting, Alan Ladwig, director of the Policy Office, explained that he wanted
to get new ideas, especially from the academic community, informing
space policy. He wondered whether a way could be found to better con-
nect NASA and the university. I subsequently offered to see what I could
do to help.

It was obvious that space policy was not a high priority on the nation's campuses. That was not due to the absence of serious issues in
space policy on the national agenda. It was because few people on campuses were paying attention to them; and NASA, as an institution, had
grown distant from the universities since Apollo. Moreover, many of the
leading space policy analysts came into the field in the 1960s, the "heroic
age" of space. The landing on the moon was a vivid memory for them and
was still an energizing force. For many younger policy analysts, however, the most striking image of space policy was the negative image of
Challenger exploding on television.

Yet as the twenty-first century arrived, it was clear that space was
again emerging as an enormously significant and potentially positive
frontier. It was being probed and used for various purposes. For example, there were aggressive efforts in the private sector to establish
markets. Earth remote sensing—long stymied by military restrictions
—was joining the information revolution as a powerful new tool. The
Space Station was finally being assembled to serve as a research labora-

tory and potential industrial facility. It was also an instrument of U.S. foreign policy as Russia, the former enemy, was now an international partner—for better or for worse. The Hubble Space Telescope had helped to trigger a revolution in space science by revealing features of the cosmos never before seen. Additional information about planets around distant stars as well as planets in the solar system suggested there might yet be some kind of life out there. At the center of the question of life beyond Earth, whether now or long past, was the quest for learning more about Mars. Would human beings someday set foot on the Red Planet?

All these issues were real, discussed among policy specialists in Washington and among space scientists and engineers elsewhere, but they were barely on the radar screen of most policy analysts with training in social science. Something needed to be done to raise the level of awareness. A symposium, jointly sponsored by Syracuse University's Maxwell School and NASA's Policy Office, seemed a timely response to the need. Some of the more senior and established scholars in the field were invited to contribute, but an attempt was made to include individuals relatively new to the field.

Discussions with NASA and academic colleagues led to a list of potential topics everyone agreed were key. With the symposium scheduled for spring 2000, we gave it a forward-looking, even prospective tone, but we kept it anchored in space history and realistic policy concerns. The general theme was civil space policy in the twenty-first century. Military aspects were important and were mentioned as relevant, but the focus was on civil issues. Also, a decision was made to include international issues in the various topics as appropriate, rather than having separate papers concerning them. As will be seen, the papers covered a wide range of civil space issues. In addition to five research papers presented at the symposium, we commissioned two papers by senior scholars in the form of general essays or "commentaries." After the symposium, certain gaps were filled by papers on the Space Station and access to space.

Any time a topic as broad as civil space policy in the twenty-first century is addressed, it inevitably raises questions of scope and depth. We started with a general plan and commissioned good researchers who made their own judgments within the parameters we set. Then additions and modifications were made for the book. Readers will find a relatively broad sweep of the issues in ensuing chapters. The book starts with policy issues that are closest in time and to Earth, then extends to those that are increasingly farther out in time and space. The chapters involve history and documented facts as well as speculation. Some are austerely neutral; others reveal an advocacy tone. The writers had great freedom, as befits a group of this kind, but in different ways all address the central questions: Where are we now in policy? How did we get here? And, most important, where are we going?

A number of individuals assisted the editor and authors in the symposium and book. Katy Howe and Jen McMahon, two graduate students in Maxwell School's Public Administration Department, were instrumental in the symposium arrangements. Agnes Gereben Schaefer, a doctoral student in political science at Maxwell, helped edit the chapters in this book. Debbie Pollock and Marlene Fowler provided secretarial assistance. We received encouragement and important suggestions for improvement from editors associated with Johns Hopkins University Press: Robert J. Brugger, Melody Herr, Julie McCarthy, and Elizabeth Yoder. Nadine Andreassen of NASA provided logistical support in Washington. To all who helped, we say, thanks. Ultimate responsibility for the product rests with me.

Space Policy in the Twenty-First Century

Introduction

W. Henry Lambright

T HOUGH Sputnik's launch in 1957 makes the Space Age more than forty years old, the most challenging years of space technology and policy lie ahead. The twenty-first century marks a transition in space policy, a shift seen in many guises. For example, the Space Shuttle, the workhorse of the U.S. space program, is getting old. What happens after the Shuttle? The International Space Station (ISS) is being assembled. Can it be used productively so as to justify the potential $100 billion cost to develop and operate over its lifetime?[1] Can the Americans, Russians, Europeans, Japanese, Canadians, and others working on ISS get along in space? To what extent can the Space Shuttle and ISS be privatized, freeing government space budgets for new ventures? What of business in space? Does it have a lucrative future? Is space a place that needs to be regulated? What are the resources in space to be exploited? Are asteroids real threats to Earth or merely the subject of science fiction movies? Will humans land on Mars in the twenty-first century? Will the search for life beyond Earth be rewarded, or will it be forever an unfulfilled quest? These and other questions are on the agenda of space policy in this century. They will not go away; rather, they will become more compelling as time goes on.

This book is built on a number of issues or themes that have been around for a long time: (1) access to space; (2) space commercialization; (3) humans in space; (4) space science; (5) Earth monitoring applications; and (6) "other." This sixth item stands for the kind of ad hoc issues that come up in space policy occasionally. The other five are recurrent, but their face changes with the times. To understand where the writers began in looking at these issues in the new century, it is helpful to consider, by way of overview and background, the faces these issues have presented to policymakers in the past.

It is possible to take a long and short view of space policy. The short view features the large and small decisions affecting the course of a program from year to year. Short-term actions can be quite important since one key battle can influence the course of a war. Then there is the long view, where the focus is on what might be called the paradigmatic shifts in a policy area. These entail changes in a policy course of the greatest scale. They affect the "mental models" of an agency charged with implementing space policy—its basic culture.[2] For space policy, the first paradigmatic change started in 1961 with the Kennedy decision to go to the moon and the transition of NASA from the small operation of post-*Sputnik* to the powerful NASA of *Apollo*. The second major shift began thirty years later, in 1991, with the dissolution of the Soviet Union, the end of the Cold War, and the emergence of globalization as a force. These milestones mark the biggest turning points in space policy thus far. They set in motion novel processes that frame debate over space policy for years. The terrorist attack of 2001 may also have a substantial impact, but that remains to be seen.

Apollo's Shadow

The first issue the United States confronted in space was access. The USSR had demonstrated a capability with *Sputnik* that America did not have. Even as the United States created a new rocket launch technology, the issue of who or what would be sent into space arose. It was resolved by the Eisenhower administration so that, in addition to having a technology for lifting machines into space, there also would be one to power human beings. However, it was one matter to send an astronaut into Earth's orbit, and quite another to send someone beyond.

In 1961 John Kennedy made the decision that the United States would engage in a race to the moon with the USSR. *Apollo* represented a great leap forward in policy, organization, and technology. The political circumstances of the time were such that there was remarkably little debate about the goal or its rationale, which was to beat the Soviet Union. The end, reaching the moon, determined the means: a new rocket, the Saturn, which was gigantic in size and cost, and which was expendable.

Apollo dominated U.S. space policy in the 1960s. It created a model of government-driven technology—the "large-scale approach"—that became embedded in NASA culture. *Apollo* also helped make available enormous sums of money that provided opportunity for activity in space concerned with space science and applications. NASA space policy was largely forged in the 1960s around three missions in this de facto order of priority: (1) human spaceflight; (2) science; and (3) applications. Each area had its own issues, although there was an overall issue of "balance" among the three fields of space activity. There has, historically, been an ongoing debate about manned space crowding out the other two missions in funding.[3]

In the 1960s there was enough money for all to prosper. The applications area featured the origins of what subsequently became another ongoing issue of space policy—the commercialization of space. Because satellite communication was a major advance over existing communication technology, the question arose whether satellite communication should be a government or a business enterprise. The debate was intense because government had spawned satellites and the communications industry was highly concentrated in power and wealth. There was worry over AT&T's capturing the fruits of taxpayer investment unless public policy created some mechanism to facilitate transfer of the technology to the private sector with certain public interests protected. The result was a new entity, Comsat Corporation, a private-public hybrid created to receive and exploit the Space Age advance.[4] The satellite communications debate showed that space policy was about more than rockets and spaceflight. The space frontier was new, but old issues (such as government-business relations) remained.

After the *Apollo* success of 1969, the major question in space policy was what human spaceflight program would be adopted as a successor. Ultimately, in 1972, Mars and a space station were rejected in favor of the Space Shuttle. Expendable Saturns were deemed not to be cost-effective. They were to be replaced by a reusable launch vehicle, the Space Shuttle. Throughout the 1970s, Space Shuttle development was the priority of U.S. space policy.

Nevertheless, space science came into its own in the 1970s. The U.S. planetary exploration program unfolded through a series of unmanned probes throughout the solar system. The most remarkable was *Viking*, a mission that observed and landed on Mars. The *Viking* mission pointed up an issue within space science: How much emphasis should Mars get relative to other planetary ventures? There was a collateral issue: To what extent should the search for life outside Earth be an explicit mission goal? Although *Viking* had such a goal, no life was detected.

Another issue that arose in the 1970s with implications for the future was the arrival of another space application with practical use—Earth remote sensing. With the launch of *Landsat* in 1972, NASA demonstrated a number of potentially valuable uses. However, unlike satellite communications, there was no industry "pull" for commercialization. Furthermore, the intelligence agencies restricted how precise the images could be lest adversaries know the resolution of spy satellite cameras. The Cold War thus had negative as well as positive impacts on civilian innovation in space. The issue of what federal policy should do or not do to encourage commercialization of Earth remote sensing was not resolved in the 1970s, and in many ways it remains an issue on the twenty-first-century space agenda.[5]

In the 1980s, as before, the issue of humans in space was at the forefront of space policy. Questions revolved around the chosen means of access—the Space Shuttle. The issue for the Shuttle was its "readiness" for routine operations. In any technological development, there is a transition from research and development to operations. When a technology achieves a certain "ripeness," the actors and rules that surround it can change. This change was seen in debates over satellite communications and Earth remote sensing. So it was with the Space Shuttle.

For those who promoted it, the Shuttle was seen to be like an airplane, capable of transporting passengers rather than only highly trained professional astronauts. After years of development and testing, in 1983 NASA certified the Space Shuttle as operational. President Reagan agreed, authorizing NASA to proceed with the "next logical step" in human spaceflight—the Space Station. The Cold War was again a factor in decision making for human spaceflight. The USSR, having failed in the moon race, had turned to space station development and was ahead of the United States.

To help pay for the Space Station—and make it a symbol of peaceful space—the president had NASA enlist the Europeans, Canadians, and Japanese as partners in its development. In a sign of the times, the foreign nations insisted on more authority as partners. They had more know-how in space in the 1980s than in the 1970s, and they expected to be listened to.[6] Power in space policy making was diffusing.

In theory, the nation would phase down spending on the Shuttle, and phase up funding of the Space Station. There was talk about privatizing the Space Shuttle. After all, it was advertised as so routine that non-astronauts, including a teacher, were going up in the mid-1980s. The *Challenger* explosion of 1986 came as a shock to everyone, especially NASA. It showed the disconnect between policy thinking and technological reality. The Shuttle was *not* like an airplane—and probably would never be. Some different model for governing this technology was needed, but no one knew quite what it should be.

Challenger caused the entire human spaceflight program to slow down. The Space Station fell behind schedule, and its projected costs soared. Even in space science, an area where NASA had done extremely well, there were troubles. The major space science activity of the decade was the Hubble Space Telescope (HST), a giant astronomical facility to be launched into Earth's orbit to see, as never before, the distant cosmos. Recovery from *Challenger* delayed Hubble's launch by the Space Shuttle until 1990, and when it went up, its vision was found to be blurred.

Only in certain aspects of space applications was U.S. space policy seemingly on target in the 1980s. The global environment was becoming a significant national and international priority. NASA adapted by combining its land, atmosphere, and oceans monitoring capability into a new Earth Observing System (EOS) scheduled for development and deployment in the 1990s. In the latter 1980s, Earth monitoring proved essential to understanding the scale and nature of the ozone hole found over Antarctica. The EOS program quickly became a new major priority of NASA. In 1989, when the first Bush administration assumed power, it embraced EOS and linked it to an interagency effort called the U.S. Global Change Research Program. The key research problem for global change, and thus for EOS, was global climate change. The budget for EOS ramped up as this particular issue gained salience.

However, the Bush administration saw the principal issue in space policy as being the absence of a long-term goal for manned space. In 1989 President Bush used the occasion of the twentieth anniversary of the *Apollo* moon landing to provide that goal. He declared that humans should return to the moon and then go on to Mars. He gave no cost or timetable, but one NASA estimate was that it could take thirty years and require more than $450 billion.[7] It became quite clear in 1990 that there was no congressional support for this expensive enterprise, which was known as Space Exploration Initiative (SEI). The nation faced a serious budget deficit, and the Bush administration and Congress agreed to sharply limit federal expenditures. This meant there would not be enough money for all the existing programs on NASA's plate, much less for SEI.

Beyond the Cold War

As the foregoing discussion shows, there was more to civil space than the Cold War. However, these other priorities—such as commercialization, science, and applications to environment—paled in comparison to that of competition. *Apollo* cast a long shadow, especially on NASA's thinking about its role and reason for existence. The clearest reference for U.S. space policy over the 1970s and 1980s was the "Evil Empire." When all else failed, at least in the dominant program of human space-flight, there was always rationalization based on what the Russians were doing. This was even true in connection with SEI. The Soviets, according to some, had their sights set on the Red Planet. The Cold War provided the comfort of long-term continuity within which incremental change was possible.

When the Cold War ended, a new rationale for space had to be constructed—especially for human spaceflight, where most public space spending took place. NASA was in deep trouble: the Space Station was behind schedule and over cost; Hubble had blurred vision; Space Shuttle launches were slowed to a trickle by a risk-averse agency and its contractors. Even the EOS was causing problems, as space officials took a "big science" approach to satellite building that put EOS on a funding profile that rivaled the Space Station.

Aware of the need for policy change, President Bush replaced the existing NASA administrator with an individual who went at the change process with gusto—and, at times, with ruthlessness. Over the 1990s, NASA administrator Dan Goldin got Hubble repaired and forced subordinates to shift from the "large-scale approach" (the *Apollo* paradigm) to one he called "faster, better, cheaper." This post–Cold War model infused microelectronic and other technical advances to produce smaller spacecraft in space science and applications. Also, while faster, better, cheaper was not readily applicable to the Space Station, this program, NASA's bellwether, was saved from demise by redesign and conversion to a new International Space Station (ISS) with Russia embraced as the principal foreign partner.

Moreover, NASA sought to get the private sector to take over much of the routine operation of the Shuttle. This move raised issues as to how far it was possible and desirable to delegate decision making from government to the private sector. Privatization (as the Shuttle process was called) had not penetrated manned space systems to this extent previously. Goldin sought progress also on the "access to space" issue through a new reusable launch vehicle, the X-33. This program intended that industry would pay partially for the experimental prototype and mostly for the operational follow-on vehicle. Also, while the manned SEI died, Mars was strengthened as a goal of unmanned space science missions. Moreover, Goldin authorized a new program, Origins, to provide a mission for space science aimed at understanding the beginnings and destiny of the universe. Both the Mars and the Origins programs had the search for life as a goal.

Both successes and failures were born of this hard-driving approach to change. In 1997 *Pathfinder* landed on Mars and was hailed as a vindication of the faster, better, cheaper approach. Two years later, in 1999, *Mars Orbiter* and *Lander* failed. Now faster, better, cheaper was criticized. In addition, the X-33 ran into technical problems that caused this government-business partnership to be terminated.

The 1990s thus increasingly revealed a sharp break with the Space Age that had existed before when the Cold War reigned. Old programs were redesigned, and new ones were established—all in an austere budget environment. Decision making was strikingly different. The Space Station was truly an international venture—to the point where decisions were made that the United States opposed—notably the Russians allowing a tourist in space for cash. International cooperation was a new space rationale, replacing Cold War competition. But there was still rivalry within the cooperative model. Control over pace, direction, and use of the Space Station was blurred. The U.S.-Russian partnership—symbolic of the biggest change in space policy—was complex and fraught with policy questions.

As the 1990s receded and 2000 came on, the post–Cold War was replaced by globalization as an overall rhetoric and frame for a new era. Viewed short term, space policy consisted of day-to-day struggles to get human spaceflight, space science, and space applications programs funded and implemented. Viewed from a long-term perspective, space policy consisted of a dramatic move from one paradigm to another whose broad outlines were just barely discernible.

The Twenty-First Century

The essays in this volume convey both concern and excitement about the potential new world of space policy. They reveal the ambiguity that accompanies the opening of an uncharted policy frontier. In examining the twenty-first-century space enterprise, the authors illuminate the interplay of space technology and public policy. Policy shapes space technology, which in turn influences policy. For example, policy makers decided to develop a space station. As the International Space Station is constructed, it produces novel policy challenges, many of which were not anticipated. Space policy leads to discovery, technological change, and broad social impacts. It also yields disappointment and even tragedy. It deals with future visions and dreams. Technological hardware is an embodiment of the human spirit. It reveals some of the best and occasionally some of the worst instincts of man. The policy process is difficult in an enterprise like space, whose goals are distant and often intangible, but whose costs are near and large.

The politics that shape policy are geared to the immediate. Politicians want instant gratification, something they can show constituents now to help themselves get reelected. In many areas of space policy—absent a Cold War imperative—justifications come across as vague. In many ways, space is the extreme example of policy making for a luxury. It is easy to show an absolute need for a Defense Department, or even an Energy Department when people worry about oil shortages. But why have a NASA? Why spend billions for a telescope in space like Hubble—and perhaps even more for its successor to pursue a program called "Origins?"

Why and how do we make policy about other planets and stars and about searching for life's beginning? Why go to Mars? Surely, say the critics, money could be more usefully spent on housing, health care, and other human needs. It is no wonder that space policy has difficulty getting the attention of policymakers. What is remarkable is that space is an established function of government at all. Moreover, there are more public and private players entering the arena of space exploration every year in the United States and abroad. The policy process is diffusing; roles and missions are in flux.

Space is both a mature area of policy, having begun decades ago, and ever young because of the substance of what it is about. The core of NASA is the development of advanced technology for discovery. As long as there is a space frontier, advanced technology will be needed to take machines and human beings to its most distant edge. Policy making for advanced technology is inherently problematic. It places human beings in space, under some of the most dangerous conditions possible. It is a testimony to humanity's innate drive to explore and the practical and psychological dividends space has provided that a space program exists. In the future, space will likely be what it has been in the past—an intensely debated realm of policy, ridiculed by some and a source of inspiration for others. Those associated with it will reap the extremes of praise and condemnation that go with high-visibility, high-risk endeavors. Great success and great failure are equally possible where space is at issue.

The contributors to this volume believe space is a critical mission for government. However, they differ about government's role in particular aspects of policy and about how much and how fast certain space enterprises should be pursued. A few writers in this book have been identified with space policy for decades; others are much newer to the field and will live out more of their lives in the twenty-first than in the twentieth century. What all of them share is a belief that space will raise policy issues in the new century that the nation and world must address.

The issues and themes mentioned earlier are addressed by the writers in their distinctive ways. The first chapter, by Roger Launius, discusses access to space. The key policy issue is how to move toward low-cost, reliable, and safe access so that spaceflight can become more truly routine. Access involves extremely difficult technological choices. Launius explores a number central policy issues involving access, including: (1) the limits of chemical rocket technology; (2) the ICBM legacy of space access; (3) the costly nature of space access; (4) the debate over public versus private development of launchers; (5) the value of reusable launch vehicles (RLV) versus expendable launch vehicles (ELV); and (6) the maintenance of international relationships with partners, as well as opposition to rivals.

Policy questions revolve around how to speed up innovation in new access technologies and the respective roles of government and industry. Launius discusses the X-33 program as a recent attempt to develop a post-Shuttle RLV through a joint government-industry activity. It was hoped that once developed, the launch vehicle prototype (X-33) would be brought to operational fruition by the contractor and then privatized as VentureStar™. The aim was for technological and institutional innovation. This particular enterprise failed, and NASA searches for alternatives. It has no choice. The policy issue—access to space—must be addressed, as Launius shows.

For Scott Pace, old issues of institutional choice take a new form. The issue is not government versus industry, but how government can facilitate a new space industry. Space commercialization policy reflects the transition from the old economy to the dynamic global economy. This new economic imperative has created considerable tension, mirroring the conflict between former and emergent values. Pace sees conflicts between economic and national security interests concerning export of controlled technologies and information derived from space systems; international conflicts over common resources (e.g., spectrum orbital locations, nonterrestrial materials); and increasing government reliance on commercial firms for access to space capabilities. All of these conflicts require policy resolution in some degree for the development of space commerce to proceed. Otherwise, uncertainties in the political and policy realm are barriers. In view of continuing policy indecision and confusion, it is not a given that the United States will maintain its competitive edge in space commerce.

Ronald Deibert deals with policy regarding applications of space technology. He holds that the politics of Earth monitoring from space has been dramatically altered by the removal of two constraints. The first includes limits by the United States and the USSR on the resolution of civilian environmental satellites. Such limits prevented the enemy from knowing how sophisticated were military spy satellites. The second constraint was the wariness of developing countries and other nations about the violation of their sovereignty by the use of Earth remote sensing to identify their resources.

Without traditional national security constraints, civil satellite systems are leaping ahead in technical acuity, thereby expanding the number of uses and users. New providers (national and private) have entered the policy arena. Much less is heard recently from developing nations about violation of sovereignty by remote sensing, in part because of their lack of unity in general, and in part because these two constraints are gone. The technology has therefore rapidly diffused. This diffusion of the technology may make it difficult for U.S. national security agencies to enforce control in a conflict situation. Also, the policy implications of diffusion are considerable in terms of getting the many providers to work, not at cross-purposes, but cooperatively around global concerns of common interest, particularly environmental change.

Karl Leib is concerned with issues relating to humans in space. He tracks the transition of the International Space Station (ISS) from a facility that is being developed to one that is assembled in space and used. This transition is well underway. When ISS will be complete is uncertain at the time of writing. However, it is likely that it will be finished in the first decade of this century and that its maintenance will heavily dominate NASA's agenda for years thereafter.

Aside from political management and technical challenges in construction, there are huge issues of utilization. Who will use ISS? For what purpose? The scientific uses are obvious—for example, to test human beings' health during long spaceflights and to conduct experiments under nongravity conditions. The economic justifications are less clear. The policy issues have to do with implementing ISS and with evaluating it as a demonstration in scientific, economic, and (especially) international cooperation.

While many issues of space policy recur, such as priority of manned versus unmanned programs, new challenges arise. Daniel Deudney examines an issue he believes will be on the space policy agenda increasingly in the future—asteroids. He sees the growing risk of asteroids as a catalyst for rethinking ways to organize the outer space regime. Traditionally, outer space is viewed by international relations scholars as analogous to the high seas, a common global resource that no nation can appropriate. However, asteroids may require a different perspective in governance. They can be threats in terms of collisions that will most likely require multilateral action by governments. However, asteroids can also be resources to be developed, a view that pushes them toward the possibility of exploitation by private or individual state actors as well as scientific investigation (potentially multistate) and military exploitation (national). Whatever the case, Deudney foresees asteroids becoming much more an object of policy in the future.

W. Henry Lambright and Debora VanNijnatten deal with the future of humans in space beyond the Space Station, specifically Mars. They begin with von Braun's vision in the 1950s and extend their analysis to the distant future, from vision to colonization. There is no question that Mars has a special place in space policy as a destiny; however, the record to date suggests that aspiration and rhetoric are not matched by resources and staying power. There is already an active robotic Mars program. What will trigger a humans to Mars program and keep it going?

Lambright and VanNijnatten suggest some possible triggers that could activate a serious Mars program. From a policy standpoint, it is essential for an expensive program concerned with human spaceflight and exploration to have a goal, even if it takes a long time and many twists and turns to realize it. The "search for life" is one reason for going to Mars. While robots can do preliminary work, only human beings can do the on-site investigation necessary to make credible determinations. In fact, the link between a scientific purpose and manned exploration may be critical as a rationale for the twenty-first-century space program.

Christopher Chyba looks at science as a space policy focus and joins Lambright and VanNijnatten in stressing the search for life as a fundamental purpose for space exploration. He goes beyond Mars to the solar system and beyond. While some writers in this volume emphasize shorter-term policy issues, Chyba takes the entire twenty-first century as his vision.

He does, however, cite some more immediate policy concerns. Specifically, while Mars currently has top priority in the search for life, he believes Europa and possibly Titan deserve attention on a par with Mars. That means a shift in policy priority within NASA's budget. Similarly, if the search for life is to be taken seriously, a reconsideration of a previous decision is needed: the congressional termination of public support for the scientific Search for Extraterrestrial Intelligence (SETI). An astrobiology program without SETI is a program with a huge gap in Chyba's view. Finally, Chyba sees the search for life inevitably coming into contact with environmental values. Bringing samples of Mars or some other planet "home" raises issues of cross-contamination. Hence, the transition to a search-for-life policy in this century requires attention to policy priorities today and raises challenges for the future.

John Logsdon's commentary paints a century that could be good or bad for NASA. His concern is greatest in connection with human space exploration, NASA's core mission. Logsdon sees space advocates in need of a better rationale for this area of space activity, in part because they are all suffering from an "*Apollo* hangover." As he notes, the political conditions that made *Apollo* possible do not exist and have not existed for a long time. The problem, as Logsdon sees it, is for NASA to find a new national purpose that is compelling enough to justify its continued relevance in the years ahead. Although he wants to believe that purpose will be forthcoming and suggests possible means, he is not sanguine.

Howard McCurdy strikes a different note. Like other writers, he speaks of transition, but his transition includes the movement from imagination to reality. He writes of how visionaries, artists, writers, and moviemakers dreamed of space futures. Some were realized in practice, but most fell far short of reality. He sees certain programs of space (such as the search for life) continuing to be dominated by government, but others (including remote sensing) becoming driven by commercial actors. Government will play a range of roles, regulation being one that will grow in importance. He sees internationalization of space as a dominant theme in the present century.

The changes of which the authors write are part of the grand transition to a twenty-first-century space program. They will not occur automatically. Their precise direction and speed depend on political forces. These forces, discussed by the editor in the book's conclusion, can be seen as tripartite.

At the first, or agency level, the most significant force for shaping U.S. space policy is NASA. Because its survival and health depends totally on the nature and direction of space policy, it is the most active force of all, most of the time, in asserting its claims on U.S. and international decisions. NASA is influenced by the larger forces in its environment. At the same time, it seeks to mold its environment to accord with its needs.

At a second or national level of political action in the United States are various domestic forces that typically collide in the executive branch and Congress over priorities. Here battles are fought over national policy choices between space and other functions of public investment. How much is enough for space versus housing, health, and veteran's affairs? Also, within the space sector itself legislators, White House science advisors, budgeters, and others contest with NASA over the relative merits of specific programs. It is at this level where the many issues of U.S. space policy—involving access, commercialization, human spaceflight, space science, Earth monitoring applications, and other concerns—are fought out.

At the third, the global level, are other nations and various institutions outside the United States who assert their claims on space policy. Globalization has meant that the forces at different levels interact. Such forces range from the most positive (e.g., concern for the planet's environment) to the most negative (e.g., transnational terrorism). Global interests provide a general setting within which national and agency space policies are enacted. However, an agency can use global forces or their actions to influence U.S. policy.

Because the United States is still key to world space policy and NASA is most critical to what the United States does in civil space, special attention is paid in the conclusion to NASA as a moving force or policy entrepreneur, acting and reacting in this tripartite context. This conclusion analyzes the politics behind space policy. It also examines NASA as an adaptive organization. Can NASA evolve with the times, responding to them so as to influence them? Leadership in the space endeavor requires an agency capable of holding to long-term strategies while making deft tactical moves in the short run. It requires an agency that relinquishes operational tasks to an ever-widening gyre of other actors in order to emphasize a core mission of frontier discovery. Paradoxically, it entails sharing power to gain power.

The interplay of various actors concerned with space policy is dynamic. It is always fascinating to observe and seek to understand because the interaction does not have predictable outcomes. Looking ahead, all the writers see a great future for increased complexity, cooperation, and conflict in space policy. While there are many challenges, opportunities for creative policy making abound in a situation so fluid. The Cold War is over, and globalization is a dominant trend in the contemporary era. Space policy in the twenty-first century will reflect continuities but also be different from what it has been.

With all the uncertainties, space policy will still be influenced most by human will and energy. The issue is which humans will prevail in policy making, and whose vision of the future will take hold.

NOTES

1. The precise cost of the ISS is difficult to discern, owing to questions of what to include (e.g., Shuttle launch costs, development versus use, how long a projection for use, etc.). The General Accounting Office (GAO) figure from 1998 is $96 billion. NASA has challenged this figure as too high, but if the ISS stays up beyond 2012, as is likely, the GAO figure could provide an underestimate. See U.S.G.A.O., *International Space Station: U.S. Life-Cycle Funding Requirements* (Washington, DC: Government Printing Office, 1998).
2. Peter M. Senge, *The Fifth Discipline: The Art and Practice of the Learning Organization* (New York: Doubleday, 1990), 8–9.
3. NASA also has had an aeronautics mission, but our focus is space. Aeronautics generally has ranked below space in the NASA scheme of missions.
4. W. Henry Lambright, *Governing Science and Technology* (New York: Oxford University Press, 1976), 69–72.
5. Ibid., 68–69. Pamela Mack, *Viewing the Earth: The Social Construction of the Landsat Satellite System* (Cambridge, MA: MIT Press, 1990).
6. The Europeans and Canadians had played a role in the Space Shuttle in the 1970s but were clearly subordinates, with NASA dominating the relationship.
7. Robert Zubrin, *The Case for Mars* (New York: Touchstone, 1997), 47.

1 Between a Rocket and a Hard Place

The Challenge of Space Access

Roger D. Launius

ACCESS. No single word better describes the primary concern of everyone interested in the exploration and development of space in the twenty-first century. Every participant in space activities—civil, military, or commercial—needs affordable, reliable, frequent, flexible access to space.[1] Unfortunately, this commodity has never existed before, and despite considerable effort, the probability of achieving it in the near term is small. Comparisons with Earth-based activities illustrate the challenges encountered in space access.

Terrestrial shipping companies deliver on a predictable schedule, function in all climates, often accept shipping orders on short notice, deliver worldwide within days if not hours of shipment, and hardly ever lose or destroy the cargo. Likewise, despite the events of September 11, 2001, passengers leave their debarkation points and arrive safely and on time to their destinations an overwhelmingly high percentage of the time. Indeed, flying is so safe that there is a greater statistical probability of being killed by a meteorite crashing to the ground from space than by dying in an airplane crash.[2] Furthermore, myths of airline travel notwithstanding, passengers' baggage almost always arrives on time and in good condition.

The same cannot be said for space launch operations. Delivery is frequently held up by technical glitches and adverse weather, flights need to be booked two to four years in advance, and reliability rates for large launchers range from about 82 to 98 percent.[3] Clearly, space launch services should not be measured by terrestrial standards, but if the grand plans of space visionaries and entrepreneurs are to be carried out in this century, the situation must improve.

After four decades of effort, access to space remains a difficult challenge in the first part of the twenty-first century. The technical challenge of reaching space with chemical rockets—particularly the high costs associated with space launch in the 20th century, the long lead times necessary for scheduling flights, and the unreliability of rockets—has demonstrated the slowest rate of improvement of all space technologies. All space professionals share a responsibility for addressing these critical technical problems. The overwhelming influence that space access has on all aspects of civil, commercial, and military space efforts indicates that it should enjoy a top priority for the twenty-first century.[4]

Of course, a key element in the spacefaring vision long held in the United States is the belief that inexpensive, reliable, safe, and easy spaceflight is attainable. Indeed, virtually from the beginning of the twentieth century, those interested in the human exploration of space have viewed as central to that endeavor the development of vehicles for flight that travel easily to and from Earth orbit. The more technically minded recognized that once humans had achieved Earth orbit about 200 miles up, the vast majority of the atmosphere and gravity had been conquered and humanity was about halfway to anywhere else it might want to go.[5]

Although it is something of an oversimplification, it seems appropriate to break down the development of launch vehicles into four specific time periods, each characterized by specific technological challenges, political and economic environments, design priorities, mission objectives, and legacies and lessons (Table 1). While a large number of questions could be explored concerning access to space, six central issues quickly emerge from any discussion of the subject: (1) the physical limitations of chemical rocket technology; (2) the ICBM legacy of space access, as well as the legacy of the Space Shuttle for human spaceflight; (3) the costly nature of space access; (4) the debate over public versus private development of launchers; (5) the value of reusable launch vehicles (RLV) versus expendable launch vehicles (ELV); and (6) the maintenance of international relationships with partners, as well as opposition to rivals. These major concerns for the next century inform the structure of the discussion that follows.

Physical Limitations of Chemical Rocket Technology

Space access has rested firmly on the shoulders of chemical rockets for boosting payloads into Earth orbit and beyond. From the first experiments by Robert H. Goddard in the 1920s through the pathbreaking V-2 missile of World War II and the mighty *Saturn V* moon rocket, to the

Access to Space in Perspective

Era	Political/ Economic Environment	Mission Objectives	Technological Challenges	Design Parameters	Lessons and Legacies
1950s	Cold War reigns, crash programs the norm, economy stable, cost no obstacle	ICBMs	Everything: is flight in space even possible?	Focus on payload miniaturization, poor launch reliability	Systems management concept, large-scale approach, funding no obstacle
1960s–1980s	Cold War heightens then wanes, government funding decreases, economy thrives in 1960s then declines, cost-benefit analysis rises	ICBM operations, ICBMs used for piloted flight, reductions of costs	Improved reliability and schedule	Move to reusability, improved reliability	Validation of systems management concept, large-scale government investment
1990s	Cold War ends, commercial space emerges, economy expands	No impetus for new military launchers, commercial needs reign	Reduction of cost to orbit, reliability of launch schedules	Incremental reduction of cost and reliability of launch schedules	Small projects the norm, less funding available, commercial investment key
Future	Space as marketplace, reconsideration of placing military weapons in space, concerns about proliferation of launch technology to hostile nations with capabilities to build weapons of mass destruction	Emphasis on multiple payloads with launcher	Reusability, single stage to orbit (SSTO), reduction of cost of access	Entirely new generation of launchers	Make space transportation more like air transportation

most sophisticated spacecraft ever built, the Space Shuttle, the basic principles have not changed.[6] However, chemical rockets are notoriously inefficient and costly to operate. In future generations, spaceflight must move beyond this technology to embrace another approach to reaching space.

With the dawn of the twentieth century, the technical developments that led to rocket propulsion made the beginning of the Space Age possible. The rocket is a reaction device based on Sir Isaac Newton's Third Law of Motion: "For every action there is an equal and opposite reaction." The action of a rocket is created by the pressure of gas inside a rocket engine that must escape through a nozzle. As the gas escapes at ever-higher velocities, it produces thrust. The reaction, therefore, propels the rocket upward. It will continue to accelerate until all of the propellant in the rocket engine is gone.[7] Unfortunately, this is an enormously simple explanation of an exceedingly complex technology. The story of space access in the twentieth century has been one of systematically applying this principle to technological systems and incrementally advancing the capabilities of those systems.

The unbroken path in rocketry from Goddard to the Space Shuttle rests on one simple mathematical equation. The product of the propellant mass flow (m) and its exhaust velocity (C) equals the thrust (T) generated by a rocket: $T = mC$. The higher the exhaust velocity, the more thrust generated per propellant mass flow. Rocketeers rate engines using two core measures. The first of these is the thrust of the rocket, which gives a rocket the kick necessary to overcome gravity and reach orbit. It is analogous to the horsepower rating used in the automotive industry. Space launch is, in essence, the heavy lifting of spaceflight, and requires achieving an escape velocity of 17,500 miles per hour (mph). The heavier the weight to be lifted to orbit, the more difficult the task of attaining that speed.

Because of the physics of our universe encapsulated in this equation, space access has relied on the staging of chemical rockets to reach Earth orbit. On the other hand, if one simply calculated the additional energy needed by a vehicle to reach orbit and were able to purchase that energy as electric power, that cost would be less than a dollar per pound. Thus, it is not the energy that is costly, but rather the inefficiencies of space launch as we accomplish it at present.[8]

Accordingly, most launch vehicles are characterized by thrust generated and by the payload mass delivered to low-Earth orbit (LEO) and to geosynchronous orbit. The Space Shuttle's three main engines, as an example, have an average thrust of 470,000 pounds and can deliver a payload of up to 53,000 pounds to LEO. Depending on exact altitude and on the inclination of the orbit over Earth's surface, payload delivery capabilities always rise or fall somewhat. Many aerospace professionals make a living calculating to multiple decimal points these critical parameters for every space launch.[9]

The second measurement used by rocketeers to rate engines is known as specific impulse (I_{sp})—the number of seconds a rocket engine can produce one pound of thrust from one pound of propellant. The I_{sp}, in effect, measures the efficiency of the rocket engine. If thrust is analogous to horsepower in an automobile, I_{sp} is analogous to miles per gallon of gas. I_{sp} is usually expressed in terms of seconds; for instance, an engine might have an I_{sp} of 300 seconds or 300 s. The best chemical rocket engines, the ones that power all of the major launch vehicles, are limited to an I_{sp} of about 500 s. As an example, the I_{sp} for the Space Shuttle main engine stands at about 455 s and represents the current state of the art in launch technology.

All launch systems, however, are dependent on the types of chemicals used as propellants in generating their I_{sp}. The hydrazine that powers many small rockets has a value of about 200 s. A combination of kerosene and oxygen—a fuel used by Wernher von Braun when developing the V-2 ballistic missile during World War II—has an I_{sp} of about 350 s, while a liquid hydrogen/liquid oxygen mixture used on the Space Shuttle can generate an I_{sp} of 450 s. Depending on the fuel system, the complexity of the engine, the efficiency of the nozzle, and a host of other attributes, engineers may be able to tinker around the edges of these chemical boundaries to deliver a slightly higher I_{sp} for any given engine.

A key issue to be wrestled with is how best to move beyond these chemical fuels to develop new types of propulsion systems that may be far more cost effective, reliable, and expeditious in operation. This may be the most important challenge facing the United States as it embraces an expansive spacefaring future. Furthermore, the crux of the problem may not be so much an inability to overcome the physical environment as it is a failure of imagination. Until the aerospace community believes that an entirely different type of space launch capability is necessary and marshals evidence to support the need to move in another technical direction, little will change.

A useful analogy illustrating this problem might be the American transition from propeller-driven aircraft to jets during World War II. American aeronautical engineers of the 1920s and 1930s had little belief in the potential of jet engines, even though the concept had been explored in a variety of research organizations and despite the fact that in retrospect no technological innovation was more significant for the development of aviation of all types than the turbojet. Americans failed to grasp jet propulsion's inherent superiority and instead focused research and development (R&D) efforts on incrementally improving propeller-driven aircraft. Although in principal a relatively simple propulsion system, the jet required a unique combination of metallurgical capability, and cooling and velocity control, as well as an unconventional understanding of Newton's third law of motion for its effectiveness to be realized. Americans had to make a crash effort in the 1940s and had to get help from the British in order to catch up with developments elsewhere.[10]

Virtually everyone dealing with the issue of jet propulsion in the United States has asked the same question: Why did the leading aeronautical nation in the world misjudge the potential of jet propulsion so badly? The answer seems to involve four interrelated factors.[11] First, few Americans were interested in tackling the jet problem because of the overall approach to aviation in the nation. Most research into the problems of propulsion was conducted by or for the engine manufacturers, and it was in their best economic interest to make incremental improvements to existing engines. Consequently, few were asking questions in the 1920s and 1930s about the potential of new propulsion technologies. When the National Advisory Committee for Aeronautics (NACA), the predecessor of the National Aeronautics and Space Administration (NASA), created a special committee under the leadership of Stanford University's William F. Durand to study jet propulsion in 1941, Durand explicitly omitted aircraft industry representatives because he believed they were inextricably wedded to the propeller.

Second, in contrast to European renegade engineers like Frank Whittle and Hans von Ohain, no American aeronautical professionals championed this unusual technology. Whittle and von Ohain were drawn to the turbojet because its simplicity and unique characteristics made it seemingly ideally adapted to flight. No one in America, it seems, grasped the potential of the turbojet until Gen. Hap Arnold returned from Britain in 1941 with plans for the Whittle engine and a collective light bulb turned on over the head of America's aeronautical engineering community.

Third, the economics of aeronautical R&D weighed against American involvement in the invention of the jet engine. The R&D establishment in the United States, most of it sponsored directly by the national government, was small and poor. Consequently, it always pursued research questions upon which it was uniquely suited to make significant contributions. NACA engineers, for example, made conscious decisions to pursue projects where they could use their world-class wind tunnels and thereby stay up-to-date with aerodynamics research. Jet propulsion research was for many of them a luxury they could not afford to pursue even if they had thought it worthwhile.

Finally, and this is by far the most significant area of concern, there was a problem of leadership among those interested in aeronautical R&D that militated against timely and effective research into jet propulsion. The principal clients of the nation's R&D organizations were the military services, and they neither appreciated the potential of jet propulsion nor asked engineers to work on the problem until they saw the Whittle engine in operation. In fact, to understand the full potential of the jet engine, individuals had to possess sensitivity to the convergence of thermodynamic and aerodynamic principles. Few military officers, even aviators, had the technical background to grasp this situation.

These factors, as well as others of a more subtle nature, came together to retard American efforts in this critical aspect of aeronautical R&D. Developments in Great Britain, however, shook the American aviation community out of its lethargy. During World War II American engineering brought significant improvements both to the turbojet and to the aircraft that they would propel, for the higher speeds necessitated significant redesigns of aircraft. It was not sufficient to strap a turbojet on an aircraft designed for propellers. Sadly, it took an international military challenge to prompt a response.[12]

Each of the factors seen in the United States in 1940 concerning jet propulsion are present today when it comes to the question of access to space. The major aerospace corporations have little economic impetus to advance into uncharted technological areas and change the status quo. The manufacturers of Atlas, Delta, and Titan launchers—Boeing and Lockheed-Martin—have honed their products to a high degree and achieved a level of maturity for their systems that they are loathe to abandon in favor of an entirely different approach to space access. NASA has been mired in Space Shuttle operations and construction of the International Space Station and lacks the resources, both intellectual and fiscal, to pursue new space access technologies aggressively. Despite a genuine desire to advance new propulsion technologies, the agency has found funding for its space launch initiative slow to materialize. Even when included in budget submissions, it was too often reduced or cut altogether by Congress.[13]

It does seem that at present there may be a failure of imagination in the public policy process in recognizing and pursuing a revolutionary new propulsion technology for American space access. But it may well be that there are some options with real potential just around the corner. These may enable space access to move beyond chemical rocket technology in the first half of the twenty-first century. They might be encouraged through a series of public policy avenues. Of course, the government may fund significant R&D in space launch, beginning with the Space Launch Initiative (SLI) included in NASA's fiscal year 2001 budget.[14] It may also stimulate innovation through prizes, more diverse research portfolios, and unusual government-industry-university partnerships in developing new systems.[15]

First, instead of the initial chemical launch, spaceflight might begin with horizontal acceleration along a track. Using magnetic levitation to eliminate friction, linear electric motors will accelerate the vehicle to more than 1,000 miles per hour before it leaves the track and fires its main engines. This MagLifter launch facility could enable space vehicles to be launched toward orbit in a more airplane-like manner. The MagLifter catapult would provide launch assistance to a variety of vehicles accelerating down a guideway for between two and five miles. Near the end of the guideway, the track would turn into an upward angle of 55 degrees, shooting the rocket on the first stage of its journey into space. Something akin to this is absolutely essential to enhance space access in this century.[16]

Second, laser-propelled craft that zip through the sky on pulses of light may offer true possibilities for space access. Scientists and engineers are setting the stage for future launches of ultra-tiny satellites into LEO. Ultimately, human-carrying spacecraft may be boosted into space using lasers. NASA and the U.S. Air Force undertook flight tests of mini-laser-propelled vehicles, dubbed "Lightcraft," in August 2000. In a demonstration, a 10-kilowatt, pulsed-carbon-dioxide laser would send Lightcraft high over the desert scenery by harnessing its energy and converting it into propulsive thrust. The laser energy would strike a parabolic condensing reflector mounted on the bottom of the Lightcraft. This area is lined with a thin coat of propellant. Struck by laser pulses, the propellant detonates and thrusts the Lightcraft upward. Interestingly, practical Lightcraft would look more like the so-called flying saucers of science fiction than like a current rocket.[17]

The Legacies of the ICBM and the Space Shuttle

Another of the major policy issues to be wrestled with concerning space access in this century is the legacy of launchers—the Atlas, Delta, and Titan—that began development as intercontinental ballistic missiles (ICBMs) in the 1950s, as well as the long shadow cast by the Space Shuttle as the raison d'être of human spaceflight in the United States since 1981. In 2001 the United States still relied on the descendants of the three major ballistic missiles for the bulk of its nonhuman space access requirements and on the Space Shuttle for all of its human missions. Even though the three families of expendable space boosters—each with numerous variants—have enjoyed incremental improvement since their first flight, there seems no way to escape their beginnings in technology (dating back to the 1950s) and their primary task of launching nuclear warheads. National defense requirements prompted the developers to emphasize schedule and operational reliability over launch costs.

The earliest ICBM, the Atlas, was first tested on June 11, 1955, and was made operational in 1959. Combined with the Agena upper stage, last launched in 1967, this rocket propelled space probes such as *Mariner* and *Ranger* to the moon and to Mars. Another variant, the Atlas-Centaur, has undergone incremental improvements since first flying in 1962. It has launched many of NASA's space probes to the planets and placed numerous military and commercial satellites into orbit. The most recent version of this powerful rocket, the Atlas IIAS, began flying in 1993 and can send 19,000 pounds into LEO at the bargain price of $105 million per flight, or about $6,000 per pound.[18]

A second ballistic missile, the Thor, also dates from the 1950s and, under the name Delta, has remained a workhorse in America's fleet of launchers, propelling smaller payloads into orbit. From 1960 to 1982, Delta underwent incremental improvements resulting in thirty-four separate configurations. The three-stage Delta II entered operational service in 1989 and can place 3,190 to 4,060 pounds into orbit, depending on configuration. Its cost is $45–50 million per launch, or about $12,000 per pound.[19]

The Titan ICBM quickly followed the Atlas and Thor into service with the U.S. Air Force in 1959 and remained on alert until the Cold War thawed in the late 1980s. Like Atlas and Delta, Titan comprised a family of rockets that has seen successive improvement since first flight. The Titan IV, the only currently operational version, is the largest, most powerful U.S. expendable launch vehicle (ELV) in use. Capable of placing

39,000 pounds in Earth orbit, it costs more than $240 million per flight. Because of these costs, operators are phasing the Atlas out of the U.S. inventory once the currently available vehicles have been launched.[20]

Movement beyond these first-generation launchers is critical for the opening of space access to wider operations. As we did with propeller-driven aircraft, we have incrementally improved launchers for the last forty years without making a major breakthrough in technology. Accordingly, the United States today has a very efficient and mature ELV launch capability that is still unable to overcome the limitations of the first-generation ICBM launch vehicles.[21]

In 1991 NASA Deputy Administrator J. R. Thompson railed at a NASA Advisory Council meeting that the launch capabilities currently in use were at best 1960s technology and that it was high time NASA moved forward to develop an entirely new system.[22] The Vice President's Space Policy Advisory Board made a similar statement in a report issued in November 1992:

> Advisory groups should be tiring of advising the government on steps to take to renew our nation's space launch capability. The basic facts haven't changed, except perhaps to worsen. We are dependent for the launch of our major payloads on the Space Shuttle and the ballistic-missile-derived Delta, Atlas and Titan launch vehicles. The latter are relatively reliable workhorses and could serve our government launch needs into the next century, albeit at increasingly uncompetitive prices, because now our international competitors will be improving the operating efficiency of their fleets. We will be paying more than we should for our own launches and will not be competitive for international commercial payloads. Complicating this will be pressure from non-market economy (NME) nations such as China and Russia.[23]

A decade later the situation remains the same. It is imperative that a national decision to expend significant resources to develop a new-generation launcher be made in the first decade of the twenty-first century.

The overpowering legacy of the Space Shuttle has also dominated the issue of space access since Project Apollo. Approved in 1972 by President Richard M. Nixon as the major NASA follow-on program to the highly successful moon landings, the Space Shuttle would provide routine, economical, and reliable indefinite access to space for the United States' human spaceflight program.[24] With the first spaceflight of the *Columbia* in 1981, NASA's human spaceflight capability became wedded to the Space Shuttle, and moving beyond that basic coupling has required twenty years. As John M. Logsdon lamented at the time of the 2000 presidential election: "Here's a sobering thought for those who anticipate that the next President is likely to make decisions and set goals that will shape NASA's future course with respect to human spaceflight. As Al Gore or George W. Bush campaigns for his *second* term in office in 2004, . . . a decision on replacing the Space Shuttle will be at least a year in the future! And that is on currently planned schedules, not accounting for any delays that may emerge over the next four years."[25]

Because of the cost of replacing the Space Shuttle as a launcher for human missions, the United States will continue to defer the decision on a replacement as long as possible. There is considerable reason to believe that because of costs and technical challenges even in 2005, when the current replacement decision is anticipated, the nation's leaders will refrain from committing to a new vehicle's development and instead put funds into upgrading and extending the usefulness of the Space Shuttle.

In addition to forestalling debate on a Shuttle replacement, the decision to build the Space Shuttle in 1972 short-circuited debate on the desirability of investment in new ELVs. At first NASA and most other space policy analysts agreed that the Shuttle would become the "one-size-fits-all" space launcher of the U.S. fleet. There would be, simply put, no need for another vehicle, since the Shuttle could satisfy all launch requirements, be they scientific, commercial, military, human, or robotic.[26] The military services at first agreed to launch all of their payloads on the Shuttle, and NASA aggressively marketed the Shuttle as a vehicle that could place any satellite into orbit.[27]

This was never a perfect situation, for during the early Reagan years the Shuttle was shouldering the responsibility for all government launches and many commercial ones. Unfortunately, it was unable to satisfy those demands. Even with the best of intentions and with attractive payload pricing policies, the Space Shuttle remained what it had been intended to be in the first place: a research and development vehicle that would push the frontiers of spaceflight and knowledge about the universe. The desire for the Shuttle to be all things to all people—research and development aerospace vehicle, operational space truck, commercial carrier, scientific platform—ensured that it would satisfy none of these singular and mutually exclusive missions.[28]

Only with the loss of *Challenger* on January 28, 1986, did this reliance on the Space Shuttle begin to change. It reinvigorated a debate over the use of the Space Shuttle to launch all U.S. satellites. In August 1986 President Ronald Reagan announced that the Shuttle would no longer carry commercial satellites, a policy formalized in December 1986 in National Security Decision Directive 254, "United States Space Launch Strategy." A total of forty-four commercial and foreign payloads that had been manifested on the Space Shuttle were forced to find new ELV launchers.[29]

For the next three years, the U.S. government worked to reinvigorate the American ELV production lines and to redesign and modify satellites to be launched on ELVs instead of on the Shuttle. The shift back to ELVs required additional government funding to fix the problems that had resulted from years of planning to retire these systems. The United States practically ceased commercial launch activities for several years, American operators conducting just three commercial satellite launches (one just prior to the *Challenger* flight) for only 6 percent of U.S. space launches from 1986 to 1989.[30]

During this period, however, two actions were initiated that enabled the emergence of a U.S. commercial launch industry. First, the Department of Defense (DOD) committed to purchasing a large number of ELVs as part of a strategy to maintain access to space using a mixed fleet of both the Space Shuttle and ELVs. This reopened the dormant U.S. ELV production lines at government expense and helped provide the economies of scale necessary to enable U.S. companies to compete effectively against commercial launches by Ariane. Second, in 1988 Congress established new insurance requirements whose effect was to limit liability for U.S. companies in case their launches caused damage to government property or third parties. The rules also established protections against government preemption of commercial launches on government ranges.[31]

As a result, the first totally commercial space launch by American firms took place in 1989—nearly five years after the insurance law was passed. Beginning in 1989, U.S. launches of commercial satellites were conducted by commercial launch companies (in most cases, the same companies providing launch services for DOD and NASA payloads as government contractors), not the U.S. government.[32]

The Costly Nature of Space Access

Lowering the cost of space access has long been the penultimate goal of rocketeers. Thus far, they have been unsuccessful in doing so to any appreciable degree. Space travel started out and remains an exceptionally costly enterprise. The best ELVs still cost about $10,000 per pound from Earth to orbit. The result is that spaceflight remains an enormously costly business. No wonder it has been the province of the government, a few high-end communications satellite companies, and other unique users.[33]

Even the most modest space launchers, placing relatively small satellites of less than 4,000 pounds into orbit, still average some $25 to $50 million per flight, or about $10,000 to $40,000 per pound, depending on the launch system, orbit altitude and inclination, indemnification, ground support, and checkout of system. The mighty *Saturn V* rocket, the most powerful launch system ever developed, had a thrust at launch of 7.5 million pounds. It could place into orbit a massive payload of 262,000 pounds, but to do so cost an enormous $113.1 million per launch ($455 million in 2000 dollars). Furthermore, those are just basic launch costs to orbit; they do not include the cost of satellite development, indemnification, boost to optimum orbit, ground support and transportation, operations, and the like.[34]

In 1972 NASA promoted to President Nixon and the American people the idea of a reusable Space Shuttle as a means of reducing the cost to orbit from $10,000 per pound to $1,000 per pound. To conduct an aggressive space exploration effort, NASA officials declared in 1972, "efficient transportation to and from the earth is required." This could be best provided, they believed, with "low-cost access by reusable chemical and nuclear rocket transportation systems."[35] Some NASA officials even compared the older method of using ELVs like the Saturn V to operating a railroad and throwing away the locomotive and box cars with every trip. The Shuttle, they claimed, would provide the United States with low-cost, routine access to space.[36]

At that time, space observers calculated that a Titan IIIC cost $24 million to procure and launch, while each Saturn IB cost $55 million. Carrying 23,000 pounds to LEO, the Titan IIIC delivered its payload at a cost per pound of about $10,000. The Saturn IB cost about $15,000 per pound to deliver its 37,000-pound payload. It was these launch costs that NASA officials sought to reduce by the much-heralded factor of ten.[37]

The Space Shuttle, therefore, became an attempt to provide low-cost access to space. George M. Low, NASA's deputy administrator, voiced the redefinition of this approach to the NASA leadership on January 27, 1970: "I think there is really only one objective for the Space Shuttle program, and that is 'to provide a low-cost, economical space transportation system.' To meet this objective, one has to concentrate both on low development costs and on low operational costs."[38] In fact, this objective held sway, becoming NASA's criteria for the program. It was an effort to deal with a real problem of public perception about spaceflight at the time: people believed that it was too expensive.[39]

A subtle but vital change occurred during the policy debate in the early 1970s over whether to build the Shuttle. This change has affected the cost of space access ever since. As a result of deliberations between NASA and the White House's Office of Management of Budget, the question of access to space shifted from "what is the least costly design for access to space" to "what design will provide low-cost access to space." As a result, NASA's rationale for the Shuttle became much narrower; and instead of talking about the benefits of the vehicle in toto, its rationale became just that it be low cost. To achieve this, NASA had to raise the projected flight rate to amortize a large development cost. This, in turn, led to policy decisions to place as many payloads as possible on the Shuttle, with consequences that were not realized until the loss of *Challenger* in 1986 and the effective grounding of the American launch capability for more than two years.[40]

NASA had originally intended to achieve cost-effectiveness on the Shuttle through economies of scale, as late as 1984 estimating that it could fly as many as twenty-four missions per year. This has proven an unattainable goal. Instead, NASA might have cut operational costs by investing more money in cost-saving technologies at the beginning of the program. Dale D. Myers, who served as NASA's deputy administrator in the post-*Challenger* era, suggests that reductions in the cost of flight operations might have been achieved "had the design team concentrated on operations as strongly as they concentrated on development."[41]

The Shuttle does not presently fly commercial payloads, and consequently there is no agreed-upon cost determination for flight per pound. Accordingly, observers have produced an enormous range of cost estimates—from $42 million per flight to estimates of more than $1 billion per mission.[42] The range of cost estimates depends, not surprisingly, on policy questions as to how much of the Shuttle's fixed costs are factored into flights.

While the goal of "low-cost, economical" access to space was appropriate for NASA, it eventually proved an embarrassment to the space program. So far, in spite of high hopes, the Shuttle has provided neither inexpensive nor routine access to space. The Space Shuttle—second to the Saturn V in both capability and cost—launches some 53,000 pounds of payload into orbit at a cost per launch of about $450 million. It is a high-end user, and the cost per flight is so great that only the government can afford it. In addition, by January 1986, there had been only twenty-four Shuttle flights, although in the 1970s NASA had projected more flights than that for every year. While the system is reusable, its complexity, coupled with the ever-present rigors of flying in an aerospace environment, means that the turnaround time between flights requires several months instead of several days. This has greatly affected the amortized cost of flying the Space Shuttle since 1981.

Since neither the cost per launch nor the flight schedule met expectations, many criticized NASA for failing to meet the promises made in gaining approval of the Shuttle program. In some respects, therefore, a consensus emerged in the last decade of the past century that the Shuttle has been both a triumph and a disappointment. The program remains engagingly ambitious and operates an exceptionally sophisticated vehicle, one that no other nation on Earth has built. In that respect, it has been an enormously successful program. At the same time, the Shuttle's much-touted capabilities remain unrealized. It has made far fewer flights and conducted far fewer scientific experiments than NASA leaders predicted.[43]

What are the most effective ways to lower the cost of space access? Is it reusability? Is it "big, dumb boosters?" Is it a design that emphasizes efficient operations? Is it something else altogether, or several "something elses?" Is it a combination of these and many other factors of a more sublime nature? Whatever the answer, it is important to take into careful consideration the legacies of these earlier research and development efforts in any future launchers.

Public versus Private Development of Launchers

One of the core questions plaguing space policy since the 1950s has been the role of the public sector in providing access to space. Should all launch vehicles be developed and owned by the federal government and operated either by it or under contract to it? Should there be some type of public-private partnership put into place to develop and operate launchers? Should the government leave launch vehicle development and operations entirely to industry, involving itself only insofar as required to assure the safety of its citizens, the regulation of orbits and frequencies, and the like? Should some entirely different model be employed to assure space access?

Initially, of course, all launch vehicles used in the United States were developed under government auspices. The first-generation launchers were all built as government projects, either as ballistic missiles or as

NASA rockets. Most were tied directly to national defense objectives, and all were justified as necessary for the continued survival of the United States. American business then found commercial spin-off uses for them. Over the years, it has been accepted as a given that some form of intensive governmental involvement is necessary to assure space access for three essential reasons: the high cost of bringing a new launcher to an operational state; the need, as a matter of industrial policy, to ensure the health of the aerospace industry; and the belief that a significant return on public investment in aerospace R&D would eventually take place.[44]

First, developing a wholly new launch vehicle is an enormously expensive undertaking. To be successful in rocket design, with its high technology base, an organization must have a vision that is multifaceted as well as clear as to its objectives and be able to stimulate and simulate change, gamble on the future, allocate limited resources, and make external allies. It must reward or tolerate risk taking and expect some failures. This is a very tall order when dealing with systems as complex and expensive as space technologies, where a corporate manufacturer would literally bet the company on the success of any new design that it might offer. Malcolm Stamper, former president of Boeing Aircraft Corporation, remarked that in this climate "locating the break-even point is like finding a will-o'-the-wisp." Caution tends to rule in that very dizzying environment.[45] The result is that there has been a very clear hesitancy on the part of corporations to undertake development of a new launch vehicle as a matter of speculation.

As a measure of governmental investment in that first generation of launchers, the Eisenhower administration undertook a study just before the Sputnik crisis and learned that through fiscal year 1957, the nation had spent $11.8 billion on space access R&D in 1957 dollars. "The cost of continuing these programs from FY 1957 through FY 1963," Eisenhower was told, "would amount to approximately $36.1 billion, for a grand total of $47 billion."[46] In 1997 dollars, for comparison, this would have represented an investment of more than $228 billion. A public investment of even 25 percent of that amount in the first decade of the twenty-first century would make possible an enormous advance of launch vehicle technology.

Second, while it is something of a truism to suggest that the United States has never developed and implemented a coherent, long-term industrial policy, nonetheless, a barely existent industrial policy has been critical in driving government investment in launch vehicle technology.[47] The aerospace arena has never been particularly profitable for private enterprise in the United States, and to help with the fielding of most new-generation aircraft and rockets, the federal government has been forced to subsidize the industry. Often it has done this indirectly. For example, the federal government has been fundamentally involved in fostering R&D aiding commercial manufacturers of air and space technologies through organizations such as the NACA and NASA.[48] More directly, as a matter of industrial policy, the United States has often placed orders for new aerospace systems at times when the industry seemed on the verge of sinking into a morass of red ink and ultimately perhaps ceasing to exist as a separate industry.[49]

The comments of one key leader come to mind in the context of the need to maintain the economic viability of the aerospace industry because of its overarching importance for the U.S. economy and national welfare:

> Only a failure of the United States government to place orders with our successful airplane designers and builders will cause our aircraft industrial strength to slip back into the position it occupied three years ago. A vital point is being overlooked by the American people. It is immediately evident that the industrial strength of the United States must be at the war strength all the time. . . . The government must stimulate and aid in the application of aircraft industrially, and also aid in foreign trade, furnishing sufficient outlet for industrial aviation and guaranteeing a continuity of production at the required rate.

Although any number of aerospace CEOs might have said this at various times in the twentieth century when there was a downturn in the market, it was actually voiced by Glenn L. Martin in 1920. He complained that the United States required a strong aerospace industry as a guarantee of national defense and should invest public dollars in it as a matter of industrial policy.[50]

Since the 1980s, moreover, it has become important to be more aggressive in ensuring this type of direct support as a matter of industrial policy because of incursions of foreign competitors to the space launch business and the direct subsidies they enjoyed from their governments. "In effect, the Federal government was limping toward a sort of industrial policy," claimed Norman E. Bowie in 1994. "Since American industry was failing to invest in sufficient research and development to bring new products to market that could compete internationally, especially with the Japanese, the government provided public funds to universities to help move the fruits of basic research in to the marketplace."[51]

During the post–World War II era, the federal government created a tremendous national infrastructure for science and innovation, expanding it even further in the mid-1980s and 1990s.[52] This came as a direct result of foreign competition. In the space launch arena, as an example, one of the major factors energizing U.S. government subsidies was the necessity to respond to the ever-present and widespread subsidization of aerospace industrial development in Europe. With the arrival of the Ariane as a commercial launcher in the 1980s, a number of questions would be frequently raised concerning the fair pricing of space launchers on the international market because of direct subsidy.[53]

Third, U.S. leaders have long believed as an article of faith that there is a significant return on investment in R&D activities. This is no truer in any other sector than for space access. In essence, political leaders have agreed—even without empirical evidence to support it—that, after accounting for labor and capital inputs to the gross domestic product (GDP), substantial advances in knowledge were also necessary to explain the economic growth of the United States in the twentieth century. A quarter-century ago, Edward F. Denison explicitly set out to examine this phenomenon, concluding that "advance in knowledge is the biggest and most basic reason for the persistent long-term growth of output per unit of input." He understood that this advance in knowledge included both "technological knowledge" and "managerial knowledge," but he also confided, "I have found no way to measure changes in the state of knowledge directly."[54]

The technologies associated with World War II and the Cold War as well as the Space Age suggested that many advances in knowledge have come from government R&D. This was evident in U.S. superiority in aircraft, medicine, and nuclear power; but even so, connections between R&D, advances in knowledge, and economic advances remain unclear at the beginning of this century. How should these advances be measured? Economist Henry Hertzfeld has examined previous estimates of the returns to U.S. space R&D. These estimates he divided into three categories: macroeconomic models, microeconomic models, and case studies.[55]

Two companies performed macroeconomic studies of the economic returns on NASA R&D in the 1970s and repeated their studies in the 1980s. The Midwestern Research Institute (MRI) study of 1971 determined that NASA R&D provided an overall 7:1 return. Essentially, for every dollar spent on R&D, seven dollars were returned to the GDP. MRI refined its study in 1988, calculating this time an even higher 9:1 return on investment. Chase Econometrics performed a more sophisticated study in 1975 that reported a whopping 14:1 return on investment.[56]

These were quite heady results, and NASA and others with a vested interest in showing "cost-benefit" results for expenditures in space used them as ammunition for expansions of their federal funding. Not everyone was so positive about the results, however. The most pointed criticism came from the General Accounting Office (GAO), which, although sympathetic to the idea that R&D at NASA generated significant return on investment, did not accept the rosy metrics presented in these studies. Despite the critics' assessments, the results became benchmark figures that have been quoted time and again in speeches by NASA officials and in various congressional testimony and publications. The results of these studies, it seems safe to conclude, have been quite inconclusive overall.[57]

Equally inconclusive microeconomic studies have also been performed for NASA. Even more important, few detailed case studies have been undertaken. In his 1992 article, Hertzfeld laments that "missing from the above discussion are the studies that document the 'big' technologies that are a direct or indirect result of the space R&D program. The most obvious examples are satellite communications, weather and remote-sensing satellites, and private space launch vehicles." In his conclusion, Hertzfeld suggests that "the most promising type of economic study for measuring returns to space R&D is the documentation of actual cases based on direct survey information."[58]

Because of the resulting confusion over the R&D return on investment for the United States, the director of the National Science Foundation (NSF), Richard Atkinson, funded a series of studies on the link of R&D investment with economic growth in the 1970s. "As late as the mid-1970s, there was no substantial economic data, no reliable economic analysis of the relationship between investments in R&D and economic development," Atkinson had concluded. He and others at the NSF realized that the lack of such information made it more difficult to gain support for research from Congress.[59] It is vital that greater understanding of this issue be gained early in this century.

Because of these three related factors—cost of launch systems, nascent industrial policy, and return in R&D investment—few aerospace firms have taken on the task of developing on their own a launch vehicle free from government involvement. There were important market reasons for this, of course. Until the mid-1960s there was no commercial market for space access. This changed slowly when commercial firms began to perceive the possibility of launching communications satellites. Even so, political realities until the 1980s suggested that launch vehicles were assets for the preservation of national security, and the government tightly controlled their use.[60]

This began to change with the Reagan administration of the 1980s. On July 4, 1982, Reagan's statement of National Space Policy made final the decision that the government would order no more Delta, Atlas, and Titan launch vehicles and would use the Space Shuttle exclusively for its space launch requirements.[61] At the same time, while allowing the Space Shuttle to launch commercial payloads, Reagan's space policy specifically encouraged private launch operations for commercial purposes. In 1984 Congress passed the Commercial Space Launch Act that established in law the desire to open space access to broader communities while assigning regulatory responsibility for commercial rockets to the Department of Transportation.[62] There followed a series of moves intended to create a commercial space transportation industry independent of the U.S. government.[63] This was largely unsuccessful through the middle part of the 1980s, in part because of NASA's opposition.

All of this changed on January 28, 1986, when the Space Shuttle *Challenger* exploded. On August 15, Reagan announced that NASA would no longer launch private satellites. This finally opened the commercial rocket market—a market that had by then been captured by the European-built Ariane launcher.[64] As a result, several entrepreneurs proposed developing new, privately financed space launch vehicles— particularly for the small satellite market niche that the Space Shuttle did not serve economically—and one of them, Conestoga I, was successfully launched in a suborbital flight. This marked the first successful flight of a privately funded U.S. launch vehicle.[65] But those efforts never had the capability to serve as replacements for the Atlas, Delta, and Titan launchers.

In part because it had now been discredited by the *Challenger* accident, NASA agreed to sponsor the development of an expansive commercial launch industry, issuing a solicitation to prospective contractors interested in commercializing NASA's Atlas and Delta launch programs. Few established firms seemed enthusiastic about the commercialization effort, and none decided to bid on contracts for it (although General Dynamics responded with a very tentative proposal to upgrade the Atlas, provided NASA were to foot the entire bill). One marketing company, Transpace Carriers, expressed interest in commercializing the Delta launcher, even though McDonnell Douglas, its manufacturer, did not.[66]

Some variants of the main launchers available in the United States started to emerge from this push during the latter Reagan years, but only after substantial government investment. The current family of commercial Atlas, Delta, and Titan launchers—all of which had their roots in the ballistic missile programs of the 1950s—first started flying in 1989, and versions of them will see service well into the present century. None of them would have been possible, however, without substantial government investment.

Any movement beyond first-generation launchers, it seemed in 1999, had to be largely a government-sponsored effort. As space policy analyst James A. Vedda suggests,

Given proper motivation and some help with risk mitigation, industry can apply adequate resources to an effort of this scope. For example, construction of the Alaska Pipeline, a project of similar magnitude, cost $8 billion (in 1970s dollars) over four years. However, the returns that can be expected from investments in new launch infrastructure are less certain than those from the Alaska Pipeline. Corporate interests cannot be confident that they will get back what they've invested within a reasonable timeframe. Some form of government support is essential and appropriate.[67]

Most agreed that the nation must make a priority investment in launch vehicle technology similar to the total dollars that were expended to develop the ICBMs of forty years ago. The Atlas, Thor/Delta, and Titan ICBMs, of course, remain the antecedents of the current ELV fleet of launchers.

Since the Reagan era, the space launch market has expanded significantly, and there is now a pressing need for new launch capability. Beginning in the mid-1990s, several start-up companies were organized to develop new vehicles in response to the promise of an expansive market for space access. In the second half of the 1990s, worldwide commercial revenues in space for the first time surpassed all governmental spending on space. Market surveys suggested that commercial launches would increase substantially in the early twenty-first century, led by telecommunications satellites.[68] In that context, many space launch advocates believed that the market had matured sufficiently that government investment in launch vehicle development was no longer necessary. Instead, they asked that the federal government simply "get out of the way" and allow the private sector to pursue development free from bureaucratic controls.[69]

This perceived "gold rush" sparked several new corporations to muscle their way into the tight conglomerate of launch vehicle companies. One of the farthest along and best financed of this new breed is Kistler Aerospace Corporation, based in Kirkland, Washington. Seeking low-cost access to space, Kistler employed Russian-built engines as a centerpiece of its K-1 reusable launcher. It was intended to deliver up to 10,000 pounds to orbit, depending on inclination. The first stage of this vehicle would fly back to the launch site; the second would orbit Earth before returning. Both stages would descend by parachute and land on inflatable air bags. Pioneer, Inc., has also been developing the Pathfinder rocketplane, an aerial propellant transfer spaceplane that accommodates a crew of two and can deliver a payload of 5,000 pounds to LEO. Lone Star Space Access, Inc. set about developing the Cosmos Mariner, intended as a prototype single-stage launch vehicle satisfying the criteria of the X-prize competition, which would award a $10 million prize to the first team to achieve a suborbital flight with a three-person, single-stage launch vehicle; return safely; and repeat the feat within fourteen days.

Among these companies the most interesting concept, albeit one that proved doomed to failure, was the Roton by the Rotary Rocket Company. Roton was intended as a fully reusable, single-stage-to-orbit (SSTO) space vehicle designed to transport up to 7,000 pounds to and from LEO. Roton planned to enter commercial service with a target price per flight of $7 million ($1,000 per pound). In 2000, Rotary shut down all of its projects. Its chief executive officer, Gary Hudson, left the company to pursue other interests, and its Mojave facility was closed after an auction of most of its contents.[70]

As of this writing, none of the myriad private efforts has yielded an operational space launcher . Perhaps none ever will, but these start-ups have been knocking on the doors of venture capitalists for the last several years without much success, seeking funds for their projects. With the failure of the Iridium Corporation in the spring of 2000, a new satellite communications system that many believed would be the vanguard of a rapidly expanding space launch market, investment for space enterprises became even more scarce.[71] In some measure because of this, although they had previously eschewed government investment and the corresponding red tape, many of these start-ups began seeking capital from NASA and the military to support their efforts. Accordingly, it seems that as the twenty-first century begins, there is still a pressing need for substantial government investment in space launch R&D.

That investment might take a different form than the standard government procurement contracts of a bygone era, however. For instance, one of the most interesting approaches was pioneered in the now discontinued X-33 development effort. NASA and Lockheed-Martin instituted a cooperative agreement to develop the X-33 beginning in 1995, and despite the termination of that particular effort in March 2001, its cooperative agreement may prove a model worth pursuing. NASA undertook this effort because over the past two decades the Space Shuttle, a partially reusable vehicle, taught its leaders that bringing down costs and reducing turnaround time were much greater challenges than originally anticipated.[72] The X-33 program was intended to meet those objectives of cost and reliability that the Shuttle had left unfulfilled. It was to have served as a technology demonstrator, but upon successful flight, Lockheed-Martin agreed to develop and fly a commercial version, VentureStar™, in the first decade of this century.

That cooperative agreement, furthermore, was at the heart of NASA's efforts to initiate so-called new ways of doing business by serving as both a procurement and a management tool. As a new procurement instrument, the cooperative agreement was part of a so-called fast track managerial approach (and of the larger "faster-better-cheaper" formula) that featured more expeditious acquisition procedures, streamlined bureaucracy, limited oversight, and less investment by NASA. It also mandated that industry share the costs of the project so that neither side placed as much at risk.[73]

Given the problems experienced on the X-33 program, with delays of more than a year because of difficulties with critical elements such as the fuel tanks, some have criticized the use of the cooperative agreement as the culprit in sidelining the project. That seems to put too fine a point on the issue, for at the end of the day, perhaps the greatest advantage of this cooperative agreement has been its fostering of shared responsibility for the funding of launcher development between the public and private sectors. The cooperative agreement also provided industry an important voice in launcher planning.

Before the X-33, the space industry had never before expended significant resources in launcher development. The industry contribution to X-33 development was $442 million dollars through 2000. In an era of declining government R&D budgets for space, the importance of that number cannot be underestimated, and it seems obvious that although sizable government investment in the development of future launchers will be required, there is a reason to pursue additional cooperative projects.[74] If a new generation of launchers is to be developed in the first part of the twenty-first century, it appears that the federal government will have to take a leadership role in identifying R&D funds and working in partnership with industry. Perhaps this may most effectively be accomplished through additional cooperative agreements.

Of course, some have condemned the overall X-33 effort as a self-deception that a single government program—even one using a new type of partnership with industry—will be able to solve the problems of space access. Unrealistic goals, coupled with impossible political demands, left the X-33 program stunned and stunted at the end of the twentieth century. As one space policy analyst concluded, "It continued to blur the line, which should be bright, between revolutionary, high-risk, high-payoff R&D efforts and low-risk, marginal payoff evolutionary efforts to improve systems."[75] The willingness to embark on this effort has been a mystery to many analysts as they review the linkage—which some called "foolish"—between the high-risk R&D of the X-33 and the supposedly operational VentureStar™.

The Value of RLVs versus ELVs

Many aerospace engineers believe that the long-term solution to the world's launch needs is a series of completely reusable launch vehicles (RLVs). A debate has raged between those who believe RLVs are the only—or at least the best—answer and those who emphasize the continuing place of expendable launch vehicles (ELVs) in future space access operations. RLV advocates have been convincing in their argument that the only course leading to "efficient transportation to and from the earth" are RLVs and have made the case repeatedly since the late 1960s.[76] Several models exist for future RLVs, however, and all compete for the attention—and the development dollars—of the federal government.

One especially important model for a next-generation RLV emerged during the Reagan administration when senior government officials began to talk about the "Orient Express," a hybrid air- and spaceplane that would enable ordinary people to travel between New York City and Tokyo in about one hour. Such a concept was quite simple in theory, although enormously complex in reality. It required developing a passenger spaceplane with the capability to fly from an ordinary runway like a conventional jet. Flying supersonic, it would reach an altitude of about 45,000 feet, whereupon the pilot would start scramjet engines, more efficient, faster jet engines that have the potential to reach hypersonic speeds in the Mach 3 realm. These would take the vehicle to the edge of space for a flight to the opposite side of the globe, from whence the process would be reversed and the vehicle would land like a conventional airplane. It never would reach orbit, but it would still fly in space; and the result is the same as orbital flight for passengers but for less time. It would even be possible, RLV supporters insisted, to build such a spaceplane that could reach orbit.[77]

One of the most significant—and perhaps least successful—efforts to develop this reusable spaceplane was the National Aerospace Plane (NASP), a joint NASA–Air Force technology demonstrator begun during the Reagan administration. This vehicle was touted as an SSTO fully reusable vehicle—one that could travel to and from Earth orbit without dropping stages once they had expended their fuel—using air breathing engines and wings. After billions spent, however, NASP never progressed to flight stage. It finally died a merciful death in 1994, trapped in bureaucratic politics and seemingly endless technological difficulty.[78]

NASA began its own RLV program after the demise of NASP, and the agency's leadership expressed high hopes for a small suborbital vehicle that would demonstrate the technologies required for an operational SSTO launcher. This was the first of a projected set of four stages that NASA contended would lead to a routine spacefaring capability.[79] But what would happen after its tests were completed remains unclear. Even assuming complete success in meeting its R&D objectives, the time and money necessary to build, test, and certify a full-scale operational follow-on version remains problematic. Who would pay for such an operational vehicle also remains a mystery, especially since the private sector has become less enamored with the joint project over the years and has eased itself away from the venture.[80]

There is also an understanding that the technical hurdles have proven more daunting than anticipated, as was the case thirty years ago with the Space Shuttle and more recently with the NASP. Any SSTO—and X-33 holds true to this pattern—would require breakthroughs in a number of technologies, particularly in propulsion and materials. And when designers begin work on the full-scale SSTO, they may find that available technologies limit payload size so severely that the new vehicle provides little or no cost savings compared to old launchers. If this becomes the case, then everyone must understand that NASA will receive the same barbs from critics who condemned NASA for "selling" the Space Shuttle program as a practical and cost-effective means of routine access to space and then failing to deliver on that promise.[81]

This is not to say that SSTO will never work or that future concepts should not be pursued. It is NASA's job to take risks and push the technological envelope. But in an effort as important as creating the next generation of launchers, technological risks must be recognized for what they are and accepted. While the goal of the RLV program has been to enable the development of a launch system that is significantly cheaper, more reliable, and more flexible than is presently available, it is possible to envision a future system that cannot meet all those objectives. Furthermore, to make progress, the federal government should be prepared to expend the resources necessary to drive R&D technology. Something approaching a $25 billion investment to achieve significant RLV advance is not out of the question. Such a public investment would go far toward bringing to fruition a next-generation launch vehicle to replace the Shuttle, supporters believe.[82]

There is an alternative position that suggests that the most appropriate approach to space access is through the use of throwaway "big, dumb boosters" that are inexpensive to manufacture and operate. While reusable rockets may seem to be an attractive cost-saving alternative to expendables because they allow repeated use of critical components such as rocket motors and structural elements, ELV advocates claim they actually offer a false promise of savings. This is because all RLV savings are predicated on maximizing usage of a small number of vehicles over a very long period of time for all types of space launch requirements. Accordingly, cost savings are realized only when an RLV flies many times over many years. That goal is unattainable, they claim, because it assumes that there will be no (or very few) accidents in the reusable fleet throughout its life span.[83]

The reality, ELV advocates warn, is that the probability of all RLV components operating without catastrophic failure throughout the lifetime of the vehicle cannot be assumed to be 100 percent. Indeed, the launch reliability rate of even relatively "simple" ELVs—those without upper stages or spacecraft propulsion modules and with a significant operational experience—peaks at 98 percent with the Delta II, and that took thirty years of operations to achieve. To be sure, most ELVs achieve a reliability rate of 90–92 percent, again only after a maturing of the system has taken place. The Space Shuttle, a partially reusable system, has

attained a launch reliability rate of 99 percent, but only through extensive and costly redundant systems and safety checks. In the case of a
new RLV, or a new ELV for that matter, a higher failure rate has to be assumed because of a lack of experience with the system. Moreover, RLV
use doubles the time of exposure of the vehicle to failure because it must
also be recovered and be reusable after refurbishment. To counter this
challenge, more and better reliability has to be built into the system, and
this must exponentially increase R&D and operational costs.[84]

NASA's goal for the next generation RLV's operational reliability has
been established at 99.9 percent.[85] No launch vehicle has ever achieved
that goal. And those who argue for ELV development note that attaining such a goal is virtually impossible. At the very least it will require a
much larger fleet than currently envisioned, and operational costs will
rise to assure reliability through redundancy. Stephen A. Book, an engineer with the Aerospace Corporation, holds that "we can pay a large
amount of money to build in very high reliability or we can pay a large
amount of money to acquire several more vehicles." There is no other
option, he contends, adding that building more "use-once, throw-away"
vehicles makes the most sense for most future launches. Certainly for
the placement of satellites into Earth orbit, Book concludes, expendable
launchers are the most economical vehicle. They may never be desirable
for human spaceflight, however.[86]

Proponents of ELV development argued that designing for one use
only simplifies the system enormously. One use of a rocket motor, guidance system, and the like means that it only needs to function correctly
one time. Acceptance of an operational reliability of 90 percent or even
less would further reduce the costs incurred in designing and developing a new ELV. Indeed, many experts believe that reliability rates cannot be advanced more than another 1.5 percent above the 90 percent
mark without enormous effort—effort that would be strikingly cost inefficient.[87]

Some provocatively suggest that new ELVs should be designed with
the types of payloads to be carried clearly in mind, accepting the risk
inherent in a space launch environment where 90 percent reliability
would be the norm. For expensive and one-of-a-kind scientific and military satellites, as well as for expensive commercial spacecraft, spacecraft
with a higher reliability rate and a higher price tag could be acceptable.
But for most payloads, especially logistics supplies and the like going to
the International Space Station, reliabilities as low as 65 percent might

be acceptable. And it goes without saying that for human spaceflights NASA's goal of 99.9 percent operational reliability is not too high a goal to seek.

As an example, Andrew E. Turner of Space Systems/LORAL has proposed development of a low-cost, high-risk, existing technology launch vehicle to ship low-cost payloads such as water or propellant to LEO. His goal is to reduce launch costs to $1,000 per kilogram, using existing technology by taking advantage of the savings inherent in a launch vehicle overall reliability of 67 percent and in the economy of scale provided by mass production of more than 1,000 units annually. His project, the Aquarius rocket, would be launched from an upright position, bobbing in the ocean wherever most appropriate for its orbital destination. Assuming a high number of launches of low-cost payloads, and accepting the loss of one in three rockets, the Aquarius proposal departs radically from other launch cost improvement schemes. Turner believes that he can reduce launch costs by up to 60 percent, depending on the concepts and cost models used with Aquarius.[88]

As another example, an interesting hybrid approach to space access has been advanced by Buzz Aldrin, the second American on the moon in 1969. Merging both RLV and ELV components, Aldrin has proposed StarBooster 200, a system that recovers the largest element of a space launch vehicle, the booster, for reflight, while the stage that enters orbit is expendable. This is the opposite of the partial reusability concept employed with the Space Shuttle. He has envisioned it as a vehicle with a fuselage cavity to house the complete first stage of the existing Atlas III ELV. Launching vertically, the vehicle would be powered by an off-the-shelf RD-180 engine. The first stage would carry its payload to a staging velocity above Mach 5 at 45 to 50 kilometers altitude. The first stage would then separate and begin a descent with two air-breathing turbine engines, cruising back to the launch site and landing like an airplane. It could then be inspected, refurbished, mated with a new payload ensemble, and reflown. The expendable second stage would fly on into orbit to deliver its payload.[89]

The feasibility of both Aquarius and StarBooster 200 might ultimately prove problematic, but they are only two of many such concepts that exist. Government investment in the most promising of the concepts will help to bring at least some of them to fruition. Picking the most promising concepts to support, however, will not be a task without difficulties.

Conclusion

The first decade of the twenty-first century promises to offer both serious challenges and enormous potential for the development of new launch vehicles that will finally achieve the long-held dream of reliable, affordable access to space. Certainly NASA leaders believe this is completely within reach in the first decade of this century. NASA envisions that it should foster this effort as one of its legitimate governmental roles in space. The policy questions loom large. Although transportation to Earth orbit is presently expensive, sustained efforts are being made to reduce the cost. One effort is to use rocket propulsion and, with new materials and clever engineering, to make a launcher that is not only recoverable but also robust. Another is to use air-breathing vehicles to enable the building of a robust launcher.

This represents a very ambitious set of requirements and schedule. One of the difficult issues to be wrestled with in space access policy is how to break the cycle of the government choosing the "one best way" to reach space and funding it. Since the beginning of the Shuttle era, such a cycle has led to the extensive hyping of systems and the resultant disappointment and loss of credibility when they fail to deliver on the promises of those advocating them. This then leads to another round of analysis and other projects. The Space Shuttle, NASP, X-33, and other concepts have all been victims of this cycle. The central reality in all R&D is uncertainty. One simply cannot guarantee success once a project is undertaken.[90]

Since human beings are at the core of any R&D project, the complexity expands to include chance and nonlinear factors endemic to the real world of people. The relationships between technological innovation; various aeronautical institutions; innovative concepts, practices, or organizations; and the people associated with each are intrinsically complex. Essentially nonlinear, these relationships no doubt allow innovation to take place, but there does not seem to be a way to guarantee it. Those who seek to command innovation find that changes in inputs to various aspects of the systems, themselves designed to yield innovative alterations, do not necessarily ensure proportionate positive developments in output. It is nonlinearity writ large.[91]

This has not yet become apparent to those involved in directing space access R&D efforts. This, despite the fact that research fields as diverse as meteorology, earth sciences, physics, space sciences, biology, and mathematics have come forward with confirmation of a position, first taken by Albert Einstein, that the universe is a relative place. Whereas before, dynamic and exceptionally small systems might have been considered deterministic in orientation, they now began to be seen as much more complex and virtually unpredictable in their long-term behavior. The rise of "chaos" theory to help explain this unpredictability fundamentally reshaped the nature of science and engineering in the latter twentieth century. Seemingly unrelated phenomena—the rise and fall of biological populations, the origin and mutation of viruses and bacteria, the behavior of the human heart, the dripping of a water faucet, the performance of a superconductor, and a host of other observable occurrences—all bespeak a fundamental unpredictability, or "chaos," in their performance. This nonlinearity seems to be the norm, for as scientists John Briggs and F. David Peat have concluded, predictable dynamics "are in fact exceptions in nature rather than the rule."[92]

Because of this basic problem, perhaps the best answer is to advocate a portfolio of R&D concepts with a diverse range of risk, cost, and potential payoff and then to make rather large investments only when justified by the potential reward. In this way, the nation might find reason to fund a tiny program in advanced antimatter research that now goes begging, while putting proportionally more funds into ensuring turbopump safety. Perhaps X-vehicles might take their place alongside these other technologies in the portfolio, and as they demonstrate new capabilities, they might be integrated into more routine operations. In this scenario, the central policy challenge would not be in "what" new overarching program to invest R&D dollars, but in "how" to make many investments in smaller efforts.[93]

One of the interesting speculative questions to be considered is how people fifty years hence will view what was accomplished in space during the twentieth century. Will the astronauts who landed on the moon and the voyages of *Apollo* be remembered as people akin to Columbus and his voyages to the Americas, as vanguards of sustained human exploration and settlement? Or will they prove to be more like Leif Erickson's voyages from Scandinavia several hundred years earlier, stillborn in the European process of exploration to new lands? No one knows, but it is incumbent on the policymakers and the public to make decisions about sustained exploration. Space access is the critical component in making the spacefaring vision a reality. Actions taken in the first part of the twenty-first century to enhance access will determine its direction for generations to come.

NOTES

1. This is the unswerving position of the Space Transportation Association. It will enable an opening of the "space frontier" to all. See Tom Rogers, "Space Tourism: A Response to Continuing Decay in U.S. Civil Space Financial Support," *Space Policy* 14 (May 1998): 79–81.

2. This claim was made in 1992 by a noted scientist in a speech to the American Astronautical Society titled "Chicken Little Was Right." Mathematical calculations confirm that every person alive today faces one chance in five thousand that he or she will be killed by some type of extraterrestrial impact during his or her lifetime since several thousand meteorites, comets, and asteroids cross Earth's orbit and many small pieces enter the atmosphere every day. One need only look at the craters on the moon to verify the fact that solar bodies make fine targets for comets and asteroids. See chapter 5 in this volume.

3. Calculated from the launch tables in Steven J. Isakowitz, Joseph P. Hopkins Jr., and Joshua B. Hopkins, *International Reference Guide to Space Launch Systems*, 3rd ed. (Reston, VA: American Institute for Aeronautics and Astronautics, 1999).

4. More than five hundred space access studies have reached this conclusion over the last forty years. See Roger D. Launius and Howard E. McCurdy, *Imagining Space: Achievements, Predictions, Possibilities, 1950–2050* (San Francisco: Chronicle Books, 2001), chap. 4; United States Congress, Office of Technology Assessment, *Launch Options for the Future: Special Report* (Washington, DC: Government Printing Office, 1984); Vice President's Space Policy Advisory Board, "The Future of U.S. Space Launch Capability," Task Group Report, November 1992, NASA Historical Reference Collection, NASA History Office, Washington, DC; NASA Office of Space Systems Development, *Access to Space Study: Summary Report* (Washington, DC: NASA, 1994).

5. This is the premise of G. Harry Stine, *Halfway to Anywhere: Achieving America's Destiny in Space* (New York: M. Evans, 1996), a book that explores the historical path of launch vehicle development in the United States.

6. Basic histories of rocketry include David Baker, *The Rocket: The History and Development of Rocket and Missile Technology* (New York: Crown Books, 1978); Frank H. Winter, *Rockets into Space* (Cambridge: Harvard University Press, 1990); Wernher von Braun, Frederick I. Ordway III, and Dave Dooling, *History of Rocketry and Space Travel* (New York: Thomas Y. Crowell, 1986); Eugene M. Emme, ed., *The History of Rocket Technology: Essays on Research, Development, and Utility* (Detroit: Wayne State University Press, 1964).

7. This section is based on *Rockets: A Teacher's Guide with Activities in Science, Mathematics, and Technology* (Washington, DC: NASA Office of Human Resources and Education, 1996); Robert Zubrin, *Entering Space: Cre-*

ating a Spacefaring Civilization (New York: Jeremy P. Tarcher/Putnam, 1999), 35–38; Isakowitz, Hopkins, and Hopkins, *International Reference Guide*.

8. Scott Pace, personal communication, 10 September 2000.

9. On Space Shuttle early history, see T. A. Heppenheimer, *The Space Shuttle Decision: NASA's Quest for a Reusable Launch Vehicle* (Washington, DC: NASA SP-4221, 1999). Specifically on the main engine, see T. A. Heppenheimer, "27,000 Seconds in Hell," *Air & Space/Smithsonian* (October/November 1998): 25–32.

10. The critical study of this subject is Edward W. Constant II, *The Origins of the Turbojet Revolution* (Baltimore: Johns Hopkins University Press, 1980). On the adoption of the jet engine in the NACA see, Roger D. Launius, "'Never Was Life More Interesting': The National Advisory Committee for Aeronautics, 1936–1945," *Prologue: Quarterly of the National Archives* 24 (Winter 1992): 361–73.

11. The following discussion is based on the observations of Alex Roland, *Model Research: The National Advisory Committee for Aeronautics, 1915–1958* (Washington, DC: NASA SP-4103, 1985), 186–94; Elizabeth A. Muenger, *Searching the Horizon: A History of Ames Research Center, 1940–1976* (Washington, DC: NASA SP-4304, 1985), 33–37; James R. Hansen, *Engineer in Charge: A History of the Langley Aeronautical Laboratory, 1917–1958* (Washington, DC: NASA SP-4305, 1987), 219–47; Virginia P. Dawson, *Engines and Innovation: Lewis Laboratory and American Propulsion Technology* (Washington, DC: NASA SP-4306, 1991), 41–63; I. B. Holley, "Jet Lag in the Army Air Corps," in Harry R. Borowski, ed., *Military Planning in the 20th Century* (Washington, DC: Office of Air Force History, 1986), 123–53.

12. John V. Becker, *The High Speed Frontier: Case Histories of Four NACA Programs, 1920–1950* (Washington, DC: NASA, 1980).

13. As an example, on May 23, 2000, the U.S. House of Representatives' Appropriations Committee marked up the NASA fiscal year 2001 budget and deleted $320 million included by the president for a Space Launch Initiative. NASA's Marshall Space Flight Center director responded, "That initiative is absolutely essential to achieving one of NASA's most critical assignments, which is to cut the cost of access to space by orders of magnitude—within 10 years to one-tenth of today's cost, then to one-hundredth within 25 years. We at the Marshall Space Flight Center have been given the lead to accomplish those ambitious goals, and we take it extremely seriously. It is the right thing to do." See MSFC Press Release 00-165, "Marshall Director Art Stephenson 'disappointed' by budget action on NASA Space Launch Initiative," 24 May 2000, NASA Historical Reference Collection.

14. Ibid.

15. NASA History Office, "Possibilities and Pitfalls of Government Offering Prizes for Technological Innovations," 27 April 1999, NASA Historical Reference Collection.

16. See Launius and McCurdy, *Imagining Space*, chap. 5.

17. Leonard David, "Riding Laser Beams to Space" (5 July 2000) at www.space. com.

18. John L. Chapman, *Atlas: The Story of a Missile* (New York: Harper and Brothers, 1960); Jacob Neufeld, *Ballistic Missiles in the United States Air Force, 1945–1960* (Washington, DC: Center for Air Force History, 1990); Thomas P. Hughes, *Rescuing Prometheus* (New York: Pantheon Books, 1998), 70–140.

19. Elie Abel, *The Missile Crisis* (Philadelphia: Lippincott, 1966); Michael H. Armacost, *The Politics of Weapons Innovation: The Thor-Jupiter Controversy* (New York: Columbia University Press, 1969); Baker, *Rocket*.

20. Isakowitz, Hopkins, and Hopkins, *International Reference Guide;* David K. Stumpf, *Titan II: A History of a Cold War Missile Program* (Fayetteville: University of Arkansas Press, 2000); Joseph T. Keeley, "The Titan Space Launch System," paper presented at Canaveral Council of Technical Societies 18th Space Congress, Cocoa Beach, FL, April 29–May 1, 1981, NASA Historical Reference Collection; Roger D. Launius, "Titan: Some Heavy Lifting Required," chap. 4 in *To Reach the High Frontier: A History of U.S. Launch Vehicles,* ed. Roger D. Launius and Dennis R. Jenkins (Lexington: University Press of Kentucky, forthcoming).

21. The ICBM technologies of the 1950s and 1960s provided an essential base on which to build an initial U.S. space launch capability at a time when only the Soviet Union had one. For instance, Europe, without an experience building ballistic missiles, was twenty years behind the U.S. and the USSR in space launch capability. Only when it successfully began launching the Ariane boosters in 1979 did it enter the Space Age in any serious way.

22. Interview with J. R. Thompson, NASA Deputy Administrator, 7 October 1999, Washington, D.C.

23. Vice President's Space Policy Advisory Board, "The Future of the U.S. Space Industrial Base: A Task Group Report," November 1992, ix, NASA Historical Reference Collection.

24. Richard P. Hallion and James O. Young, "Space Shuttle: Fulfillment of a Dream," Case VIII of *The Hypersonic Revolution: Case Studies in the History of Hypersonic Technology,* vol. 1, *From Max Valier to Project PRIME (1924–1967)* (Bolling AFB, Washington, DC: U.S. Air Force Histories and Museum Program, 1998), 957–62; Spiro T. Agnew, manager, *The Post- Apollo Space Program: Directions for the Future* (Washington DC: Space Task Group, September 1969), reprinted in John M. Logsdon, gen. ed., *Exploring the Unknown: Selected Documents in the History of the U.S. Civil Space Program,* vol. 1, *Organizing for Exploration* (Washington, DC: NASA-SP-4221, 1999), 270–74.

25. John M. Logsdon, "Getting NASA Unstuck," *Space Times: Magazine of the American Astronautical Society* 39 (September/October 2000): 23.

26. This was a powerful argument when made to the Europeans in 1971 and 1972 —thereby assuring space access on an American launcher—and prompted

them to sign up to a significant involvement in Shuttle development. Only when the United States revamped its offers of partnership did the European nations create the European Space Agency and embark on a launch vehicle of its own design, Ariane. See Roger D. Launius, "NASA, the Space Shuttle, and the Quest for Primacy in Space in an Era of Increasing International Competition," in *L'Ambition Technologique: Naissance d'Ariane,* ed. Emmanuel Chadeau (Paris: Institute d'Histoire de l'Industrie, 1995), 35–61.

27. Hans Mark, *The Space Station: A Personal Journey* (Durham: Duke University Press, 1987), 61–65; Heppenheimer, *Space Shuttle Decision,* 275–80; David M. Harland, *The Space Shuttle: Roles, Missions and Accomplishments* (Chichester, U.K.: Praxis Publishing, Ltd. 1998), 411–12.

28. Few individuals have yet discussed the competing priorities that the Shuttle was asked to fulfill. It seems more true as time passes, however, that the "one-size-fits-all" approach to technological challenges that the Shuttle was asked to solve was unfair to the launch vehicle, the people who made it fly, and the organization that built and launched it. This would not be the first time in American history when such had taken place. The Air Force had been forced in the 1960s to accept a combination fighter and bomber, the FB-111, when it recommended against it. That airplane proved a disaster from start to finish. The individuals operating the Space Shuttle soldiered on as best they could to fulfill all expectations, but the task was essentially impossible. See Michael F. Brown, *Flying Blind: The Politics of the U.S. Strategic Bomber Program* (Ithaca: Cornell University Press, 1992); David S. Sorenson, *The Politics of Strategic Aircraft Modernization* (Westport, CT: Praeger, 1995).

29. "NSDD-254," in John M. Logsdon, gen. ed., *Exploring the Unknown: Selected Documents in the History of the U.S. Civil Space Program,* vol. 4, *Accessing Space* (Washington, DC: NASA SP-4407, 1999), 4:382–85.

30. John M. Logsdon and Craig Reed, "Commercializing Space Transportation," ibid., 4:405–22.

31. "Commercial Space Launch Act Amendments of 1988," ibid., 4:458–65.

32. Isakowitz, Hopkins, and Hopkins, *International Reference Guide.*

33. Howard E. McCurdy, "The Cost of Space Flight," *Space Policy* 10 (November 1994): 277–89.

34. Isakowitz, Hopkins, and Hopkins, *International Reference Guide.*

35. NASA, *The Post-Apollo Space Program: A Report for the Space Task Group* (Washington, DC: National Aeronautics and Space Administration, September 1969), 6.

36. Roger D. Launius, "NASA and the Decision to Build the Space Shuttle, 1969–72," *Historian* 57 (Autumn 1994): 17–34; John M. Logsdon, "The Decision to Develop the Space Shuttle," *Space Policy* 2 (May 1986): 103–19; John M. Logsdon, "The Space Shuttle Decision: Technology and Political Choice," *Journal of Contemporary Business* 7 (1978): 13–30.

37. NASA, "Space Shuttle Economics Simplified," House Committee on Science

and Technology, Subcommittee on Space Science and Applications, *Operational Cost Estimates: Space Shuttle,* 94th Congress, 2nd session, 1976.

38. George M. Low to Dale D. Myers, "Space Shuttle Objectives," 27 January 1970, NASA Historical Reference Collection.

39. In January 1970, Thomas O. Paine, Richard Nixon's appointee as the NASA administrator, described a somber meeting with the president in which Nixon told him that both public opinion polls and political advisors indicated that the mood of the country suggested hard cuts in the space and defense programs. Memo by Thomas O. Paine, "Meeting with the President, January 22, 1970," NASA Historical Reference Collection; Caspar W. Weinberger interview by John M. Logsdon, 23 August 1977, NASA Historical Reference Collection.

40. Scott Pace, personal communication, 10 September 2000.

41. Dale D. Myers, "The Shuttle: A Balancing of Design and Politics," in *Issues in NASA Program and Project Management,* ed. Francis T. Hoban (Springfield, VA: National Technical Information Service, 1992), 43.

42. T. A. Heppenheimer, "Lost in Space: What Went Wrong with NASA?" *American Heritage* 43 (July 1992): 60–72; Alex Roland, "The Shuttle: Triumph or Turkey?" *Discover* (November 1985): 14–24; Roger A. Pielke and Radford Byerly, "The Space Shuttle Program: Performance versus Promise," in *Space Policy Alternatives,* ed. Radford Byerly (Boulder, CO: Westview Press, 1992), 226; NASA, "Space Shuttle Inflation History and Effects on the Agency Commitment Cost Estimates," 14 May 1979, revised 20 April 1981; "STS Non-Recurring Cost Estimates," 18 February 1981, NASA, Office of Space Flight, "Shuttle Average Cost per Flight: Based on the FY94 Budget to Congress," 1993, all in NASA Historical Reference Collection; Joseph W. Hamaker, "But What Will It Cost? The Evolution of NASA Cost Estimating," in *Issues in NASA Program and Project Management,* ed. Francis T. Hoban, NASA SP-6101, no.6 (Summer 1993): 9.

43. John M. Logsdon, "The Space Shuttle Program: A Policy Failure," *Science* 232 (30 May 1986): 1099–105; Roger D. Launius, *NASA: A History of the U.S. Civil Space Program* (Malabar, FL: Krieger, 1994), 114–15.

44. NASA Office of External Relations, Special Studies Division, "Access to Space: Issues," 13 January 1994, NASA Historical Reference Collection; Aerospace Corporation, "Future Spacelift Requirements Study," prepared under NASA contract no. F04701-93-C-0094, August 1997, NASA Historical Reference Collection; Robert S. Ryan, "Lessons and Challenges of Space Flight," n.d., NASA Historical Reference Collection.

45. The complexity of this business climate is explored in detail and with real ingenuity in John Newhouse, *The Sporty Game* (New York: Alfred A. Knopf, 1983); quote at p. 4.

46. S. Everett Gleason, "Discussion at the 329th Meeting of the National Security Council, Wednesday, July 3, 1957," 5 July 1957, 2, NSC Records, DDE Presidential Papers, Dwight D. Eisenhower Library, Abilene, KS.

47. Lewis M. Branscomb, "Toward a U.S. Technology Policy," *Issues in Science and Technology* 7 (Summer 1991): 50–55. See also Lewis M. Branscomb, ed., *Empowering Technology: Implementing a U.S. Strategy* (Cambridge: MIT Press, 1993); Lewis M. Branscomb and James H. Keller, eds., *Investing in Innovation: Creating a Research and Innovation Policy that Works* (Cambridge: MIT Press, 1999); Bruce L. R. Smith and Claude E. Barfield, eds., *Technology, R&D, and the Economy* (Washington, DC: Brookings Institution, 1996); David C. Mowery and Nathan Rosenberg, *Paths of Innovation: Technological Change in 20th-Century America* (New York: Cambridge University Press, 1998); David C. Mowery and Nathan Rosenberg, *Technology and the Pursuit of Economic Growth* (New York: Cambridge University Press, 1989); Nathan Rosenberg, *Exploring the Black Box: Technology, Economics, and History* (Cambridge: MIT Press, 1994).

48. Roland, *Model Research*, 1:4–25.

49. Roger D. Launius, "End of a Forty Year War: Demobilization in the West Coast Aerospace Industry After the Cold War," *Journal of the West* 36 (July 1997): 85–96.

50. Quoted in Lt. Col. Ellen M. Pawlikowski, "Surviving the Peace: Lessons Learned from the Aircraft Industry in the 1920s and 1930s" (master's thesis, Industrial College of the Armed Forces, National Defense University, Fort McNair, Washington, DC), 1.

51. Norman E. Bowie, *University-Business Partnerships: An Assessment* (Lanham, MD: Rowman & Littlefield, 1994), 19.

52. John A. Douglass, "A Certain Future: Sputnik, American Higher Education, and the Survival of a Nation," in Roger D. Launius, John M. Logsdon, and Robert W. Smith, eds., *Reconsidering Sputnik: Forty Years Since the Soviet Satellite* (Amsterdam: Harwood Academic, 2000), 327–63. See also Gary W. Matkin, *Technology Transfer and the University* (New York: Macmillan, 1990); Roger Geiger, "The Ambiguous Link: Private Industry and University Research," in William E. Becker and Darrell R. Lewis, eds., *The Economics of Higher Education* (Boston: Kluwer, 1992), 265–97.

53. See, for example, the Convention for the Establishment of a European Space Agency (CSE.CD [73] 19. rev.7: Paris, 30 May 1975). Article VII (I) (b) states: "The industrial policy which the Agency is to elaborate and apply by virtue of Article II (d) shall be designed in particular to: (b) improve the world-wide competitiveness of European industry by maintaining and developing space technology and by encouraging the rationalisation and development of an industrial structure appropriate to market requirements, making use in the first place of the existing industrial potential of all Member States."

54. Edward F. Denison, *Accounting for United States Economic Growth 1929–1969* (Washington, DC: Brookings Institution, 1974), 79.

55. Henry R. Hertzfeld, "Measuring Returns to Space Research and Development," in Joel S. Greenberg and Henry R. Hertzfeld, eds., *Space Economics*

(Washington, DC: American Institute of Aeronautics and Astronautics, 1992), 151–69.

56. "Economic Impact of Stimulated Technological Activity," Final Report, Midwest Research Institute, 15 October 1971, Contract No. NASW-2030; Michael K. Evans, "The Economic Impact of NASA R&D Spending," Chase Econometric Associates, Inc., Bala Cynwyd, PA, April 1976; "Economic Impact and Technological Progress of NASA Research and Development Expenditures," Midwest Research Institute, Kansas City, MO, for the National Academy of Public Administration, 20 September 1988; BDM, "Economic Return on Technology Investments Study: Final Report," 30 September 1994.

57. "NASA Report May Overstate the Economic Benefits of Research and Development Spending," Report of the Comptroller General of the United States, PAD-78-18, 18 October 1977, i–iii, NASA Historical Reference Collection; Hertzfeld, "Measuring Returns," 151–69.

58. Hertzfeld, "Measuring Returns," 166–67.

59. Richard C. Atkinson, "The Role of Research in the University of the Future" (paper presented at the United Nations University, Tokyo, Japan, November 4, 1997).

60. Jack Scarborough, "The Privatization of Expendable Launch Vehicles: Reconciliation of Conflicting Policy Objectives," *Policy Studies Review* 10 (1991): 12–30.

61. It should surprise no one that there were howls of protest inside the DOD, leading to numerous pre-*Challenger* debates over the need for a "mixed fleet" of ELVs and the Shuttle. At the time, these debates conflicted with national policy and found few advocates in the Reagan administration. Only after the *Challenger* accident did they emerge full-blown to become the official position of the government (Scott Pace, personal communication, 10 September 2000).

62. "Commercial Space Launch Act of 1984, Public Law 98-575," in John M. Logsdon, gen. ed., *Exploring the Unknown: Selected Documents in the History of the U.S. Civil Space Program*, vol. 4, *Accessing Space* (Washington, DC: NASA SP-4407, 1999), 4:431–40.

63. Space Launch Policy Working Group, "Report on Commercialization of U.S. Expendable Launch Vehicles," 13 April 1983, 3, NASA Historical Reference Collection.

64. W. D. Kay, "Space Policy Redefined: The Reagan Administration and the Commercialization of Space," *Business and Economic History* 27 (Fall 1998): 237–47; W. Henry Lambright and Dianne Rahm, "Ronald Reagan and Space Policy," *Policy Studies Journal* 17 (1989): 515–28; David J. Whalen, "NASA, USAF, and the Provisioning of Commercial Launch Services to Geosynchronous Orbit" (paper presented at symposium on "Developing U.S. Launch Capability: The Role of Civil-Military Cooperation," Washington, DC, November 5, 1999).

65. Several of these attempted private ventures are discussed in Michael A. G. Michaud, *Reaching for the High Frontier: The American Pro-Space Movement, 1972–1984* (New York: Praeger, 1986), 252–70.

66. Of course, Transpace had been seeking to expand its role in the launch for years. In 1983 the company filed a Section 301 trade complaint with the U.S. Trade Representatives (USTR) alleging unfair pricing practices for Ariane commercial launches. The Commercial Space Launch Act of 1982 had just created the licensing basis for commercial ELV firms, and Transspace used that vehicle in its complaint. The USTR decided not to pursue the complaint since the U.S. government was arguably engaging in "nonmarket pricing" itself with the Shuttle program (Scott Pace to author, 10 September 2000).

67. James A. Vedda, "Access is Job 1," *Space Times* 38 (November-December 1999): 3.

68. Tim Beardsley, "The Way to Go in Space," *Scientific American* (March 1999), special issue on "The Future of Space Exploration."

69. Craig R. Reed, "Factors Affecting U.S. Commercial Space Launch Industry Competitiveness," *Business and Economic History* 27 (Fall 1998): 222–36; Andrew J. Butrica, "Commercial Spaceports: Hitching Your Wagon to a VentureStar," *Space Times: Magazine of the American Astronautical Society* 37 (September/October 2000): 5–10.

70. Trevor C. Sorensen, AlliedSignal Technical Services Corp., "From the Earth to the Stars: The Future of Space Flight" (presentation at the University of Kansas, Lawrence, May 7, 1999); Andrew J. Butrica, "The Commercial Launch Industry, Reusable Space Vehicles, and Technological Change," *Business and Economic History* 27 (Fall 1998): 212–21.

71. Geoffrey V. Hughes, "The Iridium Effect," *Space Times: Magazine of the American Astronautical Society* 39 (March/April 2000): 23.

72. On the Space Shuttle as a launch vehicle, see Dennis R. Jenkins, *Space Shuttle: The History of Developing the National Space Transportation System* (Marceline, KS: Walsworth, 1996); Ray A. Williamson, "Developing the Space Shuttle," in Logsdon, ed., *Exploring the Unknown*, 4:161–91.

73. Stephanie A. Roy, "The Origin of the Smaller, Faster, Cheaper Approach in NASA's Solar System Exploration Program," *Space Policy* 14 (August 1998): 153–71; Tony Spear, "NASA FBC Task Final Report," March 2000, 1–2; DC-X Evaluation Team, "DC-X as a Demonstrator for SSTO Technologies" (briefing to NASA Administrator, March 1, 1994), 17, 31; NASA Office of Inspector General, "Review of National Aeronautics and Space Administration Cooperative Agreements With Large Commercial Firms," P&A-97-001, 22 August 1997, 4–5; all in NASA Historical Reference Collection.

74. Andrew J. Butrica, "The NASA-Industry Cooperative Agreement as a Tool for Reusable Launcher Technology Development" (paper presented at the Society for History in the Federal Government annual meeting, March 16, 2000, Washington, DC).

75. Scott Pace, personal communication, 10 September 2000.

76. This was the argument made to obtain approval for the Space Shuttle. See *The Post- Apollo Space Program: A Report for the Space Task Group* (Washington, DC: National Aeronautics and Space Administration, September 1969), 1, 6.

77. Fred Hiatt, "Space Plane Soars on Reagan's Support," *Washington Post,* 6 February 1986, A4; Roger Handberg and Joan Johnson-Freese, "If Darkness Falls: The Consequences of a United States No-Go on a Hypersonic Vehicle," *Space Flight* 32 (April 1990): 128–31; Linda R. Cohen, Susan A. Edelman, and Roger G. Noll, "The National Aerospace Plane: An American Technological Long Shot, Japanese Style," *American Economic Review* 81 (1991): 50–53; Roger Handberg and Joan Johnson-Freese, "Pursuing the Hypersonic Option Now More Than Ever," *Space Commerce* 1 (1991): 167–74.

78. Carl H. Builder, "The NASP as a Time Machine," RAND Internal Note, August 1989, copy in possession of author; Roger Handberg and Joan Johnson-Freese, "NASP as an American Orphan: Bureaucratic Politics and the Development of Hypersonic Flight," *Spaceflight* 33 (April 1991): 134–37; Larry E. Schweikart, "Hypersonic Hopes: Planning for NASP," *Air Power History* 41 (Spring 1994): 36–48; Larry E. Schweikart, "Managing a Revolutionary Technology, American Style: The National Aerospace Plane," *Essays in Business and Economic History* 12 (1994): 118–32; Larry E. Schweikart, "Command Innovation: Lessons from the National Aerospace Plane Program," in *Innovation and the Development of Flight,* ed. Roger D. Launius, ed. (College Station: Texas A&M University Press, 1999), 299–323.

79. These stages may well be viewed as hubris in future years. In the spirit of the 1960s, each new vehicle represents a major, dramatic advance over its predecessor. It is all very linear. Unfortunately, the advances of technological systems rarely are so simple. This lack of a steady evolutionary approach is based on a continuing assumption—which may be warranted—that access to space will continue to remain predominately a government activity. This becomes a significant, but perhaps unstated, policy assumption that affects how federal R&D dollars are allocated.

80. Frank Sietzen, "VentureStar Will Need Public Funding," *SpaceDaily Express,* 16 February 1998, NASA Historical Reference Collection.

81. Greg Easterbrook, "The Case Against NASA," *New Republic,* 8 July 1991, 18–24; Alex Roland, "Priorities in Space for the USA," *Space Policy* 3 (May 1987): 104–14; Alex Roland, "The Shuttle's Uncertain Future," *Final Frontier* (April 1988): 24–27.

82. James A. Vedda, "Long-term Visions for U.S. Space Policy," background paper prepared for the Subcommittee on National Security, International Affairs, and Criminal Justice of the House Committee on Government Reform and Oversight, May 1997.

83. Barbara A. Luxenberg, "Space Shuttle Issue Brief #IB73091," Library of Congress Congressional Research Service Major Issues System, 7 July 1981, NASA Historical Reference Collection; *Economic Analysis of New Space*

Transportation Systems: Executive Summary (Princeton, NJ: Mathematica, Inc., 1971); General Accounting Office, *Analysis of Cost Estimates for the Space Shuttle and Two Alternate Programs* (Washington, DC: GAO, 1973); William G. Holder and William D. Siuru Jr., "Some Thoughts on Reusable Launch Vehicles," *Air University Review* 22 (November-December 1970): 51–58; Office of Technology Assessment, *Reducing Launch Operations Costs: New Technologies and Practices* (Washington, DC: U.S. Congress, Office of Technology Assessment, 1988).

84. Stephen A. Book, "Inventory Requirements for Reusable Launch Vehicles," paper presented at Space Technology & Applications International Forum (STAIF-99), copy in possession of author.

85. T. A. Heppenheimer, "A Technological History of the Space Shuttle," August 2000, book manuscript at NASA History Office, Washington, DC.

86. Book, "Inventory Requirements," 13.

87. B. Peter Leonard and William A. Kisko, "Predicting Launch Vehicle Failure," *Aerospace America* (September 1989): 36–38, 46; Robert G. Bramscher, "A Survey of Launch Vehicle Failures," *Spaceflight* 22 (November-December 1980): 51–58.

88. Andrew E. Turner, "Aquarius: A Low-Cost, High-Risk, Existing Technology Launch Vehicle to Orbit Low-Cost Payloads," December 20, 1999, paper in possession of author.

89. Buzz Aldrin, "Evolution from Today's Space Shuttle to a Next Generation Infrastructure," paper presented in Paris, May 7, 1999, copy in possession of author.

90. I have discussed this at length in "Introduction: Patterns of Innovation in Aeronautical Technology," in *Innovation and the Development of Flight*, ed. Roger D. Launius (College Station: Texas A&M University Press, 1999), 3–18.

91. The complexity of nonlinearity in historical study has been discussed in its larger context in Bryan D. Palmer, *Descent into Discourse: The Reification of Language and the Writing of Social History* (Philadelphia: Temple University Press, 1990), 188–206; Brook Thomas, *The New Historicism, and Other Old-Fashioned Topics* (Princeton: Princeton University Press, 1991), 24–50; Peter Novick, *The Noble Dream: The "Objectivity Question" and the American Historical Profession* (New York: Cambridge University Press, 1988), 415–628.

92. John Briggs and F. David Peat, *Turbulent Mirror: An Illustrated Guide to Chaos Theory and the Science of Wholeness* (New York: Random House, 1989), 110.

93. Scott Pace, personal communication, 10 September 2000.

2   The Future of Space Commerce

Scott N. Pace

THE FIRST age of space development, characterized by the race to the moon and the first explorations of the solar system, is over.[1] NASA continues to send out planetary probes and is building the International Space Station, but commercial ventures are an increasingly important part of U.S. and global space activities. The main competitor to the United States in space is no longer the Soviet Union, but other market economies. The Cold War fault lines have given way to the forces of economic globalization, leading to both new risks and new opportunities from the proliferation of advanced technologies and information.[2]

The idea of space commerce has been a part of visions of future space activity for decades. In the 1940s, popular articles predicted communication satellites—sometimes as part of manned space stations. In the 1970s, popular articles and congressional hearings examined the creation of solar powered satellites that would beam electricity to Earth and lessen the use of fossil fuels.[3] There were predictions of space industrialization, with the Space Shuttle helping to build factories in space that would process new materials in the unique environment of space.[4]

Government spending has been crucial to the creation of space technologies and systems that are the basis of commercial growth.[5] However, the government has not had a good record at directing or even predicting that growth. Relative to flat or declining government budgets for space activities, commercial space revenues are continuing to grow.[6] These revenues are being driven by new and unexpected applications, not by the realization of formal plans and projections. Older aerospace industries, comfortable with government contracting, are being joined by and changed by information and market-driven companies.

As the saying goes, "the future is not what it used to be." In contrast to images of a new industrial revolution in space, there has been an information revolution on Earth that has extended into space. A new "skin" of communication satellites, navigation satellites, remote-sensing satellites, and environmental satellites has been deployed around the Earth. This skin is an integral part of the information infrastructure that is critical to the global economy. On the other hand, there are no hotels or factories, regular tourist flights, or even routine package delivery services in space. Commercial space industry is not characterized by a few large companies or government corporations, but instead by firms of many sizes and countries, some with government ownership and many more without.

The reality of space commerce has resulted in new and unique public policy conflicts. These conflicts arise from the possible military uses of space technology (known as "dual-use"), the spread of information made possible by space systems, government reliance on commercial space capabilities, and disputes over the use of space resources (e.g., orbital positions and spectrum). The most well-known conflicts are those involving export controls, such as accusations that Loral and Hughes provided information on restricted satellite technologies to China or that Boeing provided missile-related information to its Ukrainian partners in the Sea Launch vehicle program.[7] The global nature of space commerce, in which satellites and launch vehicles are matched up wherever the best deal can be found, is in conflict with other global efforts to stem the spread of technologies that can be used to deliver weapons of mass destruction.

Political and strategic interest in limiting the spread of "dangerous" technologies is not limited to physical objects such as satellite components and missiles. There are those who see information itself—whether bits, pictures, or derived reports—to be a potential weapon that should be controlled if it comes from space. This was demonstrated in the case of congressional restrictions on the allowable resolution of commercial satellite images taken of Israel.[8] In times of war or national crisis, U.S. commercial operating licenses for remote-sensing satellites allow for "shutter control" in which imaging over specific areas could be delayed or prohibited. A more subtle issue is how will the intellectual property rights of remote-sensing firms be protected internationally—whether by copyrights or by software-like use licenses.

In parallel to fears of undesirable access to space technology and information, there are policy concerns over increasing government reliance on commercial space capabilities. The United States already meets much of its unmanned space transportation needs by using commercial services, and it uses a commercial operator for the Space Shuttle. Increases in commercial launch activity are creating problems for shared facilities such as launch bases and government ranges. To date, commercial uses have paid only the marginal cost for using excess capacity on government launch facilities. However, since commercial launches now exceed government launches, some analysts have argued that commercial firms should pay the average cost of use plus some amount for capital maintenance. Not surprisingly, commercial firms resist paying for capabilities that were not and are not optimally designed for their needs.[9]

Use of commercial sources has the potential to lower costs in meeting government needs, but government agencies are concerned about the dependency on commercial industry that this creates. The Defense Department hopes to make greater use of commercial satellite communications such as the Globalstar network, as well as imagery from commercial remote-sensing satellites.[10] NASA is seeking to buy commercial data to support global change research and possibly to have a nongovernmental entity manage the International Space Station—in a partial analogy to the way the nonprofit Space Telescope Institute operates the *Hubble Space Telescope*.[11] When commercial firms perform functions previously provided by government agencies, this is more precisely termed *privatization* as opposed to *commercialization*. It remains to be seen how well this will work, and policy debates are continuing over how far it can be extended. Some questions are, Is there a need for the same institutional infrastructure as existed during the Apollo program? Could a space-oriented Defense Advanced Research Projects Agency (DARPA), which contracts for all research and development (R&D) and services, function just as well? What critical core skills need to be retained within NASA?

Finally, despite the physical vastness of outer space, there are conflicts over how to use its resources. These conflicts, in turn, have implications for the conduct and feasibility of commercial space activities. The International Telecommunications Union (ITU), for example, requires the coordination of satellites wanting to use specific geosynchronous orbital slots. Every two or three years, the ITU hosts a massive month-long international conference to negotiate the international allocation of radio spectrum. Particularly contentious issues involve spectrum for broadcast satellite services (BSS) in which countries seek to manage the television and radio broadcasts from space that can reach their citizens. The agreement of many more countries is required compared to ground-based fixed services such as traditional TV and radio stations.

Another area of potential conflict is the creation of space debris and how to manage or minimize it. Technical studies of space debris have been underway for many years, and voluntary practices by spacefaring nations have served to reduce the creation of it by, for example, placing satellites in higher "safe orbits" at their end of life and venting remaining on- board fuel to prevent future detonations.[12] Some believe these voluntary measures will be sufficient, while others advocate the creation of new legal requirements or even market-oriented approaches (e.g., deposit refunds for spent upper stages) to reduce space debris.[13] In addition to the potential costs of complying with new "environmental" regulations, commercial space firms are concerned that the regulations may not be uniform and may thus provide a cost advantage to competitors in other countries.

Ultimately, the growth of space commerce may lead to the private exploitation and use of nonterrestrial materials such as water at the southern lunar pole or volatiles from Earth-crossing asteroids. The 1967 Outer Space Treaty forbids claims to "celestial bodies" by sovereignty but is silent about private ownership. Thus, the legal regime is uncertain, and this—in addition to the obvious technical and financial challenges— could be a potential impediment to developing real property in space. The 1999 Third UN Conference on Space (UNISPACE III) adopted as part of its "Vienna Declaration" the statement that "as exploitation of outer space resources and those of celestial bodies becomes more likely, international law must also examine issues such as ownership and access."[14]

In the following sections, I will briefly highlight the key trends and policy challenges in the major sectors of space commerce today. While there is much good news in the health and strength of space commerce, there are also disturbing signs of vulnerability as a result of government failure to adapt to a rapidly changing environment.

Growth of Commercial Space Markets

Space commerce has grown dramatically in the last decade, driven by international communications and other information technologies. Global space activity has been estimated to have revenues of more than $100 billion in 1999. Worldwide employment is more than one million people and expanding.[15] Major sectors and annual revenues for this industry consist of:

- Infrastructure (e.g., satellites and launch vehicles, ground, and space facilities), $57.8 billion;
- Communications (e.g., fixed and mobile satellite services, and direct broadcast services), $37.4 billion;
- Space applications (e.g., remote sensing, geographic information systems, and satellite navigation applications), $6 billion;
- Support services (e.g., financial services, insurance, consulting, and publishing), $4 billion.[16]

Overall, space commerce is showing a compound annual growth rate of 9 percent. Sales of infrastructure are growing most slowly, while space telecommunications is the largest growth area. GPS and remote-sensing applications are much smaller today compared to telecommunications, but they are growing the most rapidly. After decades of predictions, direct broadcasting of television from space has reached global commercial acceptance, and direct broadcast radio services for developed and developing countries appear imminent.

The composition of space commerce is much different today than was predicted as recently as the mid-1980s. At that time, NASA was promoting the use of the Space Shuttle for commercial payloads and anticipating the need for new space-based facilities to support commercial enterprises. One notable forecast was done by the Center for Space Policy (CSP) in 1985. They predicted that in 2000 the major commercial space market segments and associated revenues would be:

- Communications, $15.3 billion;
- Materials processing in space (MPS), $17.9 billion;
- Remote sensing-$2.5 billion;
- Total commercial revenues of $51.3 billion dollars.[17]

Commercial activity was seen as being directly enabled by government support for on-orbit infrastructure and R&D, especially in materials processing. Criticized at the time for being overly optimistic, the CSP projection turned out to be conservative in toto. On the other hand, this projection is also notable for major misses. It was too optimistic on the prospects for materials processing in space, and it completely missed commercial applications of the Global Positioning System (GPS). Commercial remote sensing and mobile satellite communications were both identified, but the impact of rapidly changing information technology on both was underestimated.

Space commerce is even more market-driven today than the CSP projection anticipated. In part this is due to the size of commercial revenues but also because such commerce is less dependent on active support from government facilities. Materials processing, for example, was expected to rely on the use of space-based facilities such as human-tended platforms or a government space station. In contrast, the most government-reliant commercial space sectors today are GPS applications that exploit the same navigation signals needed by government users. The government does nothing special to enable commercial use except for maintaining and protecting a satellite system it already needs for national security and public safety purposes.

As might be expected, the character of the space industry is changing as commercial revenues outpace government funding. The percentage of space industry revenues that could be attributed to commercial activity was estimated at 64 percent for 1998. In 2002 this percentage was expected to be 75 percent according to the International Space Business Council. While governments are a major source of revenue, high industry growth rates are being driven by commercial activity. This is changing the relative mix of public and private revenue sources for virtually all space firms. Space commerce is being driven by information markets, not by government contracts for aerospace hardware; by agile responses to changing demands, not by fulfillment of long-term development plans. As a result, the needs of capital markets are felt much more keenly today than ever before; and commercial space ventures are sensitive to the needs of those markets for predictable government policies, transparent accounting, and the free flow of information necessary to manage investment risk.

Rather than a government-driven revolutionary development, the growth of space commerce has been a market-driven evolutionary one. Given the current cost of access to space, it is not surprising that the primary "cargo" being moved between Earth and space are weightless photons carrying bits of data. But these bits are part of a larger global information infrastructure composed of undersea and underground cables, microwave relays and cellular phone towers, and orbiting satellites. The space segment of the Global Information Infrastructure (GII) includes communication satellites in low-Earth and geosynchronous orbit, GPS satellites in medium-Earth orbits, and remote-sensing satellites in low-Earth polar orbits. More than ten years ago, President Reagan noted the implications of commercial space-based information technologies: "Linked by a network of satellites and fiber-optic cables, one individual with a desktop computer and a telephone commands resources unavailable to the largest governments just a few years ago. . . . Like a chrysalis, we're emerging from the economy of the Industrial Revolution."[18]

The implications of this growth affect all areas of space operations. For example, new mobile satellite communication services create demand for more space launches, which increases the ability to raise private capital for improving the performance and capacity of those launchers. Increasing commercial use of satellite navigation and remote-sensing data helps drive down the price of related equipment and services. On the other hand, these same space-based information systems can also be used by adversaries and thus create the need for military and diplomatic countermeasures.

The growth of space commerce has encouraged new ideas about how to move beyond the idea that space development should focus on public goods. There is wide agreement on the importance of reducing the cost of access to space and the value of multiple approaches (e.g., expendables, reusables, government research, and private prizes). If space transportation becomes inexpensive and reliable enough, new commercial markets will be enabled, leading to incentives for even better space transportation. Rather than *Apollo*-like efforts to create space infrastructure, there is an increasing appreciation of the power of private demand, such as space tourism. Even if space tourism does not occur for many years, the space segment of the GII is here to stay and will continue to evolve and attract investment.

Given the track record of previous predictions of commercial space activity, one can be skeptical with respect to predictions about specific markets but optimistic about the future of space commerce. Shuttle launch rates of 40–60 flights per year have not occurred, but there is now a strong international market in space launch services. Large geostationary antenna farms were never built, but fleets of small satellites seek to provide mobile communication services. Materials processing in space has yet to show a viable commercial product, but commercial GPS receivers are widely available as car navigation devices.

On the other hand, it is also possible to be deeply concerned about the future of space commerce based on recent trends. Among the danger signs are increasing rates of launch and satellite failures; delays in the development of next-generation, reusable launch vehicles (RLVs); poor space-related stock performances and major bankruptcies; and, for the United States, a decline in historical market shares. Some of these problems are the result of poor business plans and commercial quality-control problems—factors that can and should be punished by the market. Others, such as difficulties faced by almost all space ventures in raising private capital in the aftermath of the Iridium and ICO Global bankruptcies, are derivative of those problems. Most difficult to manage are dangers resulting from government policies such as the imposition of restrictive satellite export controls by the United States in 1999. In addition to crimping satellite exports to traditional markets, the new controls also restricted the flow of information needed by international satellite insurance firms, which in turn lowered the available worldwide insurance capacity for commercial satellite projects.

Past predictions about space industrialization assumed the need for government spending to build the necessary infrastructure. Even though such spending did not happen to a large degree, other commercial activities grew anyway. Threats to the future of space commerce are more deep-rooted than a series of individual failures and business model shortcomings. Space commerce is at risk, not from technology and markets alone (although Iridium is a cautionary tale[19]) but from government policies seeking to control the flow of space-related information and to tilt international competition in favor of "national champions." Today's space commerce depends on enlightened government policies supporting innovation and competition, and restrained shaping of the international environment for free and fair trade. As will be discussed, such actions are turning out to be more difficult to secure than is increased government spending.

Space Launch

It is a truism that access to space is necessary to all space commerce. The United States was the first country to promote and license commercial space launch operations as a result of the 1984 Commercial Space Launch Act. After the loss of the Space Shuttle *Challenger* in 1986, however, commercial payloads were taken off the Shuttle and became a market for commercial launch services.[20] This also resolved complaints from commercial providers that prices for shuttle launches had been so low as to constitute unfair competition. In the same period, the European launcher Ariane became increasingly competitive, gaining market share against U.S. launchers.[21]

As the Cold War was ending, launchers from "nonmarket" economies such as China, Russia, and later Ukraine came onto the market, seeking to compete for commercial payloads. The United States was concerned about the potential for market disruption from launch service providers who did not have the pricing discipline of market economies. As a result, a series of launch trade agreements were negotiated with China, Russia, and Ukraine that set limits on the number of commercial launches that could be conducted by vehicles from these countries and required that launches be priced on par with Western launch services.

The demand for commercial space launches strengthened in the 1990s as a result of new commercial ventures, particularly low-Earth orbit (LEO) constellations of communication satellites. In May 1999, the Federal Aviation Administration (FAA) estimated that, on average, 51 commercial space launches a year will occur worldwide through 2008, an increase of more than 40 percent from the 36 commercial launches conducted in 1998.[22] Overall, a total of 1,210 commercial payloads are projected to be deployed to geosynchronous (GSO) and nongeosynchronous (NGSO) orbits on 514 launches through 2008. The projected payload demand is dominated by the high number of LEO payloads expected to be launched for LEO communications constellations, which fluctuates considerably year to year.[23] Conservative estimates are that the United States will capture about 40 to 50 percent of available commercial payloads, which is about the same market share held over the past three years. (In 1998, U.S. launch providers conducted 17 of the world's 36 commercial launches for a 47 percent commercial market share.)[24]

Unfortunately, these projections may not pan out, due in large part to assumptions on the viability of LEO constellations providing mobile voice, data, and related communication services. During the 1990s fiber optic, cellular, and wireless communication networks expanded worldwide at a rapid rate. In addition to providing expanded coverage, this growth also helped drive down the costs of equipment and services compared to satellites. There still may be a viable market for services from LEO constellations, but the demand for launch services will likely decrease as a result of ground-based alternatives. Lower launch demand, in turn, ripples back into the business justification for developing new vehicles or even improvements to existing vehicles. There is already an excess number of launchers in comparison to expected demand, and the situation will worsen as new foreign vehicles come onto the market.

The U.S. government has historically funded the development of new launch vehicles but is having increasing difficulty doing so. This has led some to argue that commercial industry should have the lead for developing new vehicles, perhaps with government support in the form of R&D and future contracts for launch services. Developing new launch vehicles is very capital intensive, however, and uncertain demand directly affects the amount of commercial funding that can be raised. Joint government-industry investments are possible in existing expendable launch vehicles if industry is able to share in profits from savings. More advanced systems, such as single-stage-to-orbit (SSTO) vehicles, are likely to remain a government activity. Private operators might be attracted if there were a large, stable government market such as providing routine logistics support to the International Space Station.

A related problem for government funding is range modernization. The United States built space launch ranges on the East and West Coasts to support military and civil missions during the Cold War. Commercial launch providers have had access to the ranges on a "marginal cost" basis; that is, they pay only for the direct costs of using the facilities. This made sense when commercial launches were in the minority compared to government launches, but today commercial launches are in the majority. Unfortunately, the launch base infrastructure and range systems are showing signs of deterioration. While the U.S. Air Force has been modernizing these facilities, it has had difficulty sustaining sufficient funding levels beyond that needed to support the Department of Defense (DOD) and NASA requirements. As the number of commercial launches continues to increase, the infrastructure will be increasingly stressed, raising issues of roles, responsibilities, and funding between the private sector and the U.S. government.

Adding to the problems of uncertain demand and limited government funding is competition for launch contracts from foreign government-supported launchers. The strongest competition comes from Europe's Arianespace, which conducts launches of the *Ariane 4* and *Ariane 5* launch vehicles from the Guyana Space Center in Kourou, French Guyana. As part of a strategy to maintain their dominant market position, the French government and the European Space Agency (ESA) offer Arianespace a mix of government supports and risk-sharing arrangements that include launch vehicle technology and development, launch infrastructure development and maintenance, and range and payload processing services. Ariane vehicle developments are funded entirely by the French and other European governments before being turned over to Arianespace for commercial operation. Funding for Kourou is approximately $150 million annually, of which ESA pays two-thirds and Centre National d'Etudes Spatiales (CNES), the French space agency, pays one-third.[25]

Perhaps the most important aspect of the relationship between Arianespace and the French government is that they act as a team in a seamless manner to secure customers. Arianespace is a consortium of fifty-three European shareholders including forty-one manufacturers from twelve countries, eleven banks, and the French government through its space agency, CNES. French participation in Arianespace amounts to more than 55 percent, with Germany's participation second at 18.6 percent.[26] CNES is a member of ESA and manages launch vehicle development on behalf of ESA. Several of the French companies that are shareholders of Arianespace are also partially owned by the French government.

Next to Europe, launch vehicles from the former Soviet Union are the most serious competitors for commercial launch services. Since the breakup of the Soviet Union in 1991, the Russian economy has struggled as it attempts to adapt to market principles. However, the cost of labor and materials used in the construction of launch vehicles remains far below Western market levels even today, although these costs have risen gradually over the past decade. In 1993 the United States and Russia signed a commercial space launch trade agreement allowing Russian launch providers to allocate commercial launches on the worldwide market. Since the agreement was signed, Russia has conducted commercial launches on several launch vehicles including *Proton, Soyuz, Cosmos,* and *Start.* A similar agreement was signed with Ukraine allowing the use of the former Soviet *Zenit* and *Cyclone* launch vehicles.

A number of international joint ventures have been formed to market launch vehicles from the former Soviet Union. In 1993 Lockheed-Martin formed a joint venture with Russia's Khrunichev and RSC Energia to conduct launches of the *Proton* launch vehicle. As of this writing, the *Proton* has had twenty-one commercial launches since its first in 1996, representing a major presence in the commercial launch services market. In 1995 Boeing formed the Sea Launch joint venture with Russia's Energia, Ukraine's Yuzhnoye, and Norway's Kvaerner to develop and launch Yuzhnoye's *Zenit* with Energia's Block-DM upper stage from a sea-based platform in the Pacific Ocean. Sea Launch's first launch, of a satellite simulator, was successfully conducted in March 1999. In 1996, France's Arianespace and Aerospatiale formed the Starsem joint venture with the Russian Aviation and Space Agency (RKA) and Russia's Samara Space Center to market the *Soyuz* launch vehicle. Starsem conducted its first three commercial launches in early 1999.[27]

The most government-dominated "commercial" launch services are those provided by China. The Chinese government owns and operates all launch site infrastructure, including the facilities for launch vehicle processing, payload processing, launch operations, and range control.

The launch vehicles are designed and built by the government through the China Academy of Launch Vehicle Technology and other government institutes. While China benefits from the same nonmarket economic factors as does Russia, the poor reliability of Chinese launch vehicles has been a major factor in preventing China from becoming a major commercial launch provider.

The 1996 National Space Policy calls for transitioning to a free and fair trade environment for space launch services that does not use quotas as found in launch service trade agreements with China, Russia, and Ukraine.[28] It would seem politically unrealistic to simply drop quotas entirely, given concerns with missile proliferation by China and Russia in particular. An alternative approach would be to develop a comprehensive trade agreement that would define "rules of the road" for space launch services. If a launch provider could meet certain requirements for market-based competition, then no quotas should be applied. The difficult issue would be agreeing on the types of allowable government supports. Research into new technologies would likely be more acceptable than operating subsidies, but there are many variants in between that would make for complex negotiations.

Commercial space launch services face severe challenges that will require serious attention from senior government policymakers. Public funding will be needed to develop new, lower-cost launch technologies—even if commercial firms have the leading role in actually operating new launch systems. Public-private cooperation will be needed to maintain and modernize space launch facilities. Finally, government leadership will be necessary to craft an international trade environment to foster market-based competition among launch vehicles from countries with vastly different degrees of government involvement.[29]

Satellite Communications

Communication satellites were the first commercial space success and are today the largest single source of commercial revenue in the space industry. The total revenue generated by the manufacture of satellites in 1998 was about $9.6 billion, of which communication satellites represented slightly over 60 percent ($5.75 billion) of the total.[30] This revenue comes not only from the sale of satellites themselves but from sales of ground stations and transponder time as well. These sales in turn stimulate the purchase of launch services, insurance, and related services. Thus, the health of the commercial satellite or "comsat" sector is central to the health of many other space businesses.

The most common type of communications satellites for decades has been voice and data services via geosynchronous (GSO) orbit. As fiber optic cables spread around the world in the 1980s and 1990s, becoming more price-competitive with satellites, new satellite systems have been proposed to serve users that cable cannot. Such users are typically mobile and/or are located in remote, low-density population areas that are not economical to serve by fixed ground infrastructure. These new systems can be grouped into three general categories:

- "Big LEO" systems in the 1–2 GHz range that provide voice and data communications, especially mobile telephone service (e.g., Iridium, Globalstar);
- "Little LEO" systems operating below 1 GHz and providing data communications such as e-mail, two-way paging, and messaging to remote locations (e.g., Orbcomm, Starsys);
- "Broadband LEO" systems that provide high-speed data services such as videoconferencing and high-end Internet access, using primarily the Ka-Band (e.g., Teledesic, Skybridge).

A relatively new service, but one that has been discussed for decades, is Direct Broadcast Satellites (DBS). In 1999 DBS added millions of subscribers for commercial services such as DirectTV and millions of homes throughout the world receive satellite TV broadcasts from legal (and illegal) receivers. Another emerging system is Direct Audio Broadcast (DAB), in which numerous digital radio channels are broadcast to receivers on the ground. Services such as Sirius Satellite Radio (formerly CD-Radio) and XM Satellite Radio are targeting affluent markets in order to provide nationwide radio programs such as commercial-free music, talk shows, and news. Stereo manufacturers such as Alpine, Clarion, and Panasonic will offer after-market satellite receivers. Other services, such as Worldspace, seek to serve poor developing countries by offering government-supported education as well as commercial entertainment services through low-cost radio receivers.

The year 1999 was a rough one for mobile satellite services (MSS) due to low demand for the large phones and costly service compared to ground-based wireless cellular systems. Globalstar began providing service in the United States in January 2000, and it remains to be seen how the market will respond compared to Iridium. On one hand, Globalstar is simpler and more closely tied into local telephone services, and it provides coverage in areas cellular services do not reach. On the other hand, it is not clear that the high development and operating costs of any

Big LEO system can be recovered in competition with ground-based systems, even with less coverage. Penetration rates of MSS into cellular and Personal Communications Service (PCS) markets are typically estimated at 1–1.5 percent, which means the service is largely a niche feature.[31] Advocates point to countries such as China, Vietnam, and Pakistan who need the "instant infrastructure" of satellites without taking the time and expense of building a ground infrastructure. That may be true, but it is not clear that such countries represent enough of an addressable market to justify a commercial investment.

Broadband LEO systems have similar problems in competing with ground systems, with satellite service often being oversized for rural areas and undersized for urban areas. Looking further ahead, companies such as SkyCache, iBeam Broadcasting, and Edgix propose to use satellites to distribute Internet content and streaming media, bypassing congestion on major Internet backbone lines. Again, these ideas will face competition from digital subscriber lines (DSL) and cable modems for delivering broadband access to fixed sites. The most attractive markets—North America, Europe, and Japan—will already have many alternatives, but success in niche markets may be possible. Efforts by Craig McCaw to combine Iridium, ICO Global, and Teledesic indicate that the market for new satellite services is being fundamentally restructured.

The current problems experienced by new mobile satellite services point to even more serious problems with the traditional GEO communications. In the longer term, the GEO comsat market for fixed services appears fundamentally threatened by fiber. Areas where this is not the case tend to be niche markets such as island chains (e.g., Indonesia) or remote, thinly populated areas (e.g., Russian Far East, parts of interior Africa). The rising rates of data transfer on global information infrastructure are so large that, in comparison, voice traffic will soon be "free" and bandwidth will be priced as a commodity, not a scarce resource. As a result, the satellite industry is mounting several business responses. Major satellite builders such as Hughes are expanding their offerings of satellites to serve mobile users (e.g., Thuraya). At the same time, these manufacturers are looking to enter the services market, which promises higher margins than the increasingly commodified hardware market. The Lockheed effort to purchase COMSAT is an example of service market entry by acquisition.[32] The Hughes sale of its satellite business to Boeing is an example of shedding a core capability to focus on new service businesses.

Political considerations have been part of communication satellite policy and regulation since the first launches. Intelsat was created in part to counter the spread of Soviet propaganda to developing countries. Arguably, one of its Cold War high points was the broadcast of the first U.S. lunar landing to almost every country on Earth. Today's political considerations are more difficult, if less lofty. Separately developed technologies such as telephones, TV, and the Internet are converging across many different transmission media, from satellites and cellular networks to fiber optic cable and even traditional copper wires. Regulatory systems have had difficulty keeping up with the rapid "convergence" of technologies, given the very different institutional histories of each. The cultures of regulated monopoly (cable TV), privatized competition (telephone), and decentralized consensus (Internet) are not easy to bridge.

Not surprisingly, as satellite communications face new technical and market challenges, they also face novel regulatory challenges. The protected monopolies of Intelsat and Inmarsat are being privatized, and companies like PanAmsat have been competing with Intelsat for years. At the same time, new services such as DAB face resistance from traditional license holders as represented by the National Association of Broadcasters and the Internet.[33] Exports of satellites have been held up pending licenses from the State Department, which is required to treat them as "munitions" in light of concerns that sensitive technology was flowing overseas. Export license delays not only affect the final sale of the satellites themselves but also hinder technical discussions with potential customers and insurance firms. This in turn gives competitive advantages to foreign firms that do not have such regulatory burdens.

However, the most difficult regulatory challenges are based on access to the basic "real estate" of satellite communications-radio spectrum. The International Telecommunications Union (ITU) is the forum for decisions on global allocations of radio spectrum and geosynchronous orbital slots. The growth of satellite communications, especially proposals for new constellations of nongeosynchronous satellites, has placed great strains on the multilateral processes of the ITU. Foremost is the problem of spectrum crowding, with more satellites seeking use of the same geostationary slots and frequencies suitable for satellite communications. The creation of global networks makes the problem more severe as countries around the world have to agree on the necessary spectrum allocations versus local networks that are provided in only one country or region and thus require less coordination.

The competitive pressures for spectrum at the ITU has led to firms' filing applications for spectrum for which they may or may not be able to get financing and final regulatory approval. Nonetheless, these "paper satellites" are part of the internal coordination process and can delay actual decisions. Further complexity is created when new systems seek to "share" spectrum already allocated to existing services by means of complex arguments about geographic separations and power flux density limits. This is the case, for example, with the proposed French LEO constellation Skybridge, which seeks to use spectrum now allocated for GEO satellites such as those used by Intelsat. In other cases, sharing between dissimilar services, such as mobile satellite communications and GPS, is shown to be infeasible only after years of international study. The timelines of the ITU spectrum process are vastly longer than the product cycles of current information technologies.

The future growth of satellite communications is at risk from competing technologies and existing regulatory institutions. The declining costs of fiber and terrestrial wireless systems are challenging both traditional (e.g., GEO) and new (e.g., LEO) satellite services. There is increasing competition for spectrum from the public and private sectors and regulatory barriers to the convergence across satellites, cable, and wireless media. Policymakers are challenged domestically in balancing security concerns with international competitiveness in export controls, and internationally in balancing safety and security objectives with commercial pressures to share or use spectrum needed by government systems.

Global Positioning System

The U.S. Department of Defense operates a constellation of twenty-four satellites in twelve-hour orbits that transmit precise time signals. Receivers in view of multiple satellites can use knowledge of the signals to calculate their positions and velocities anywhere in the world. These satellites make up the space segment of the Global Positioning System (GPS). The most precise signals, or P-Code, are reserved for U.S. military and other authorized users (e.g., allied militaries) by encryption key. A less precise set of signals, the C/A code, can be used by anyone. The continuous, free, global availability of these latter signals has led to hundreds of applications for precise navigation, positioning, and timing.

GPS is a crucial utility for U.S. transportation infrastructure, global air traffic control networks, and advanced high-speed communications, especially in mobile applications when precise timing and location are needed. The commercial GPS equipment industry began with land survey services in the mid-1980s when only a few GPS satellites were operating. The industry has grown and is growing rapidly, with billions of dollars in equipment sales. Civilian and commercial sales are outstripping defense procurement of ground equipment; and the user equipment industry is being driven by commercial competition in electronics packaging, manufacturing, and software technology. Japan is the second largest manufacturer of GPS systems after the United States.[34] The only comparable foreign system is the Russian GLONASS, but political instability and poor satellite reliability have hindered its international acceptance.

The Clinton administration issued a comprehensive GPS policy statement in March 1996. In defining specific roles for agencies such as the Departments of Defense, Transportation, and State, the policy seeks to promote GPS as a global standard, maintain the military advantages of GPS, and enable U.S. firms to benefit from growing commercial markets. There are American and international proposals to augment GPS signals for aviation and maritime applications by installing additional beacons on the ground or in space to provide signal integrity monitoring and differential corrections for even greater accuracy than the P-Code signal (i.e., less than one meter). In fact, some commercial firms broadcast encrypted differential corrections and charge a fee for access to the encryption key in a manner reminiscent of cable television. The FAA, the U.S. Coast Guard, the U.S. Army Corps of Engineers, and the Department of the Interior are all either creating or studying their own systems for providing differential GPS (DGPS) services for public safety purposes.

While GPS provides many economic benefits to the world, potential providers of mobile satellite services (MSS) covet the spectrum it uses. At the 1997 session of the World Radiocommunications Conference (WRC), where international spectrum allocation decisions are made, a coalition of European and Asian spectrum authorities advanced a proposal that would have allowed MSS to operate in a portion of the GPS band. This proposal was opposed by the United States as an interference threat to GPS signals and a threat to the use of GPS for safety of life services (e.g., international aviation and maritime navigation). The proposal was deferred to study only after a major U.S. diplomatic effort involving the highest civilian and military levels. GPS came under attack, not in a military sense, but as part of the intense international competition for spectrum in which billions of dollars are routinely at stake. The United States cannot assume that its current spectrum allocations will always be available because it does not have a veto over international spectrum decisions such as those made at WRC-97.

As a result of extensive educational outreach efforts and technical studies showing the harm that would result from overlaying powerful MSS signals on the relatively low-power GPS signals, an international consensus grew for protecting spectrum used by GPS. This consensus was reflected in the final acts of the 2000 WRC held in Istanbul in May 2000. A major development since 1997 was the decision by the European Commission to pursue studies of building its own satellite navigation system, called Galileo. In addition to an open, free service like GPS, the European concept envisions two levels of controlled-access services for commercial and security-related applications.[35] This should provide continuing incentives for U.S.-European cooperation in protecting the spectrum needed by GPS, Galileo, and GLONASS.

The Galileo program will likely create difficult trade and security issues that will have to be resolved in direct discussions between the United States and Europe. The United States sees GPS and related augmentations as being capable of meeting user needs. Europe believes that it needs its own system to ensure independence from the United States and secure economic benefits from space-based positioning, navigation, and timing. This last point has been the subject of some debate in that "the money is on the ground, not in space." That is, commercial revenues come from sales of ground equipment, not from the satellites themselves or services.

The United States is committed to providing GPS signals free of charge, and it is difficult to see why commercial customers would pay for a Galileo signal unless it provided some unique value-added feature. Doubts about the viability of "public-private partnerships" for Galileo have fed U.S. concerns that Europe may seek to mandate use of Galileo in Europe, for example, for air traffic management or vehicle navigation. Not surprisingly, this would create trade frictions with the United States. Similarly, any requirements for European militaries to use Galileo in preference to GPS will create interoperability problems within NATO. It is certainly possible that the addition of Galileo signals would benefit current GPS users. On the other hand, conflicts over GPS interoperability and regulatory requirements might slow the market growth of GPS equipment sales and services.

The United States is adding two additional civil signals to GPS to provide greater accuracy for aviation and other users. These signals will be added to future GPS satellites as part of military modernization efforts (e.g., adding new secure signals, increased power).[36] Unfortunately, the 106th Congress chose not to fund the civil portion of GPS modernization but did fund most, if not all, of the military portion. As a result, the DOD is moving to add at least one civil signal while proceeding with military modernization and delaying the next generation of GPS satellites. Civil GPS augmentations have also not faired well in Congress. The FAA's Wide Area Augmentation System (WAAS) has been delayed and funding cut. As a result, there may be an opportunity for privatized WAAS, or regional space-based GPS augmentation systems such as proposed by Lockheed and Boeing. Careful coordination with GPS will be needed as well as clear spectrum that is not shared or subject to interference.

The United States is in a strong competitive position with respect to GPS, but its future may be at risk as a result of decisions by U.S. and foreign governments. Decisions at the 2000 WRC to protect current GPS spectrum and allow for new signals required complex technical and political negotiations. Future decisions may be needed to address how to best protect GPS signals from unintentional interference by services in nearby bands, such as mobile satellite phones or ultrawide band radars.[37] Funding for GPS modernization, especially new civil signals, will enable more accurate, more rapid navigation—for example, submeter accuracy position fixes in real time. Such improvements will help promote greater international acceptance of GPS as it evolves to meet user needs. Finally, U.S. and European policymakers will face multiple technical, trade, and security questions as the Galileo program proceeds.

Remote Sensing

Space-based remote sensing for both surveillance and reconnaissance activities had its U.S. beginnings with government aircraft, balloons, and even interplanetary probes.[38] Today the most important factors driving space-based remote sensing are the simultaneous decline in support for traditional Cold War missions and the growing prospects for commercialization. The passage of the Land Remote Sensing Policy Act of 1992 and the release of presidential guidance on operating licenses for private remote-sensing systems on March 10, 1994, have encouraged several U.S. companies to enter the competition for remote-sensing markets.[39] This is a competition to provide remote-sensing services, but not to export satellites and especially not to export the underlying technology that remains subject to the restrictive export controls applied to munitions.

The ill-fated effort to privatize the Landsat program in the 1980s caused many to believe that the remote-sensing market as a whole could not be commercially profitable. This led to calls for government support for civil remote sensing as a public good.[40] In the late 1980s, technical advances by DOD and the Department of Energy (DOE) opened up the prospect of smaller, lighter, more selective, and less expensive remote-sensing systems. At the same time, computer costs were dropping rapidly, and the market for geographic information systems was growing rapidly. With the costs of entry dropping and new markets for specialized remote-sensing data appearing, the potential for truly commercial remote-sensing systems brightened. This led the Department of Commerce (DOC), which was responsible for Landsat and other forms of private remote sensing, to support streamlining the licensing process. As a result, several firms received licenses and were able to raise private capital. These ranged from small firms, such as WorldView Imaging (later EarthWatch), which received the first operating license since Landsat; to medium-sized space firms, such as Orbital Sciences; and large defense contractors with a long heritage of military remote sensing, such as Lockheed (now as Space Imaging).

The launch of the first high-resolution commercial system, *Quick-Bird-1,* on a Russian *Start-1* booster, was successful, but the satellite subsequently failed on-orbit. Another high-resolution satellite, *Ikonos-1,* was lost due to a failure of its Lockheed *Athena 2* booster. With the successful launch of a duplicate *Ikonos* satellite in 1999, the first commercial 1-meter resolution imagery became available on the market. Images of cities such as Washington, London, and Beijing are now available on public web sites as well as images of North Korean missile launch sites. While national security uses for such imagery are obvious, the growing use of geographic information systems (GIS) has stimulated demand for updated remote-sensing images to serve a wide variety of civil government, nonprofit, academic, and commercial purposes. Global revenues for raw and processed data have been estimated at about $600 million in 1999, not including value-added information products and services.[41] Satellite firms need to "move down the food chain" into value-added applications and acquire strategic allies in applications. Sales of raw data alone are not sufficient to justify the costs of building and operating remote-sensing satellites.

Competitors to space-based imagery have not been idle while commercial satellites were developed. Airborne remote sensing has become increasingly sophisticated with the use of digital cameras, stabilized platforms, and GPS-based geo-location (that can eliminate the need for ground control points). Airborne systems can respond rapidly to cover small areas, while satellites provide repeatable coverage of wide areas. The supply of airborne imagery has grown greatly in the last decade, aided by the same information technologies that have stimulated use of satellite imagery. As a result, the remote-sensing and GIS markets in general are not dependent on satellites, but satellite imagery will require these broader commercial markets to be successful.

As with other markets for information technology and services, the market for remote sensing is a complex and evolving one. Initial buyers are, not surprisingly, government agencies that are already comfortable with using remote sensing and that can afford to pay premium prices for unique data. The largest government markets are for national security and environmental management and research.[42] As remote-sensing data become integrated into commercial GIS applications, businesses are using more remote-sensing data—and are willing to pay based on productivity benefits. The large consumer market is largely untapped at present because prices have not yet fallen to a point where remotely sensed data is affordable, save as a form of wall art. In addition, the manipulation and management of remotely sensed data is a difficult skill that requires professional training.

A natural result of evolving remote-sensing markets is that customers will become indifferent to the source or the data, whether from air or space-based platforms or from foreign or domestic sources, but will care about price, quality, reliability, and ease of use. Data, like desktop computers, will increasingly become a commodity, with consequent pressure on achievable profit margins. One commercial response will be to offer new and different sources of data such as radar and hyperspectral imagery in addition to high-resolution panchromatic imagery. This is in fact happening, with commercial license applications having already been submitted for these more technically advanced forms of space-based remote sensing. Another response will be to expand into higher-margin services where specialized skills and customer knowledge can be exploited in concert with processed data. A critical need in order for either response to succeed is agreement on standards, definitions, and interface protocols to enable the integrated use of data from widely varying sources.

The excitement of seeing high-resolution commercial imagery on the market, however, can mask a number of underlying threats to its future. The markets for commercial remote sensing are certainly real and, like communications, will survive any number of failures by space-based ventures. An important challenge, however, is whether firms competing to put up space systems will be able to make the cultural transition from aerospace companies to information companies. It has been a truism for commercial remote-sensing firms to stress that they see themselves in the information business (with consequently higher price-to-earnings multiples on future stock prices) and not aerospace. Such statements have not yet been matched with actions in developing new applications and attracting users that are comparable to the understandably high levels of effort involved in putting the satellites in orbit. Even supportive efforts by government agencies to buy data, not information products, can be counterproductive in reinforcing aerospace industry habits that focus on building hardware.

Government policy changes have been crucial in creating a stable environment in which commercial remote sensing could emerge. U.S. policy, as reflected in presidential decisions and law, has been stable at the highest levels, but its implementation has been confusing and inconsistent. Eight years after the passage of the 1992 Land Remote Sensing Policy Act, the government finally issued an interim final rule on implementing regulations.[43] This delay was not the result of inattention, but rather of intense interagency conflicts between the Departments of Defense, State, and Commerce and the intelligence community on how to protect national security interests while fostering the growth of commercial industry. These policy differences extend to different interest groups within agencies as well. For example, there are tensions in the Department of Defense between the acquisition, policy, and operational communities. The acquisition branches are interested in possible cost saving from using commercial data and products; the operators are looking for any new tool that will give them a military advantage; and the policy offices are concerned with retaining influence over long-term political-military developments in a world where space-based remote sensing is widely available.

New commercial possibilities, such as radar and hyperspectral data have come along before the government had adjusted to the reality of high-resolution imagery. As a result, there has been uncertainty and conflict over whether and how to license these new types of systems. Industry efforts to establish international financing and distribution arrangements have been seen as deeply threatening to government officers used to having control over high-quality space imagery. On the other hand, proposed government-to-government partnerships in sharing government remote-sensing data have been seen by industry as hostile competition, intended to create an international monopoly in space-based remote sensing. Complaints from Israel about potential imaging by hostile neighbors led to restrictions on the resolution levels allowed over that country. This, in turn, has led other countries such as India and France to consider seeking similar limits. After championing the virtues of openness and transparency during the Cold War, the United States now finds itself under pressure to limit commercial activities that enhance global transparency.

The United States enjoyed a major technical lead in remote sensing as a result of prior government investment.[44] It adapted quickly at the end of the Cold War to remove policy barriers to new opportunities in commercial remote sensing. It has then arguably wasted several years in internal bureaucratic debates, giving uncertain signals to U.S. industry and allowing other countries to expand and enhance their government-funded programs in order to compete commercially. In particular, disputes over export controls for satellites have affected remote sensing. For example, temporary licenses for airborne remote-sensing platforms traveling overseas have been delayed where they were once routinely granted. In other cases, commercial firms have been denied export license for ground equipment similar to that already provided by the U.S. government. Some export control officers have tried to restrict environmental data about the Earth gathered from space on international science programs; others have tried to extend technology controls to cover information produced by unclassified, privately owned systems. The misuse of export controls is not only deplorable for its impact on constitutional rights and freedom of information, but it also creates a chilling effect on private-sector investment in direct contradiction to the intent of the president and Congress.

The benefits of remote-sensing applications are becoming more widely appreciated, while the future of commercial space-based remote sensing remains fragile. This commercial sector lacks a large, traditional customer base as is the case for satellite communications. It also lacks a secure base of government support for its space systems as is the case for GPS. Space-based remote sensing comes out of an aerospace industry culture, but it is not likely to be viable without adapting the flexible, open, rapid innovation cultures of information industries. The attractions of being a safe government contractor can be a strong incentive not to risk change. At the same time, inconsistent policy implementation in the United States, especially with regard to export and operating licenses, is raising the perceptions of political risk in this sector. Finally, the United States has not done much internationally to advance its traditional support for the free flow of information and to promote greater global transparency by private means. If commercial firms vanish, the United States will not see the end of remote sensing from space but will be faced with a market dominated by quasi-government and government-owned firms based overseas.

Space Commerce at Risk

Compared to traditional technical, market, and financial risks, political risks are typically the most difficult to manage for commercial ventures. Space commerce is based on many technologies that were first developed during the Cold War and are now being used to compete in a global economy. The dual-use heritage of these technologies leads to contentious policy debates over how to integrate national security and economic interests. These debates create uncertainty and risks for private investors and make raising private capital more difficult for space ventures as compared to other areas of the economy. An understanding of the interplay of advanced dual-use technologies, policy debates, and private financial markets is necessary to understanding space commerce and why government policy decisions pose the greatest risk to its future growth.

The momentum begun in the 1980s to explicitly encourage commercial space carried through the end of the Cold War into the early 1990s. The Clinton administration continued many procommercial positions and made notable advances in areas such as remote sensing and GPS. However, the long arc of procommercial space policies begun under Reagan and his successor, George H. W. Bush, has stalled and may have ended.

• While quotas remain on launches from Russia and China, the United States is barring transfers of commercial satellite data to NATO allies;

• While GPS is an increasingly vital part of global information infrastructure, its spectrum is threatened by domestic and international commercial pressures for reallocation;

• Commercial remote sensing is facing uncertain government regulatory decisions affecting current and proposed space systems;

• Satellite communications are facing international regulatory delays in providing truly global services while competition from ground-based alternatives is increasing.

Policy debates over space commerce reflect deep conflicts between public and private sector interests. In some cases, the information requirements for international finance and insurance are in conflict with technology export control regulations. In other cases, the global marketing of space-based communications, navigation, and remote-sensing capabilities is seen to be undermining the control of information previously held only by governments. In effect, U.S. companies are at times discouraged or even barred from offering advanced capabilities or accessing foreign markets, while at the same time, domestic markets alone are insufficient to justify the investments needed for new space systems. As a result, space industries seek government supports that are resisted by government agencies faced with tight budgets of their own.

This is not to say that the U.S. government and its agencies are opposed to space commerce. They are, in fact, increasingly reliant on commercial space products and services and benefit from them.[45] But the widespread availability of space capabilities and the importance of private capital markets are unsettling to traditional habits and assumptions of government agencies. They are given conflicting directives on how they should apply regulations and use their resources with a limited to nonexistent sense of overall national interests. At the same time, private-sector space capabilities are increasingly independent of traditional government programs. The resulting conflicts are typically treated on a case-by-case basis that makes it difficult for the administration and Congress to define common approaches to national interests affected by space activity. At an even more fundamental level, the interagency decision-making process, the lack of a National Space Council or similar White House staff mechanism makes it difficult to resolve conflicts, elevate those issues requiring presidential attention, and assign accountability for policy implementation.

Obviously, government has many important roles to play in the future of space commerce. It supports basic and applied R&D that creates new space technologies for public purposes such as national security and science. It may be a first buyer or a major sustaining customer for space products and services. Government provides the regulatory environment to enforce contracts as well as to protect public interests such as national security and safety. It also shapes the international environment for trade, investment, technology transfer, intellectual property rights, spectrum, and so forth—all of which are part of the foundation for high technology business.[46] Unlike some foreign governments, the U.S. government (typically) does not go into business for itself or take equity positions in commercial firms.

The definition of just what constitutes space commerce can be difficult as a result of unclear public- and private-sector roles. One common problem is confusion between "commercialization" and "privatization" referred to earlier. Truly commercial activities are carried out with private capital at risk and are driven by nongovernment markets. Privatized activities are formerly government functions that are now accomplished by the private sector but where the government is the dominant customer and where both market and financial risk are limited. Privatized activities may be conducted more efficiently as a result of private firms competing to perform them, but they should not be confused with the existence of commercial markets. The Space Shuttle and International Space Station are both examples of space activities that may be privatized at some point. They may enable commercial activities to occur, but they are not likely to be commercialized due to high costs at current levels of technology. Very costly and risky commercial activities require large markets to justify them. Merely having a private firm engaged in a space activity does not make that activity commercial.

The thinking about space commerce is subject to the same intellectual trends as in other areas of economic policy.[47] There was a time when the idea of space commerce was considered science fiction. Later, it was thought that government would create space commerce through funding of large-scale infrastructure such as shuttles, solar powered satellites, and even space colonies and lunar mining facilities. These technocratic models of government-led "space industrialization"—so common in NASA advanced planning from the 1970s and '80s—are not taken seriously anymore. The government has neither the resources nor the agility to create commercial markets alone. But recognition of what does not work has not been replaced by a common sense of what government should and, just as important, should not do.

Adding to the complexity is the fact that space commerce is a global activity and that international organizations play an increasingly important role in shaping it. These organizations, unlike the European ESA or the Japanese NASDA, are not very well known to traditional space communities because they are not space agencies. Rather, they are specialized technical agencies of the United Nations. For example:

• The International Telecommunications Union (ITU) is where global spectrum and orbital slots, necessary to satellite communications and GPS, are allocated and regulated.

• The World Meteorological Organization (WMO) influences the data policies of space-based weather monitoring systems, including issues such as encryption and user fees. Some government agencies, seeking to meet budget shortfalls, closely resemble business competitors.

• The World Intellectual Property Organization (WIPO) is developing the intellectual rules for protecting intellectual property such as software and databases, integral to commercial remote sensing business models.

• The World Trade Organization is currently silent on the particular issue of space transportation services, but one can easily imagine trade disputes over government subsidies and market access restrictions being taken up.

The same sort of inattention and failure to anticipate change that happens in policy making generally becomes even more acute when complex technical issues are decided in international bodies that the United States is already pledged to abide by. One only has to look at U.S.-European conflicts over issues such as encryption and privacy to imagine how decisions in foreign capitals can affect the structure of commerce in space-based information.

This issue of the respective roles of the public and private sectors is especially critical now precisely because government cannot "do it all." The health of commercial space industries is necessary to sustaining national space capabilities, and policy failures—however unintended—can and do harm those capabilities. Support for space commerce does not mean agreeing to whatever commercial interests ask, since such interests cannot speak for public concerns such as protection of national security and public safety.[48] It can be argued that in being overly restrictive on satellite export controls and overly permissive on GPS spectrum interference, the government is failing to protect public interests as well as private ones.

Support for space commerce does mean ensuring there are senior-level policy mechanisms that bring a sense of the larger national interest to complex space policy issues and do not allow agencies to pursue parochial agendas by default. Support means continual attention to the faithful implementation of existing policies—not just press releases, but administration and congressional oversight of responsible agencies. Finally, based on these foundations, support for space commerce can then be extended to innovative thinking about new policy initiatives and reform. Reasonable people can certainly disagree about the merits of particular policy questions, but taken as a whole, the pattern of the last few years has not been encouraging.

The globalization of the economy means that capital flows where it finds the most inviting home. Among the signs of a promising home for investment is the existence of intelligent government—not anarchy or oppressive controls, but a government that understands how to balance competing interests, set stable and predictable policies, and faithfully execute those laws and policies.[49] The United States has been failing to demonstrate such intelligent government in space commerce, and the outflow of capital and talent may not be far behind.

Policy Precepts for Space Commerce

To be in hell is to drift: to be in heaven is to steer.
—*George Bernard Shaw,* Man and Superman

The size and diversity of space commerce has been impressive, and its future growth is vital to the space capabilities of all spacefaring nations, especially the United States. There are many risks facing the future of space commerce, such as unreliable technologies, weak market demand, and more attractive financial returns in other areas of the global economy. The most important risk category and the most difficult to manage, however, is political risk from inconsistent and counterproductive government policies. No single government program or policy change can remove or mitigate the political risks, but some propositions—such as those described below—may help in thinking about how to manage them.

EVOLUTION, NOT REVOLUTION

For the immediate future, space commerce is about enabling terrestrial trade through space-based information systems. It will not be about goods and services being traded between the Earth and space destinations, much less trade between space settlements or interplanetary bases. Depending on future technical and market developments, space tourism and products processed in the space environment may emerge. With the price of raw materials continuing to fall, it is hard to imagine the case for importing nonterrestrial materials to the Earth, although space-generated electricity might become attractive compared to fossil fuels on environmental grounds. Thus, space commerce will represent a continuing evolution of the global economy to include locations in Earth orbit. It will not be about revolutionary quantum advances such as the rapid creation of government-funded factories and settlements in space.

TENSIONS AT THE PUBLIC-PRIVATE INTERFACE

The implications of space commerce cut across many different interest groups, and conflicts between the public and private interests will be at the center of commercial space policy disputes. Conflicts over issues such as missile proliferation in space launch and hostile uses of commercial remote-sensing data will overshadow other policy conflicts between government agencies or among private firms. These conflicts will not be solvable by government funding alone but will require careful thought about what government regulation and international agreements should and should not do.

GARDENING, NOT ENGINEERING

As a philosophical approach to government space policy, enabling the future growth of space commerce will be more akin to gardening than engineering. Unlike the Apollo program, the Space Shuttle, or even the International Space Station, space commerce is not a defined, single result. Rather, it is a process with multiple, unpredictable outcomes such as the rise of GPS applications and the competitive success of cellular networks against mobile satellite phones. Government policy toward space commerce should not try to pick winners and losers or craft a space industrial policy. Rather, it should support R&D (plant), buy commercial space goods and services to the greatest extent feasible (nurture), and remove unnecessary government competition to private industry (weed).

INTERNATIONAL ARENAS SHAPE SPACE COMMERCE

The need for both global markets and global financing means that international rules, not just domestic ones, will determine the policy environment for space commerce. These rules will not be created in one international forum, but in several fora that reflect the multifaceted character of commercial space activities (e.g., spectrum, intellectual property, trade rules for goods and services). As space commerce grows and becomes more sophisticated, international agreements will be needed to recognize and protect private property rights, contracts, and other commercial concerns beyond the Earth. The outcome of debates now occurring in places like Geneva, Brussels, and Washington will determine what balance will be struck between public and private interests in the future policy environment for space commerce.

Spacefaring countries such as France, Germany, Japan, Israel, India, Russia, China, and Brazil have economies that run the gamut in terms of being market-driven or government-driven. As with other areas of foreign policy and trade, the United States will be engaged in cooperation and competition on many issues with these same countries. The end of the Cold War meant the end of one kind of political struggle and the emergence of others. Struggles continue over national self-determination, ethnic and religious conflict, and the role of the state in private lives and commerce. Space commerce, like any other area of international relations, cannot be separated from those struggles. The task for U.S. space policy analysts and policymakers will be to craft alliances and strategies that advance critical values—free markets, limited government, private property, and human rights—as human activities of all kind expand into space.

Alternative Futures

Discussions of space policy, perhaps more than other areas of public policy, are about alternative futures. That is, space policy is perceived as being about creating an imagined future in addition to meeting immediate goals of scientific exploration, defense, and economic growth. Perhaps one of the most striking differences between space commerce and the old Wernher von Braun visions of space development is that space commerce is less predictable, less technocratic, and less amenable to centralized planning.

How might space commerce develop in the years ahead? While acknowledging the risks of any projections, especially for individual markets and firms, three general types of futures can be envisioned. Over the next ten years the most optimistic scenario might be termed "roses." In this case, the sky is dark with commercial satellites providing global communications, images of the Earth, and navigation. Improvements in space launch technology and increased commercial traffic have resulted in dramatically lower costs for access to LEO. This, in turn, has enabled new markets in space tourism as increasing numbers of people take short trips to small commercial stations. The growth of commercial infrastructures providing power, fuel, and life support have enabled governments to support more ambitious exploratory efforts beyond Earth orbit, including a return of humans to the moon. While human missions to Mars are still too difficult and expensive, a "virtual presence" has been established on all the planets and linked by an interplanetary Internet.

A more modest scenario could be termed "grass," in that space commerce is mature but is only a complement to terrestrial activities. Fiber and wireless networks increasingly displace satellite communications, but satellites still serve many developing countries that lack local infrastructure. Similarly, satellite remote sensing is an important adjunct to airborne remote sensing, but satellite systems are dependent on government subsidies and purchases. Space launch technology improvements have been gradual and not dramatic. Space transportation remains difficult and expensive, of interest to governments and large corporations but not to the general consumer. Government spending on space activity is driven by military needs and a few large civil space projects such as a second-generation Space Shuttle and maintenance of the International Space Station. Commercial investments in information technology and biotechnology provide more attractive rates of return than aerospace—drawing capital and skilled new workers away from space projects.

Finally, if events go badly, one can imagine a scenario of "bramble," in which space commerce is effectively crippled. Governments seeking to control the impact of space-based information and protect domestic industries from the effects of globalization create heavier regulatory burdens on private industry. Global roaming of satellite phones becomes effectively impossible. Private funding for satellite remote sensing dries up due to concerns that such ventures risk being nationalized in a crisis. Increasing interference from terrestrial communication devices continues to pollute the spectrum used by GPS, driving away civilian users and forcing military users to use costly anti-jamming equipment even in peacetime. Fewer satellite launches and the collapse of international insurance markets due to stringent export controls result in no private R&D for improvements to space launchers. These limitations drive industry to become partners with government agencies who still need them, nationalized in all but name. Activities revert to the patterns of the 1960s, in which large government contracts and subsidies determine the structure of domestic and international space industries. Military and scientific missions continue to be flown, but with increasing pressures on government budgets, human spaceflight comes to an end.

It is impossible to say which scenario will occur, for each depends on technologies, markets, and, most importantly, on policy choices by public and private organizations. Barring a global nuclear conflict or biological disaster, humans will continue to make use of space for a multitude of government purposes—especially scientific, military, and political ones. However, there are no assurances that humans themselves or nongovernmental activities will persist or grow in space. These activities are more fragile and depend on a supportive political and regulatory environment. As with any frontier or new opportunity, the choices are up to us.

NOTES

1. William E. Burrows, *This New Ocean* (New York: Random House, 1998).
2. David C. Gompert, *Right Makes Might: Freedom and Power in the Information Age* (New York: Foreign Policy Association, June 1998).
3. T. A. Heppenheimer, *Colonies in Space* (New York: Warner Books, 1977).
4. G. Harry Stine, *The Third Industrial Revolution* (New York: G. P. Putnam's Sons, 1975).
5. Walter A. McDougall, . . . *The Heavens and the Earth: A Political History of the Space Age* (New York: Basic Books, 1985).
6. Aerospace Industries Association, *Aerospace Facts & Figures 1999–2000* (Washington, DC: Aerospace Industries Association, 1999) contains a table of federal space activities outlays in constant collars.
7. Interview with Clay Mowry, Satellite Industry Association, Washington, DC, 22 October 1999.
8. U.S. Congress, "Prohibition on Collection and Release of Detailed Satellite Imagery of Israel and Other Countries and Areas," amendment 4321 to the 1997 National Defense Authorization Act, also known as the "Kyl-Bingaman Amendment" (1996).
9. Executive Office of the President, *The Future Management and Use of U.S. Space Launch Bases and Ranges* (Washington, DC: Office of Science and Technology Policy and the National Security Council, February 2000). After an extensive interagency review, the U.S. government decided to retain the current direct cost approach.
10. Timothy M. Bonds, et al., *Employing Commercial Satellite Communications: Wideband Investment Options for the Department of Defense*, MR-1192-AF (Santa Monica, CA: RAND, 2000).
11. Interview with Mark Uhran, NASA Headquarters Space Station Utilization Planning, 9 February 2000.
12. Executive Office of the President, *Interagency Report on Orbital Debris* (Washington, DC: National Science and Technology Council, 1995).
13. Expendable launch vehicles often leave their final stage in space after they separate from the payload. Residual fuel in these stages can, over time, lead to detonation of the stage and the creation of more space debris.

14. United Nations, *Vienna Declaration on Space and Human Development*, UNISPACE III Conference, Vienna, Austria, July 30, 1999.
15. International Space Business Council. *1999 State of the Space Industry*, with KPMG Peat Marwick (Arlington, VA: Space Publications, 1999).
16. Ibid.
17. Center for Space Policy Associates, *Commercial Space Industry in the Year 2000: A Market Forecast* (Cambridge, MA: Center for Space Policy Inc., June 1985).
18. Ronald Reagan, "Speech at Moscow State University, May 31, 1988," reprinted in *The American Reader*, ed. Diane Ravitch (New York: Harper-Collins, 1990), 364–65.
19. The Iridium project was a large constellation of communication satellites in LEO that was to provide global mobile phone service. During the time it took to come to market in the 1990s, the rapid expansion of ground-based wireless services took much of the market targeted by Iridium. The project ended in bankruptcy in 2000.
20. Executive Office of the President, *National Space Transportation Policy–NSTC 4* (Washington, DC: Office of the Press Secretary, 4 August 1994).
21. NASA, *Pocket Statistics* (Washington, DC: NASA, January 1996) contains a historical table of all worldwide launches by vehicle type and launching state.
22. U.S. Department of Transportation, *1999 Commercial Space Transportation Forecast* (Washington, DC: FAA Office of Commercial Space Transportation, May 1999).
23. In the same forecast, deployment of LEO satellites is expected to reach a low of 64 payloads in 2001 and a high of 192 payloads only two years later in 2003. By contrast, the number of GSO spacecraft projected to be launched does not fluctuate as much, with a high of 39 in 2001 and a low of 29 in 2003 and 2004.
24. International Space Business Council, *1999 State of the Space Industry*.
25. Executive Office of the President, *Future Management*. See Annex D.
26. Ibid.
27. U.S. Department of Transportation, *1999 Commercial Space Transportation Forecast*.
28. Executive Office of the President, *National Space Policy* (Washington, DC: National Science and Technology Council, 19 September 1996). The quota arrangement with Ukraine was terminated by mutual agreement on 5 June 2000. The agreement with Russia was terminated by mutual agreement on 31 December 2000. The agreement with China expired on 31 December 2001 and has not been renewed.
29. Patti Grace Smith, "Implications of Changing Government Role in Space Transportation," (Washington, DC: FAA Office of the Associate Administrator for Commercial Space Transportation, November 1998).
30. International Space Business Council, *1999 State of the Space Industry*.

31. Ibid.

32. After a long legal process, the sale was completed in August 2000.

33. Rather than paying for premium radio services, consumers in industrialized countries may choose to download music from the Internet and create their own compact disks with new, lower-cost computer technology.

34. U.S. Department of Commerce, *Global Positioning System Markets* (Washington, DC: ITA Office of Telecommunications, September 1998).

35. Galileo Program Office, www.galileo-pgm.org/ (2000).

36. In addition to new civil signals, the United States decided in May 2000 to refrain from degrading current civil signals. The removal of "selective availability" resulted in immediate accuracy improvements, from about 100 meters to less than 10 meters.

37. Ultrawide band devices can use signals that spread across 1–10 GHz of spectrum. Domestic regulatory decisions on commercial use of this technology are under debate, and it may be several years before international discussions are appropriate.

38. Merton E. Davies and William R. Harris, *RAND's Role in the Evolution of Balloon and Satellite Observation Systems and Related U.S. Technology,* R-3692-RC (Santa Monica, CA: RAND, 1988).

39. U.S. Congress, *The Land Remote Sensing Policy Act of 1992*--P.L. 102-555; Executive Office of the President, *Remote Sensing Licensing and Exports— PD 23* (Washington, DC: Office of the Press Secretary, 10 March 1994).

40. Pamela Mack, *Viewing the Earth: The Social Construction of Landsat* (Cambridge: MIT Press, 1990).

41. International Space Business Council, *1999 State of the Space Industry.*

42. U.S. House of Representatives, *Commercial Remote Sensing in the Post-Cold War Era,* joint hearings before the Committee on Science, Space, and Technology and the Permanent Select Committee on Intelligence, 9 February 1994.

43. U.S. Department of Commerce, "Licensing of Private Land Remote-Sensing Space Systems, Interim Final Rule," *Federal Register,* 15 CFR Part 960, vol. 65, no. 147, 31 July 2000, 46822–37.

44. William O. Studeman, "The Space Business and National Security," *Aerospace America* (November 1994).

45. Bob Preston, *Plowshares and Power: The Military Use of Civil Space,* Institute for National Strategic Studies (Washington, DC: National Defense University, 1994).

46. Dana J. Johnson, Scott Pace, and C. Bryan Gabbard, *Space: Emerging Options for National Power,* MR-517 (Santa Monica, CA: RAND, 1998).

47. Virginia Postrel, *The Future and Its Enemies* (New York: Touchstone, 1998).

48. Johnson, Pace, and Gabbard, *Space.*

49. Gompert, *Right Makes Might.*

3 Unfettered Observation
The Politics of Earth Monitoring from Space

Ronald J. Deibert

O F ALL of the technological characteristics of the so-called information revolution, the one that has arguably the greatest potential global implications and yet the least social and political analysis is
space-based Earth remote sensing. Such an omission has a variety of
sources. Because satellites operate in space and are practically invisible
to the naked eye, they lack the immediate intrusiveness that might otherwise capture academic and public curiosity. More significant has been
the fact that the most sophisticated remote-sensing technologies have
been shrouded in secrecy for much of the twentieth century, their product being largely monopolized by the military and intelligence organizations of the United States and the former Soviet Union.

Yet the information derived from space-based remote-sensing satellites has obvious importance for global politics. Satellites equipped with
advanced sensing technologies provide an almost unparalleled vantage
point from which to view the entire Earth. The ability to observe and
map the planet from space in a variety of spectral modes and resolution capabilities confers power on those who have the capability to do
so. Today the most advanced military satellites can resolve objects as
small as several centimeters, can detect minuscule heat and radioactive
emissions, and can operate in all weather and day/night conditions. The
strategic benefits of such technologies are clear. It was precisely because
of this power that the United States and the Soviet Union went to great
lengths to conceal and preserve their control during the Cold War.

Space-based Earth remote sensing is important to global politics in
a less dramatic, more practical sense as well. The information derived
from satellite remote-sensing systems is increasingly integrated into
countless applications and activities on Earth. For example, space-based
remote-sensing products are now found in weather forecasting and gen-

eral meteorological sciences, disaster relief operations, urban planning, development projects, forestry practices, environmental management and Earth sciences, agricultural management, peacekeeping, arms control and disarmament, refugee support, fire-fighting, fishing, and safety and rescue operations. Given such wide-ranging applications, how such technologies and the information derived from them are developed, managed, distributed, and otherwise controlled is of vital importance to the nature and character of global governance.

Such extensive applications point to another aspect of contemporary space-based Earth remote sensing that warrants further analysis: like other technology-related areas, satellite remote-sensing practices are currently undergoing a profound transformation. Part of this transformation is related to technological change itself, which has at once both dramatically lowered the costs, and increased the sophistication and potential applications of such systems. The other part of the transformation is derived from changes in the world political landscape since the end of the Cold War that set the parameters within which such technologies now operate. These changes have had the effect of altering well-established constraints on such aspects of satellite remote sensing as the relationships between military and civilian remote sensing, the potential sophistication of commercial remote-sensing products, and the possibilities of international cooperation.

In this chapter, I probe the consequences for world politics of recent developments in satellite Earth remote sensing and suggest some ways that it might be fruitful to begin to organize such activities as part of the larger context of global democratic governance.[1] There are two broad sets of constraints that limited the use of Earth remote-sensing technologies during the Cold War period: national security constraints and natural resource sovereignty constraints. These constraints have gradually dissipated with an accompanying proliferation and expansion of uses of space-based remote-sensing technologies.

My assumption is that, given the awesome surveillance and destructive powers of communication and information technologies today, the best strategy to preserve the Earth's biosphere while furthering global liberal democracy is to prevent the centralization of these technologies in a single node through dispersed control. While contemporary trends show significant movement in the latter direction, the continuation of those trends is not guaranteed. The possibility of a reversion to the status quo ante still exists. In this chapter I identify interests that could upset and reverse these trends and conclude by sketching out several policies that should be promoted to shore up and ensure the continued trajectory of recent developments toward unfettered and dispersed observation of the Earth.

Constraining Satellite Remote Sensing

Technological research and development does not take place in a vacuum but is embedded within a complex of social forces and institutions that shape and constrain its evolution. The history of technological development in the area of satellite remote sensing is no different. The basic theories of rocket propulsion explored by the early-twentieth-century American scientist Robert Goddard, for example, remained obscure for decades until World War II, when German research into the *V2* rocket spurred on American interests that in turn gave a boost to Goddard's research. While such social forces can push technological development in this way, they can also constrain it.[2] Two very different constraints—one derived from the world of military-intelligence, the other from concerns over sovereignty and control of natural resources—channeled and limited satellite remote-sensing applications from the 1960s to the 1990s.

COLD WAR MILITARY-INTELLIGENCE CONSTRAINTS

From its origins, satellite remote sensing has had potential for both military and civilian applications. The modern history of civilian remote sensing from space can be traced back to 1954, when the International Council of Scientific Unions, looking forward to the International Geophysical Year of 1957–58, adopted a resolution calling for artificial satellites to be launched to map the Earth's surface. President Dwight D. Eisenhower initially had high hopes that satellites would be used for peaceful scientific and educational purposes, and many others shared his views. These hopes were dashed, however, by the successful Soviet launch of *Sputnik* in 1957, by the obvious military applications derived from such technology, and by the increasing tensions associated with the Cold War, in particular the May 1, 1960, downing of Gary Powers' U2 flight over the Soviet Union.

As early as 1946, when the Rand Corporation undertook a study entitled a "Preliminary Design for an Experimental World Circling Spaceship," the military had begun to explore the use of space-based technologies for military reconnaissance.[3] By 1958 two separate projects for satellite photographic reconnaissance, headed by the U. S. Air Force and the Central Intelligence Agency (CIA) respectively, were under development. The CIA project, based on recording images of the Earth on film, ejecting the canisters from the satellite, and then retrieving them with a large net strung behind an airplane, was the first of the two to be implemented.[4] Code-named "Corona," the first CIA satellite was launched in February 1959. Not until August 18, 1960, however, was a satellite successfully put into orbit and a film capsule recovered on the following day.[5] Shortly thereafter, on August 25, 1960, the responsibilities for managing the U.S. space-based reconnaissance program were transferred to a new unit, the National Reconnaissance Office (NRO), where the program has remained until the present time.[6]

In 1995 President Clinton signed an Executive Order directing the declassification of intelligence imagery derived from the Corona series, some 800,000 images of the Earth's surface taken from 1960 to 1972. Although the contemporary significance of this declassification will be discussed below, for now what is noteworthy is how revealing the imagery is in terms of the benefits for military intelligence for the time in which they were taken. The imagery provided unprecedented illumination of key Soviet military programs, including missile complexes and test ranges, submarine deployments and operation bases, bombers and fighters, and atomic weapons storage installations.[7] Adding value to the imagery was the fact that the satellites were far less vulnerable to being shot down than were U2 and other aerial reconnaissance missions. The very first image taken from the Corona satellite was on August 18, 1960. Although the grainy image of the Soviet airfield may seem unimpressive by today's standards, the remote acquisition from space of such sensitive information was, for those in intelligence circles, revolutionary. Given the intense level of hostilities between the superpowers and the unprecedented intelligence benefits, it is not surprising that it became an imperative to guard closely the sophistication of the technologies as they developed and the information derived from them.

From the early 1960s onward, therefore, the development and application of space-based remote-sensing technologies operated within the tight confines of the national-security complexes of the two superpowers. The most sophisticated technologies were set beneath a deep shroud of secrecy and were used exclusively for military reconnaissance, while civilian applications were strictly controlled and limited. The first Corona satellites, designated KH-1, carried a single panoramic camera and had an approximate ground resolution of 25 feet. By the time of the KH-4 series, the ground resolution had been improved to 6 feet. By comparison, not until 1978 and the launch of the French satellite SPOT would there be a civilian satellite with anywhere near the ground resolution capability of even the first-generation KH-1. The American *Landsat* (then known as the Earth Resources Technology Satellite), which was launched with great interest in 1972, for example, had a best visible ground resolution of 80 meters.

The secrecy surrounding the Soviet space program is understandable, given the authoritarian nature of the regime and its strict control over technological research and development. No less severe, however, was the level of secrecy that surrounded the operations of the NRO, the main agency that oversaw military and intelligence satellite reconnaissance operations for the United States. Like other parts of the U.S. intelligence complex, the institutions associated with satellite reconnaissance have been governed by a deeply pervasive secrecy that informs every aspect of daily routines and operations. In fact, so pervasive is the secrecy that the central organization in charge of satellite reconnaissance, the NRO, was not even officially revealed as existing until 1992. Information about systems and operations is tightly controlled and compartmentalized, blanketed by levels-upon-levels of classification and opaque jargon, such as the vague euphemism "national technical means" to refer to surveillance systems. This deep insecurity and secrecy extends beyond the strict confines of the NRO itself to include the operations of the numerous defense contractors and image-processing agencies that orbit the intelligence community and that together form a kind of secret inner sanctum. As William Burrows puts it, "There is a kind of reconnaissance club, an unofficial secret society composed of 'black hats' from the various contractors, military services, and the intelligence agencies and divisions, all of whom carry the appropriate clearances and are scrupulous about remaining in deep shadow."[8]

Although the NRO has, since the end of the Cold War, made some minor adjustments toward greater openness, this pervasive secrecy had the effect during the Cold War of tightly restricting access to sophisticated satellite systems and constraining civilian research and development (R&D). Examples can be found as early as 1962, when the United States was sponsoring a United Nations resolution calling for international cooperation in space, including formal notification of space launches. While the resolution was being pushed in the United Nations, the U.S. military undertook a formal policy of secrecy regarding the registration of its military satellite launches, effectively nullifying any comprehensive effectiveness that might have been achieved by the proposal.[9] Formal U.S. regulations prohibited the development of space-based remote-sensing technologies beyond 30-meter ground resolution throughout the Cold War in spite of the much greater level of sophistication of military satellites. And of course very little about the technology was shared with other countries or the public at large.

SOVEREIGNTY AND NATIONAL RESOURCE ISSUES

The Cold War security constraints, while clearly the most important, were complemented by a less significant constraint—the resistance among many countries, particularly in the Third World, from being surveyed from space. In the early years of the Space Age, the resistance centered largely on resolving how the novel activities in outer space were to be reconciled with the principle of national sovereignty. As Lincoln Bloomfield noted in 1962, "Where are the boundaries of space? Where does outer space begin? How high up can nations exercise their traditional rights of sovereignty, and what are the rules above that height?"[10] At the same time as these questions were being asked, the practical benefits of space-based remote sensing were still largely theoretical. Not long afterward, however, the question of national sovereignty over information derived from space would become intertwined with the very real and much larger concern shared among developing countries over information inequality in the global system.

By the late 1960s and early 1970s, many developing countries were joining together in an alliance to push for structural changes in the global political economy under the rubric of a New World Information and Economic Order (NWIEO).[11] The gist of the NWIEO was to redress the disparities between the North and South populations by instituting transfers of technology and capital and by ensuring more equitable access to and control over global media, information, and communication technologies. Most of the concern centered on traditional media of communications such as television, radio, and newspaper and sought ways to counter Western hegemony in such areas. Reflecting this sense of urgency, a 1976 Non-Aligned Symposium concluded that "since information in the world shows disequilibrium favoring some and ignoring others, it is the duty of the non-aligned countries and other developing countries to change this situation and obtain the decolonization of information and initiate a new international order in information."[12]

In the area of space-based remote sensing, the resistance among developing countries concerned the use of information derived from satellite systems operated and controlled by the West, in particular by the United States. While the existence of military and intelligence satellites outlined above were known, the objections focused largely on the information derived from the civilian *Landsat* satellite, first launched in 1972. Debates in the Outer Space Committee of the UN General Assembly of the time focused on the greater sophistication of data analysis expertise in the United States and the fear that this would generate a gradual loss of control over natural resources. It was felt, for example, that the ability conferred by these technologies to monitor crop production and make forecasts on yields would give the United States a monopoly advantage in setting world food prices.[13] Karen Litfin elaborates on the type of concerns raised:

> Even when information is made available at no cost to developing countries, which is by no means always the case, remote sensing is still a technology that is likely to benefit industrialized countries the most. Research agendas are largely set in the West, space and computer technologies are owned by the North, and the results are published in English. When satellite data reveals mineral deposits in the Third World countries, U.S. and European multinational corporations quickly arrive on the scene to "develop" the resources.[14]

The proposals designed to rectify these issues ranged from technical solutions that would have had imaging systems turned off and on over countries that consented to being surveyed, to a U.N.-based system of centralized control of all satellite remote-sensing systems—or at least those related to nonmilitary applications.[15] Not surprisingly, most of the proposals were nonstarters, with the objections made largely moot in the face of technological developments and Western state and corporate control.[16] The resistance did, however, have the effect of limiting the acceptance and use of space-based remote-sensing technologies and information by a large segment of the global population. Creative ideas designed to exploit space-based remote-sensing technologies within the context of the United Nations would, for much of the 1970s and 1980s, be met with suspicion and even resistance from countries concerned about losing autonomy over their natural resources.

Together, these two political or social forces acted as a constraint on the development of space-based remote-sensing technologies. The United States and the Soviet Union, joined later by China, actively pursued the most advanced applications of satellite technologies but restricted the information derived from them to a limited circle and used it exclusively for military-intelligence purposes. Both also went to great lengths to ensure that they monopolized the technology, only rarely sharing imagery with other allied countries and virtually never sharing or selling the technology itself. Nor did they permit potential civilian applications to exploit the technologies, keeping satellite systems buried beneath a shroud of secrecy. For their part, many developing countries saw satellite remote-sensing technologies as largely a threat rather than an opportunity, and as part of a complex of technologies controlled by the West that needed to be resisted.

Unraveling Constraints

The end of the Cold War with the collapse of the Soviet Empire is perhaps the single most important event contributing to the changing context of the space-based remote-sensing issue. It made it less defensible for national security arguments to be used to maintain rigid controls over access to sophisticated satellite technologies, particularly when Soviet imagery was made commercially available. High technology firms operating in the United States who had been previously reliant on defense and intelligence contracts have put increasing pressure on the government to allow them to offer their goods and services to a wider commercial market unbridled by stifling national security constraints. As a consequence of this pressure, the U.S. government has gradually relaxed a variety of policy restrictions.

The consequences flowing from the end of the Cold War have joined together with more long-term evolutionary processes of change in the international political and economic environment that have had similar repercussions for Earth remote sensing. Over the last several decades, the applications and uses of space-based remote-sensing information have gradually widened and deepened. The sources of remote-sensing information have proliferated as well. Although it is possible that these social forces would have been powerful enough to overwhelm the national security constraints on their own, the end of the Cold War created a window of opportunity through which these forces have been released.

Three related areas have contributed to the proliferation of space-based remote-sensing technologies: expansion of uses, expansion of sources, and technological advances.

EXPANSION OF USES

When space-based remote-sensing technologies were first theorized and employed, the potential uses included the obvious military and intelligence applications as well as weather surveillance, but little else. Over the last thirty years, however, the number of applications for which space-based remote-sensing technologies have relevance has mush-roomed beyond expectations. Military, intelligence, and weather fore-casting are still very important users of the technology, but they now only comprise a small proportion of the total applications.

Perhaps the fastest-growing use of space-based remote-sensing tech-nologies is in planetary environmental monitoring and earth sciences—fields of investigation that have intensified over the last several decades due to the global environmental crisis. The systems that exist today for environmental remote sensing are numerous and complex, and include a plethora of national, regional, and global organizations. A glance at some of the activities undertaken by these organizations, however, gives some indication of the many different uses of space-based Earth remote-sensing technologies. For example, these technologies play a vital role in the various studies of global climate change, including disease vector surveillance, land cover mapping, desertification and deforestation, car-bon dioxide and aerosol emissions, and ozone depletion. They are used extensively in the area of global ocean monitoring, including marine pol-lution, sea-level and wave-height measurements, and ice mapping. The same technologies are used in studies of the human impacts of global change, including human population growth and migration patterns. In just about every area of environmental monitoring, which in and of itself is expanding rapidly, space-based remote-sensing technologies likely play a role. Given the increasing concerns over global environmental degradation, it is almost certain that such applications will continue to expand.

Of these various uses, the one that is likely to generate the greatest need for satellite monitoring technologies in decades to come is studies of global warming and climate change. Briefly, this issue centers on whether the human-induced buildup of various greenhouse gases in the Earth's atmosphere—primarily carbon dioxide, nitrous oxide, and methane—is, in turn, contributing to an increase in global temperatures, otherwise known as the "greenhouse effect." It was largely in response to this and other pressing environmental issues that NASA launched its Mission to Planet Earth (now known as the Earth Science Enterprise) and its centerpiece Earth Observing System (EOS) series of satellites, the first of which, EOS *Terra,* was launched in December 1999.[17] One of the first results from *Terra* was the confirmation that there was much less snow cover than normal in North America during the winter of 1999–2000, data that fall in line with global warming projections.

The causes of, impacts of, and potential solutions to, global warming and climate change are all hotly contested political issues involving both developed and developing countries.[18] While most scientists and environmentalists are of the opinion that the potential impacts of global warming are serious and that their causes are directly attributable to human social and industrial practices, a minority of skeptics disputes these claims. Much of the contention centers on climate change projections and/or estimates of potential impacts.[19] Although the details of this debate are outside the scope of this chapter, what is relevant is that dispute itself will only likely further add to the incentives to deploy space-based technologies to help resolve the disagreements and to make more accurate projections. For example, one dispute centers on the reliability of surface-based measurements of global temperature changes—a dispute whose resolution points in the direction of employing space-based monitoring techniques instead. Global warming and climate change, including all of its multifaceted political and scientific controversies, in other words, will be one of the most potent forces contributing to an expansion of uses of space-based monitoring technologies.

Although environmental and earth science monitoring applications are growing the fastest, space-based remote-sensing systems are used in a variety of other applications as well. More traditional weather forecast images that show cloud-cover patterns, for example, have been augmented by imagery from thermal, radar, and infrared sensors and are complemented by systems used to study lightning, hurricanes, and tornado storms.[20] In a similar vein, such technologies have now become crucial to disaster relief operations such as those in floods, droughts, and winter storms. They are also used to detect oil spills and oil slicks.[21]

Space-based remote-sensing technologies are now used extensively for business applications, including the mining, forestry, agricultural, tourism, automobile, and fishing industries. They are also employed for purposes of urban planning, development, and civil engineering. A growing number of academic sciences employ satellite remote-sensing technologies to aid in their research, such as geology and archaeology.[22] Satellite imagery finds its way into the computer games and simulation industry. It is also sporadically used in multilateral arms control verification as well as in peacekeeping and peace-enforcement missions. Such technologies have been employed for refugee resettlement, humanitarian aid, and war crimes investigations as well.[23]

This expansion of uses of remote-sensing imagery has contributed to an explosion of the secondary market for what are called "value-added" services. Around the world, thousands of private companies now provide services that include satellite imagery analysis in such areas as change detection and visual mapping. In short, since space-based remote-sensing systems were first developed, the number of potential uses and applications has grown exponentially. It is likely, moreover, that such uses will continue to expand as the technologies proliferate and become more sophisticated.

EXPANSION OF SOURCES

During the Cold War, the United States and the Soviet Union closely guarded satellite reconnaissance technologies. Few other countries had the technological expertise, national strategic incentives, or capital resources to build their own. Gradually, however, the number of countries with autonomous space-based remote-sensing technologies has grown considerably. Alongside Russia and the United States, today China, Israel, India, and France (with support from Italy, Germany, and Spain) all own and operate military-capable reconnaissance satellites. A number of other countries have emerged as imagery providers for civilian and commercial purposes (i.e., not strictly military), including Canada, Japan, India, and Brazil.

Perhaps most importantly, commercial imagery that is coming close to being on the level of sophistication as military imagery is now available from several different sources in different state jurisdictions, with more in store for the future. As mentioned above, the first commercial satellite imagery systems were limited to a best resolution of 10 meters. However, that began to change with the limited sale of Soviet imagery beginning in 1987 and then expanded in sophistication and reliability in 1992 through the U.S.-based company, Central Trading Systems. Imagery from these systems were on the order of 1.5- to 2-meter resolution, a level of sophistication that called into question the logic of U.S. government restrictions. As Gerald Steinberg has argued, "Industry leaders claimed that the Soviet military threat had been replaced by a commercial threat from French and Russian companies that were preparing to enter the high-resolution market in which sales had already reached $700 million in 1994."[24] Public media advocates simultaneously pressured the U.S. government as well, arguing that the restrictions violated the First Amendment. In the face of this pressure, President Clinton issued Presidential Directive 23, which permitted private firms to develop and sell high-resolution satellite imagery within certain limitations.[25] Since then, several firms have applied successfully for licenses, with the first successful launch and operation by Space Imaging Corporation in April 1999.[26]

TECHNOLOGICAL ADVANCES

Partially driving the proliferation of these different uses and applications of space-based remote-sensing systems have been advances in technology. From the very first photographic image systems, space-based remote-sensing technologies have advanced to provide data in a wide variety of spectral modes, such as thermal, infrared, and radar. Some of these new imaging systems have opened up potential applications that would have been unavailable with a purely optical spectral mode. Synthetic aperture radar images, such as those from the *ERS-1* and *Radarsat* satellites, provide all-weather and day/night resolution capabilities. Multispectral and hyperspectral scanners can provide evidence of changes in vegetation patterns, for example, while new kinds of analytical software integrated with geographic information systems have provided three-dimensional spatial mapping data for urban planners and developers.[27] Advances in computer graphics have allowed the integration of satellite imagery into detailed three-dimensional digital terrain models, which in turn has opened up markets for satellite imagery in a variety of nonmilitary and intelligence areas. And of course none of these uses could be achieved without the powerful advances that have been made in computer processing and information storage capabilities that have permitted a "desktop" remote-sensing capability to thrive.

An even greater impetus to the expanding uses and applications of these technologies has been the integration of satellite data into the Internet. Today many companies make sample and commercial imagery and data available over the World Wide Web, which, in turn, has increased the number of potential users. Perhaps the most intriguing effort is the partnership between Microsoft and several imagery providers to create the Terraserver Web site, which provides increasing coverage of North America, Europe, and other parts of the world using 1-meter imagery derived from Russian and other data sources.[28] Such developments on the Internet will be further fueled by sites that promote "open source" algorithms, code, and technologies related to remote sensing, such as the Open Source Remote-Sensing Effort Web site.[29] Recognizing the importance of this shift, space industry representatives have talked about the need to speak of products from space imagery as "information services" rather than as exotic space technologies in order to capture the reorientation underway and further widen the customer base. As the president of SPOT Image Corporation recently noted, "The convergence of technologies, such as powerful work stations, the Internet as a data delivery system and improved software tools, is transforming the remote-sensing business *into an information business.*"[30] Such a coupling of remote-sensing technologies with the Internet in these ways will deepen and expand further the number of potential applications and users.

A Reversal of Constraints?

As outlined above, the numbers, uses, and sophistication of civilian and environmental Earth-monitoring systems have exploded over the last decade. Many more states, nongovernmental organizations, international organizations, and private corporations from around the world are now increasingly involved in Earth-monitoring missions from space, either through R&D or through use of information. The growing concerns over environmental degradation have spurred yet further interest and investment in Earth-monitoring systems. Nontraditional applications in areas such as refugee monitoring, peacekeeping, and disaster relief have been proposed as more people become aware of their utility. The information derived from space-based systems is being increasingly integrated into the Internet and World Wide Web, which in turn has expanded the user base. As a consequence of these factors taken together, a growing and dispersed constituency of private and public actors from around the world in a variety of sectors now depends on, and has a stake in, space-based Earth-monitoring systems.

As Earth-monitoring technologies are integrated into the economic, environmental, and social practices of societies around the world in this way, will a return to the status quo ante become increasingly unlikely? In other words, will the widespread and dispersed centers of planetary surveillance that have emerged increasingly act as a constraint of their own on various social, military, and political practices? Evidence that this constraint now operates is already beginning to emerge. For example, in 1999 the United States eliminated Canada's long-standing exemption from U.S. export licensing requirements in the area of defense technology. One of the consequences of the new restriction was that Canada's application with the U.S. company Orbital Sciences to provide the launch system for its *Radarsat-2* satellite was delayed for eight months. Rather than having no choice but to wait, as would have been the case in the past, Canada simply turned to alternative European suppliers.[31] One can imagine similar scenarios arising not just in satellite production but also in data supply and acquisition. A kind of "Internet-effect" could emerge, whereby access to information in foreign juris-dictions allows suppliers to sidestep their own national restrictions. As noted above, remote-sensing data is now commercially available from several different national sources. The European Union plans to develop its own Global Positioning System (GPS), which would provide an alter-native to the present United States GPS system.[32]

A real "test" of an Internet-effect to answer the questions above with certainty would require, for example, a non-U.S. private company offer-ing to sell satellite imagery that is prohibited within the United States. As it stands now, the only private companies with resolution strong enough to present such a scenario are U.S.-based. These companies are now subject to U.S. national security "shutter controls" that prohibit sales of data under certain circumstances or to certain foreign nation-als.[33] If push came to shove during a crisis in which the United States were involved, in other words, these companies' services would likely be controlled or altogether suspended. During the recent NATO action in the Balkans in the late 1990s, for example, there was some discussion concerning whether such controls would be imposed. None were, how-ever, most likely because there was no massing of troops for a ground assault, the positioning of which commercial high-resolution satellite imagery could compromise.[34]

There are examples of the type of cross-checking inherent in mul-tiple sources of imagery that, while not prohibited by the U.S. govern-ment, show how commercially available imagery can begin to act as a constraint in ways hypothesized above. Most of these examples are the work of a U.S.-based nongovernmental organization, the Federation of American Scientists (FAS), which has employed commercially available imagery and intelligence in a wide variety of "government watchdog" projects.[35] Recently, for example, a FAS project used high-resolution commercial imagery to raise questions about the significance of the North Korean missile program. The analysis touched off a sensitive de-bate over U.S. national security policy, calling into question the justi-fication for the controversial anti-ballistic missile program and forcing an official response from the government.[36] A similar type of situation occurred several years earlier when Peter Zimmerman, working under contract for the *St. Petersburg Times,* employed Russian imagery to de-termine after the fact that the Bush administration had exaggerated the overall Iraqi troop buildup leading up to Operation Desert Storm.[37] To test the limits of the present restrictions, the FAS has ordered, through

Space Imaging Corporation, imagery of Area 51, the military base known to UFO buffs as a suspected UFO storage facility.[38] Though within the boundaries of acceptability for U.S. government regulations so far, these examples nonetheless suggest the type of constraints against controls that will begin to emerge as alternative sources of data and imagery proliferate. It is reasonable to assume that, given present trends, more probes of the present restrictions will occur.

Could the trends outlined above be reversed? Could the dispersion and proliferation of multiple sources of data and imagery for Earth monitoring be reconsolidated and checked? With respect to the national resource/sovereignty constraint outlined above, there is very little possibility that such a check from this direction could be imposed. First, the constraints emanating from this area were not formidable even at their peak, doing little to stem the development of Earth remote-sensing technologies. Since that time, the strength of this social force has dissipated enormously. There is very little prospective unity among developing countries. Concerted resistance against infringements to national sovereignty over resources has now been abandoned in favor of policies designed to cope with, or adapt to, globalization.

The possibilities of a reconsolidation through national security constraints, on the other hand, are much more formidable. As has been mentioned, there are presently government regulations that establish "shutter controls" on high-resolution commercial imagery. To date there has been no crisis—including the terrorist attack of 2001—where the limits have been put to the test, but should such a global crisis occur in which the United States is involved, the movement in the direction of reconsolidation could be swift. Such a possibility is even more realistic in light of two recent trends that counter those outlined earlier: First, United States defense strategies now openly speak about the need to be able to achieve "total space control" in the event of a conflict. Indeed, one could say with relative certainty that such a capability is now merely latent and awaits activation in the event of a serious global conflict. Second, a gradual blurring of "security" and "nonsecurity" surveillance missions has occurred since the end of the Cold War in spite of the proliferation of environmentally dedicated satellite systems around the world.[39] One aspect of this blurring can be seen in the expansion of U.S. military reconnaissance toward environmental missions.[40] Driven by shrinking defense budgets, intelligence agencies in the United States have shed their initial aversion to recent reconceptualizations of the "security" paradigm to take on new missions, including environmental ones. The once-secret U.S. NRO now monitors everything from coastlines to forests in addition to top-secret missile installations and other traditional security targets.[41]

Further blurring can be seen in trends in the production of new satellite systems. Increasingly, economic efficiency arguments are being used to argue for the consolidation of military and civilian/environmental R&D and operations, especially in the United States. As one U.S. Office of Technology Assessment report argued, "This increased use of CTIB [commercial technology and industrial base], dubbed civil-military integration (CMI), can take many forms, including purchasing commercially available goods and services, conducting both defense and commercial research and development in the same facility, manufacturing defense and commercial items on the same production line, and maintaining such items in shared facilities."[42] For example, until an inter-agency squabble between NASA and the DOD over system design derailed co-production, *Landsat 7* was to have been operated as a joint military-civilian satellite.[43] Likewise, in May 1994 the Clinton administration announced a proposal to "consolidate" the polar-orbiting meteorological programs of National Oceanic and Atmospheric Administration (NOAA) and the DOD and to coordinate both to avoid overlap with the programs of NASA's EOS.[44] More recently, several U.S. corporations won a prized contract to build the Brazilian Amazon Surveillance System (what Bill Clinton, who was president at the time, called a model environmental project) that will monitor everything from regional crises and territorial defense to forests and oceans.[45] Without a separation of activities, such a blurring of environmental and military/intelligence systems would allow for a much speedier reconsolidation of Earth-monitoring activities in the event of a global military crisis.

In sum, the trends toward dispersion of remote-sensing activities have not reached a point where a return to the status quo ante is completely out of the question, especially given concerns with international terrorism. The present configuration of social forces and interests, particularly within the U.S. intelligence and defense spheres, could reconsolidate control over Earth remote-sensing activities in the event of a global military crisis. In other words, the view that "the U.S. government is trying to maintain a kind of export control over a technology that has long since proliferated beyond U.S. borders" may be an overstatement.[46] Short of such a crisis, however, the interests in favor of the proliferation and dispersion of Earth remote-sensing activities to multiple sources and uses will continue to mount. Although we have not yet reached a point of no return, it is reasonable to anticipate that for the foreseeable future world politics will take place within an umbrella of multiple and overlapping, inward-focusing surveillance systems.

World Politics in an Environment of Enclosed Encounters

The preceding discussion suggests that while we are in the midst of a major transformation in the area of space-based remote-sensing technologies, there is still a great deal of fluidity in terms of how such activities and technologies will be controlled and governed. As a consequence of this fluidity, much more attention should be paid to different ways in which the various forms of contemporary and future Earth remote sensing—from environmental to civilian to commercial to military/intelligence—should be organized as a whole. Ironically, such analyses of comparative architectures of Earth surveillance were much more prevalent early in the Space Age when the technologies were in their infancy, but they have fallen out of favor now that they are most advanced. Such analyses need to be resurrected, paying greater attention to the ways in which the many disparate existing remote-sensing activities relate to each other and to different forms of global governance. These analyses would fall into a relatively new category of world political theorizing and might include questions such as those following.

What are the consequences of increasing privatization and commercialization of Earth remote-sensing activities? Over the last several decades and picking up momentum since the end of the Cold War, the space industry has been moving in the direction of greater commercialization of services. The commercialization of high-resolution satellite images noted above is a good example. While privatization and commercialization may remove arcane government restrictions and open up the technology to new users, how far can such commercialization go without becoming a detriment to the provision of public goods in remote sensing? Not all consumers of Earth remote-sensing data stand to benefit from such a regime. Already many scientific researchers, NGOs, and relief organizations worldwide are feeling the squeeze of more rigid applications of property rights, data access, and pricing policies as suppliers of Earth remote-sensing data increasingly adopt or conform to commercial distribution standards.[47] This sizable global "public goods" lobby would likely constrain the development of a full-blown market-driven regime for imagery and data in areas like meteorological remote sensing, where "market failures" and a strong norm of cost-recovery pricing access exist. But in many other areas, a free-market regime for

Earth remote-sensing data would still put developing countries without the capital and expertise at an enormous disadvantage relative to the North. Essentially, as Florini and Dehqanzada point out, the issue revolves around the dividing line between private and public provision of Earth remote-sensing data:

> When should satellite imagery be treated as a public good, to be provided (or controlled) by governments, and when is it a private good to be created by profit-seekers and sold to the highest bidder? Who gets to decide? Is it possible to reconcile the public value of the free flow of information for such pressing purposes as humanitarian relief, environmental protection, and crisis management with the needs of the industry to make a profit by selling that information?[48]

In short, there needs to be greater discussion about the desired relationship between, as Mansell and Paltridge put it, "public sector objectives in the Earth observation data market and the economic interests of Earth observation data producers."[49]

What are the consequences of consolidating military and environmental remote-sensing activities? As mentioned above, another notable trend in the United States and around the world has been to seek areas in which environmental and military/intelligence remote-sensing activities could be consolidated. Most often justified on the basis of reducing overlap and cutting costs, Earth remote-sensing platforms catering to both military and civilian/environmental clients are now common. While most applaud such developments, some (including myself) have questioned the wisdom of integrating environmental and military missions. Among other reasons, such consolidation could call into question the integrity of environmental data drawn from military sources and could hamper the openness and international cooperation necessary for long-term environmental rescue, given the secrecy surrounding the organizations involved in intelligence and military monitoring. A more long-term concern would center on the lack of separation between these two central spheres of Earth monitoring, which, in the context of global democratic governance, would remove a significant constraint against possible global consolidation of planetary surveillance.

Multilateral regimes for monitoring the environment are now prevalent. What would be the potential benefits of organizing similar regimes for security, arms control, and peacekeeping? If we were to divide all of the existing planetary surveillance systems roughly into those that focus on "security" and those that focus on "nonsecurity" issues, we would see two starkly different operational norms or modes of governance. Non-security satellites have been embedded in, and operated through, several overlapping and increasingly robust *multilateral* regimes. These include the Committee on Earth Observations Satellites (CEOS), the Earth Observation International Coordination Working Group (EO-ICWG), and the World Weather Watch of the World Meteorological Organization (WMO/WWW), which in turn are coordinated through the Integrated Global Observing Strategy (IGOS) of the UN EarthWatch Program.[50] Additionally, production and operation of these systems has been increasingly transnational, with collaborative joint ventures among several states becoming the norm for both R&D and long-term missions and operations. NASA's EOS is a case in point, involving the cooperative efforts of several countries.[51]

In the security sphere, however, satellite surveillance has been primarily *unilateral*. While there has been a rapid expansion in the number of multilateral security regimes since the end of the Cold War, and while numerous studies have shown ways in which space-based surveillance will play an indispensable role in their operations, *no formal provisions have been made for satellite surveillance in any multilateral security regime*. Instead, the practice to date has been that the United States has supplied imagery to these various multilateral security regimes in an ad hoc way. Consider, for example, the extent to which the policing operations of the Gulf War and ensuing United Nations Special Commission in Iraq were dependent on the vastly superior intelligence and surveillance capabilities of the United States.[52] Or consider the extent to which relief, peacekeeping, and peace-enforcement operations in Bosnia were dependent on the supply of United States' intelligence and imagery. Or consider the reliance of the International Atomic Energy Agency (IAEA) on imagery and data supplied by the United States in its disciplining and sanction of North Korea.[53] Or, more recently, consider the supply of U.S. satellite and aerial data to the UN High Commission on Refugees in determining the size and flow of refugees between Zaire and Rwanda.[54]

Certainly, in the cases mentioned above, the interests of the international community, the United States, and these multilateral security regimes were all more or less congruent. But such a neat intersection should not be counted on to persist indefinitely. There may be times, in other words, when the United States could use its leverage over surveillance to sway the operations of such regimes toward its more parochial concerns. Rather than ensure a balance of power, such unilateralism could actually lead to the *institutionalized imbalance* of influence by a

single state over the operations of existing and future security regimes—
an imbalance that could potentially undermine the viability and legitimacy of the wider principles of multilateralism on which such regimes
now rest. The accusations levied by North Korea of the IAEA being a
"tool of the U.S.A." because of its use of U.S. satellite imagery may provide a glimpse of such a possible deterioration.[55] To counter this imbalance and foster multilateralism, much more attention should be paid to
the ways in which multilateral arms control verification and peacekeeping regimes can make autonomous use of satellite remote-sensing data.

*What is the relationship between the possible weaponization of
space and Earth remote-sensing activities?* The extent to which outer
space technologies are now considered vital to modern war fighting, particularly in the United States, is increasingly well known. Integral to the
Revolution in Military Affairs (RMA), outer space technologies provide
the "high ground" essential to communicating information around the
world, coordinating force movements, rehearsing simulated interventions, and targeting attacks. Since the dawn of the Space Age, a multifaceted regime has existed that has prevented the placing of weapons
in outer space or using space as a theatre of war. Although there are
several treaties and agreements of relevance here, the most important
is the 1967 Outer Space Treaty, which, among other things, outlaws the
placement of weapons of mass destruction in outer space and the use of
the moon or other celestial bodies for military purposes. The 1972 Anti-
Ballistic Missile Treaty (ABM) also bans the development, testing, and
deployment of ABM systems in a number of environments, one of which
includes outer space. In addition to these agreements, there have been
several principles and resolutions of the UN General Assembly and the
Committee on the Peaceful Uses of Outer Space (COPUOS) that have
formed the basis for this regime.

According to many observers, however, this regime (which has
always been a tenuous one at best) is now in danger of disintegrating.
The United States has recently announced its withdrawal from the ABM
Treaty. Although there are numerous reasons for the withdrawal, it is
widely considered that one of them was that the United States needs
to develop an effective war-fighting capability for outer space, which
would include an anti-missile capability component. Some go so far
as to suggest that the United States acquire "total space domination."[56]
Reaffirming the regime that prevents the weaponization of outer space
would help create safeguards against such a potentially dangerous and
normatively dubious bid.[57] By preventing the tools (AntiSatellite, or

ASAT, weapons) necessary to acquire military dominance in space, it would create safeguards against any one state attempting to acquire space hegemony and thus preserve the present multicentered Earth-monitoring system.

Conclusion

As described above, for much of the Cold War era the story of satellite remote sensing was of strong constraints against autonomous development, mostly emanating from the military and intelligence apparatuses of the Soviet Union and the United States. A separate, much less powerful constraint existed from the concerns over national resource sovereignty from developing countries. Over the last several decades, and especially since the end of the Cold War, however, these constraints have gradually been removed. Today the Earth is blanketed by a dense web of inward-focusing surveillance systems, operating in numerous spectral modes and resolution capabilities and controlled by several states, regional agencies, and international organizations for a variety of tasks. The commercial market for high resolution satellite imagery is perhaps the pinnacle of these developments, providing access to data that in the past was monopolized by a small elite of intelligence officials in the United States and the Soviet Union.

The number of uses for, and interests in, remote-sensing technologies has mushroomed to such an extent that this dispersed web of surveillance is beginning to act as a constraint of its own should any attempt be made to reconsolidate Earth remote-sensing activities. What might be called an Internet-effect can be seen to be operating in the area of Earth remote-sensing, where prohibitions against use are being sidestepped through the multiple suppliers that now exist in several state jurisdictions. One possible scenario by which such a reconsolidation could take place, however, is in the event of a global military crisis involving the United States where access to space-based technologies by hostile foreign powers would compromise U.S. war fighting capabilities. Short of such a crisis, however, the trends described above will likely continue with increasing movement in the direction of a widening and deepening of access to, and provision of, Earth remote-sensing data.

Such a development of enhanced global transparency and 24-hour Earth surveillance presents a radically different environment for global governance than that which has existed for much of human history. Seen in light of the increased attention to issues of global governance in the early twenty-first century, the existence of this technological web shifts the security problematic from an international to an "intra-planetary" context. Like so much else related to new information and communication technologies, satellite remote-sensing systems are pushing us increasingly in a direction of "world domestic politics." In such a context, questions of a normative nature involving the comparative benefits and drawbacks of alternative architectures of planetary surveillance become especially potent and worthy of attention by those interested in world politics and global governance.

NOTES

1. Although such probes are rare today, they were much more common early in the "Space Age." In a sense, this analysis mirrors a question asked more than twenty-five years ago by Klaus Knorr: "How much will advancing space technology and development affect the intentions and/or capabilities of actors in the [world] system, and hence, perhaps, also the operation of the system itself?" ("The International Implications of Outer-Space Activities," in *Outer Space in World Politics,* ed. Joseph Goldsen (New York: Praeger, 1963), 115–16.

2. For a study of the social pressures constraining and directing technological change, see Brian Winston, *Media, Technology and Society: A History From the Telegraph to the Internet* (New York: Routledge Press, 1998).

3. The U.S. military involvement in satellite reconnaissance affected U.S. participation in the International Geophysical Year outlined above. In a portent of things to come, U.S. scientists wanted U.S. participation to be as open and unclassified as possible but were blocked by military officials. For a discussion, see Joseph M. Goldsen, "Outer Space in World Politics," in *Outer Space in World Politics,* ed. Joseph M. Goldsen (New York: Praeger, 1963), 7.

4. See Jeffrey Richelson, *America's Secret Eyes in Space* (New York: Harper & Row, 1990).

5. The best history of the Corona program is found in Dwayne A. Day, John M. Logsdon, and Brian Latell, eds., *Eye in the Sky: The Story of the Corona Spy Satellites* (Washington, DC: Smithsonian Institution Press, 1998).

6. See Jeffrey Richelson, *The U.S. Intelligence Community* (Cambridge, MA: Harper & Row, 1989), 27–29.

7. An excellent overview of the Corona program can be found at the Federation of American Scientists Web site: www.fas.org/spp/military/program/imint/corona.htm. See Day, Logsdon, and Latell, eds., *Eye in the Sky,* 8, for some details on the early Corona pictures.

8. William J. Burrows, *Deep Black: Space Espionage and National Security* (New York: Berkeley Books, 1986), viii.

9. Goldsen, "Outer Space in World Politics," 21.

10. Lincoln Bloomfield, "The Prospects for Law and Order," in *Outer Space:*

Prospects for Man and Society, ed. Lincoln Bloomfield (New Jersey: Prentice Hall, 1962).

11. For a discussion of the politics of international communications, see Hamid Mowlana, *Global Information and World Communication: New Frontiers in International Relations* (London: Sage, 1997).

12. Cited in Philip M. Taylor, *Global Communications, International Affairs and the Media Since 1945* (London: Routledge, 1997), 47.

13. For a review of these issues, see John V. Granger, *Technology and International Relations* (San Francisco, W. H. Freeman, 1979), 158–60.

14. Karen Litfin, "The Gendered Eye in the Sky: A Feminist Perspective on Earth Observation Satellites," *Frontiers* 18, no. 2 (1997): 26–47.

15. Ibid.

16. At best, the concerns of developing countries found concrete manifestation in the U.N. General Assembly resolution on "Principles Relating to Remote Sensing of the Earth from Space," and in particular several principles giving sensed states the right to access remote-sensing data of their own territory "on reasonable cost terms."

17. For a useful examination of the administrative pressures and constraints that led to the creation and then modification of NASA's Mission to Planet Earth, see W. Henry Lambright, "Administrative Entrepreneurship and Space Technology: The Ups and Downs of 'Mission to Planet Earth,'" *Public Administration Review* 54, no. 2 (March/April 1994): 97–104; and W. Henry Lambright, "Downsizing Big Science: Strategic Choices," *Public Administration Review* 58, no. 3 (May/June 1998): 259–68.

18. Good background on the politics of global warming and climate change can be found in John Houghton, *Global Warming: The Complete Briefing,* 2nd ed. (Cambridge, UK: Cambridge University Press, 1997).

19. One rather extreme and heavily U.S.-centric example of the latter is Thomas Gale Moore, *Climate of Fear: Why We Shouldn't Worry about Global Warming* (Washington, DC: Cato Institute, 1998).

20. See Joseph Rose, "Solving the Mysteries of Twisters," *Wired News,* 3 June 1999. See the Lightning and Atmospheric Electricity Research Center at the Global Hydrology and Climate Center Web site at www.thunder.msfc.nasa. gov/.

21. See, for example, the Automated Ship and Oil Slick Detection site at the Canada Centre for Remote Sensing Web site, www.ccrs.nrcan.gc.ca/ccrs/ tekrd/radarsat/images/nfd/rnfd01e.html.

22. See the NASA Observatorium Education site's description of "How Remote Sensing Helped Find a Lost City," www.observe.ivv.nasa.gov/nasa/exhibits/ ubar/ubar_0.html.

23. See the ReliefSat Web site at www.fram.nrsc.no/reliefsat/.

24. Gerald M. Steinberg, "Dual-Use Aspects of Commercial High Resolution Imaging Satellites," *BESA Security and Policy Studies* 37 (February 1998): 11.

25. See the White House, Office of the Press Secretary, "Foreign Access To Remote Sensing Space Capabilities," 10 March 1994. The restrictions include, as outlined in number 7: "During periods when national security or international obligations and/or foreign policies may be compromised, as defined by the Secretary of Defense or the Secretary of State, respectively, the Secretary of Commerce may, after consultation with the appropriate agency(ies), require the licensee to limit data collection and/or distribution by the system to the extent necessitated by the given situation."

26. See William J. Broad, "Private Spy in Space to Rival Military's," *New York Times,* 27 April 1999; and William J. Broad, "Giant Leap for Private Industry: Spies in Space," *New York Times,* 13 October 1999.

27. See Steward Taggart, "Digital Mapping Paying Off in South Australia," *Wired News,* 19 September 1997.

28. www.terraserver.com/.

29. www.remotesensing.org/.

30. As quoted in Leonard David, "Panelists Say Remote Sensing Industry Must Shift Focus From Space to Information," 4 November 1999 at www.space news.com/isba/panel5coverage.html; italics added.

31. Edward Alden, "Canada Seeks Satellite Suppliers," *Financial Times,* 12 August 1999.

32. Bob Brewin, "EU to Launch Homegrown Satellite Navigation System," *CNN News,* 17 March 1999.

33. See President Decision Directive-March 23, 1994 at www.fas.org/irp/offdocs/pdd23-2.htm.

34. William J. Broad, "Private Spy in Space to Rival Military's," *New York Times,* 27 April 1999.

35. See the FAS Web site at *www.fas.org/*. See also Gary Stix, "Public Eye," *Scientific American* (August 1996): 18.

36. See William J. Broad, "Spy Photos of Korea Missile Site Bring Dispute," *New York Times,* 11 January 2000; Joseph Anselmo, "Commercial Images Detail North Korean Missile Site," *Aviation Week and Space Technology,* 17 January 2000; and Bob Drogin, "Sale to Public of Satellite Photos Debated," *Los Angeles Times,* 15 January 2000. The official response was made by Kenneth Bacon, Assistant Secretary of Defense for Public Affairs on January 11, 2000. See the news briefing at www.fas.org/nuke/guide/dprk/facility/t01112000_t0111asd.htm.

37. See Stix, "Public Eye."

38. Paul Bedard, "Uncle Sam, Show Us the UFOs," *U.S. News and World Report* 24 January 2000.

39. See Joanne Gabrynowicz, "The Promise and Problems of the Land Remote Sensing Policy Act of 1992," *Space Policy* (November 1993): 319–28. As Gabrynowicz notes, "The dovetailing" of national security and environmental monitoring activities may become more common in the future.

40. This section draws from Ronald J. Deibert, "From Deep Black to Green? De-

Mystifying the Military Monitoring of the Environment," *Environmental Change and Security Report* 2 (January 1996); and Ronald J. Deibert, "Out of Focus: U.S. Military Satellites and Environmental Rescue," in *Contested Grounds,* ed. Deudney and Matthew (Albany: SUNY Press, 1999).

41. See William J. Broad, "U.S. Will Deploy Its Spy Satellites on Nature Mission," *New York Times,* 27 November 1995.

42. *Assessing the Potential for Civil-Military Integration: Technologies, Processes and Practices,* United States Office of Technology Assessment Report ISS-611, September 1994.

43. See Joanne Gabrynowicz, "Promise and Problems," 319–28.

44. See *Civilian Satellite Remote Sensing: A Strategic Approach,* United States Office of Technology Assessment Report ISS-607, September 1994, esp. chap. 3, "Planning for Future Remote Sensing Systems."

45. "Brazil Signs $1.4 Billion Satellite Contract with U.S. Companies," *Associated Press/News and Observer,* 1 June 1995.

46. Ann Florini and Yahya A. Dehqanzada, "No More Secrets? Policy Implications of Commercial Remote Sensing Satellites," *Global Policy Program, Project on Transparency: Working Paper Number 1,* Carnegie Endowment for International Peace, July 1999.

47. For a discussion, see Ray Harris and Roman Krawec, "Some Current International and National Earth Observation Data Policies," *Space Policy* (November 1993): 273–85; and Ray Harris and Roman Krawec, "Earth Observation Data Pricing Policy," *Space Policy* (November 1993): 299–318. As Harris and Krawec note, "It has been estimated that in the USA a typical global change research grant is approximately $150,000 for one year, of which about $20,000 may be available for the purchase of data. This would allow, for example, the purchase of four Landsat Thematic Mapper geocoded digital scenes, which is unlikely to be adequate for a global change research project" (p. 302).

48. Florini and Dehqanzada, "No More Secrets?"

49. Robin Mansell and Sam Paltridge, "The Earth Observation Market: Industrial Dynamics and their Impact on Data Policy," *Space Policy* (November 1993): 286.

50. See the Earthwatch homepage at www.unep.ch/earthw.html.

51. For an overview of EOS, see "Special Issue on ISY: Mission to Planet Earth," *IEEE Technology and Society Magazine* (Spring 1992). The primary forum for international coordination of EOS is the Earth Observation International Coordination Working Group, involving the United States, Europe, Japan, and Canada.

52. See Steven Mataija and J. Marshall Beier, eds., *Multilateral Verification and the Post–Gulf War Environment: Learning from the UNSCOM Experience* (Toronto: York University Centre for International and Strategic Affairs, 1992).

53. See David Fischer, "The Safeguards System of the International Atomic En-

ergy Agency after Iraq and North Korea," in *Verification 1994,* ed. J. B. Poole and R. Guthrie (London: Brassey's, 1994).

54. See "REFMon-Refugee Monitoring Using High Resolution Imagery," a project undertaken at the Nansen Environmental and Remote Sensing Center, Bergen, Norway, for information on using satellite imagery to determine refugee flows, at ww.nrsc.no:8001/~einar/UN/refmon.html.

55. Fischer, "The Safeguards System," 53.

56. See the U.S. Air Force *Report 2025* (August 1996), found at www.au.af.mil/au/2025/, which makes the case for the abrogation of the ABM Treaty as well as the necessity of the United States' acquiring "total space domination." As the authors of that report argue, "The successful integration of information, air, and space will provide increased capabilities by enhancing the capabilities of each individual area as well as the combination of them. Utilizing them will allow the U.S. to achieve dominance in air and space to protect the nation, its assets, and its citizens around the globe."

57. On the verification of the prevention of outer space weaponization, see William J. Durch, "Verification of Limitations on AntiSatellite Weapons," in William C. Potter, ed., *Verification and Arms Control* (Toronto: Lexington Books, 1985); Joseph Pilot, "Prospects for Space Arms Control," in *Space Without Weapons* (Montreal: McGill University Centre for Research of Air and Space Law, October 1989); and Donald Hafner, "Verification of ASAT Arms Control," in *Verification and Compliance: A Problem- Solving Approach,* ed. Michael Krepon and Mary Umberger (Cambridge, MA: Ballinger, 1989).

4 Entering the Space Station Era

International Cooperation and the Next Decade
in Human Spaceflight

Karl A. Leib

A DOMINANT image of the Space Age is the astronaut, encased
in technology, boldly crossing the new frontier, whether that frontier is Earth orbit, the moon, or some more distant vista. Human spaceflight has remained a preoccupation of the public and of decision makers
in part because of the emotional power of this image. However, adven-
tures like the Apollo moon landings have been primarily driven by political considerations of national interest and pride.[1] Within that basic
framework, the political rationale of the U.S. space program has dramatically changed from its roots in the 1950s. The end of the Cold War
eroded the value of international competition as a political justification.
Increasingly, space programs are rationalized for their economic benefits. International cooperation has also emerged as an important political
rationale, especially for the International Space Station (ISS), the largest
contemporary space project.[2]

Nominally a scientific project, the Space Station has been most
clearly defined by its political rationale. That rationale has been linked
to American foreign policy interests and has shifted dramatically over
time. Begun by President Ronald Reagan, the American-led multilateral
Space Station was presented as a peaceful project of "free world" countries necessary to counter the Soviet "lead in space stations."[3] The Space
Station even had a good Cold War name, *Freedom*. By 1993, entering its
third presidential administration, long overdue, and with no hardware
in orbit, the Space Station faced a new political environment. Emerging
from a major redesign process, the Space Station, with post-communist
Russia as a partner, was reinvented as the ISS, the premier science project of the post–Cold War world.

The unfolding story of the Space Station is significant because, for
good or ill, it provides a model for future international cooperation in

science and technology. Domestically, the Space Station offers several insights into space and international relations. It also suggests some of the perils inherent in large-scale science and technology projects. With the end of the Cold War, international cooperation is the most politically acceptable rationale for human spaceflight. Human explorers may only reach the Holy Grail of space, the planet Mars, through an international endeavor like the ISS. Finally, the ISS is likely to be the sole human spaceflight program the United States will attempt for a decade. The Space Station is therefore an important test case for international cooperation and possibly a harbinger of the future for the American space program.

The Space Station Project

The history of the Space Station project is reminiscent of an adventure serial with many perilous encounters, twists of fortune, and narrow escapes.[4] The major domestic peril facing the Space Station has been its spiraling and unpredictable cost. When the program began in 1984, NASA estimated the cost of designing and building the Space Station to be $8 billion.[5] However, by 1993, $10 billion had been spent on research and development with little hardware built and none launched into space.[6] Presently, NASA estimates the cost of building the current ISS design at $24–26 billion, with an additional $13 billion in operating costs during the project's 10-year life span.[7] However, these estimates appear less and less plausible, despite budget caps, and the final cost of the Space Station is still a matter for dispute. For example, the Government Accounting Office (GAO) has placed the final cost of construction and operation at $94 billion.[8]

Technical complexity is another peril that has dogged the Space Station project. The assembly process will be long and difficult. The scale of the project is unprecedented: the completed ISS will be the largest object ever assembled in space. The ISS will be approximately the size of a football field—108 meters (356 feet) across and 80 meters (262 feet) wide—and will have a mass of 454,000 kilograms (1 million pounds). Three to six crewmembers will staff the Space Station when assembly is completed, sometime around 2006.[9] Approximately fifty separate launches by the United States and Russia will be required to place ISS components in orbit.[10] Numerous difficult and dangerous Extra-Vehicular Activities (EVAs), or "space walks," will be required to assemble and maintain the ISS. The success of the ISS remains dependent on many different technical and managerial systems functioning properly over an extended period of time.

Justifying this expense and risk has been a persistent problem for Space Station supporters. From the beginning of the program, the Space Station was touted as a multipurpose facility that would serve many different functions, from pure research to commercial production. Presently, a major goal of the ISS is to learn about the effects on human beings of long-duration spaceflight, which is critical if piloted missions to Mars are to be attempted. In addition, medical and other scientific research will be conducted in the Space Station's laboratory modules, exploiting the microgravity environment of space.

Budgetary and technical limitations forced several redesigns to the Space Station, resulting in fewer missions and a smaller facility. The assembly of large orbiting structures and the repair of satellites are two mission categories originally proposed for *Freedom* but not part of the current ISS. Automated research modules in independent orbits and small craft to service them also fell victim to budget cuts. The current Space Station is also planned for a shorter life span. The *Freedom* was projected to operate for thirty years, whereas the ISS is projected to operate for only a decade, although operational duration could potentially be extended.

Beyond these perils lie the difficulties of international cooperation. The promotion of international understanding and cooperation is an often stated, if ill-defined objective of the project. The Space Station has been variously presented as a means to "strengthen peace," to "forge new partnerships with the nations of the world," and to "promote international cooperation."[11] Although primarily an American program, the international dimension has been critical for the evolution and survival of the ISS.

With sixteen countries participating to one degree or another, the ISS is truly an international undertaking.[12] However, cooperation in space on this scale is new. The ISS partners operate through a variety of multi- and bilateral agreements that address many but not all of the potential problems the project may face. Satisfying the policy goals of all the partners has been a persistent challenge. Relations between the United States and the original partners (Canada, the European Space Agency, and Japan) have never been smooth. The incorporation of Russia into the program created as many problems as it alleviated. Some American officials have been uneasy about cooperation, fearing the transfer of economically sensitive technology. It remains to be seen how the political and cultural dimensions of cooperation will shape the ISS.

History and Development

BACKGROUND

The space station idea goes back to the earliest spaceflight visionaries of the late 1800s.[13] Before the electronic revolution, it was widely assumed that space-based telecommunications, Earth observation, and weather forecasting would require inhabited space stations. Space stations were also viewed as the first step toward deep space. In the 1950s, Wernher von Braun envisioned a giant wheel-like space station that would be an orbiting laboratory and a staging post for flights to the moon and Mars.[14] The 1968 film *2001: A Space Odyssey* visualized a gracefully rotating space station as a way station to the moon and planets.

While early concepts were influential in defining for the public what a space station was supposed to look like, the demands of the Cold War "space race" between the United States and the Soviet Union necessitated a different path. *Apollo* reached the moon without a space station. In addition, by the 1960s automated satellites began providing those space-borne services that were most profitable and valuable.

However, the space station idea still had its proponents. NASA sought a permanent space station as part of its post-*Apollo* proposal that included a fully reusable Space Shuttle and human missions to Mars. When the Space Station was rejected by President Richard Nixon for budgetary reasons, NASA settled for a partially reusable Space Shuttle and a temporary space station, *Skylab*.[15] Derived from leftover *Apollo* hardware and launched in 1973, *Skylab* was used successfully by three separate crews. However, no follow-up station was launched, and *Skylab* ungraciously reentered the Earth's atmosphere in 1979, a symbol to the public of a space program adrift. No Americans flew in space between July 1975 and April 1981 as NASA focused on building the complex and expensive Space Shuttle system.

THE FREEDOM PROJECT

The U.S. space program never existed in a purely national environment, and despite winning the so-called race to the moon, many Americans still saw the Soviet Union as a rival in space. It was, in fact, the Soviet Union that launched the first space station two years before *Skylab*. Called *Salyut 1,* it was followed by six additional space stations with the same name over the next decade. A larger, modular space station, *Mir,* was launched in 1986. Abandoning its lunar program after *Apollo 11* landed on the moon, the Soviet Union concentrated on space stations and developing an impressive infrastructure for operations in Earth orbit, including reliable launchers, automated supply ships, and techniques for supporting a crew for up to a year in space.

The Soviet "lead" in space station operations was a hook that could be used to rejuvenate the dream of an American space station. Within NASA, the space station idea had never died, and after the first Space Shuttle flights in 1981, the agency began to promote a space station as "the Next Logical Step" in space.[16] Shuttle flights had heightened public interest in space, and NASA believed President Ronald Reagan would be supportive.[17] NASA presented the Soviet Union as having established a permanent presence in space, with implications for American technological, symbolic, and military leadership. Capitalizing on this (and Cold War fears), NASA offered the Space Station as a counter to the Soviet "threat" as well as a boon to the American economy and national prestige. When NASA presented its case for the Space Station to Reagan in a 1983 meeting, Administrator James Beggs and his lieutenants promised numerous benefits, including a challenge to the USSR and the unleashing of America's latent technological power.[18]

Supporting NASA's proposal, the president announced his decision in his 1984 State of the Union address. Echoing John Kennedy's initiation of *Apollo* decades earlier, Reagan announced that he was "directing NASA to develop a permanently manned Space Station and to do it within a decade." He claimed that "[a] space station will permit quantum leaps in our research in science, communications, in metals, and in lifesaving medicines which could be manufactured only in space . . . strengthen peace, build prosperity and expand freedom for all who share our goals."[19]

The decision was not universally popular. Reagan actually embraced the Space Station over the objections of many of his key advisors, including Defense Secretary Caspar Weinberger and Budget Director David Stockman.[20] The birth of the Space Station was rooted in Cold War competition and Reagan's own faith in the power of American technological ingenuity. According to Beggs, Reagan was fascinated by the Space Station's potential for science and national prestige.[21] The size and scale of the project also reflected Reagan's proclivity toward asserting U.S. power through large-scale technology.

However, from the beginning the Space Station was also conceived to be a cooperative venture with American allies. This was welcomed by NASA, which had been informally canvassing potential partners for almost two years.[22] The partners' contributions would expand the capabilities of the Space Station and give it a broader political rationale; moreover, it could be presented as a cost-saving measure, while still maintaining American dominance. By 1988, NASA had negotiated formal agreements with the European Space Agency (ESA), Canada, and Japan that governed the construction and operation of the Space Station, now formally named *Freedom*. The project at this time involved twelve countries.[23]

Several difficulties derailed the original ten-year development and assembly schedule of the Space Station. The 1986 *Challenger* accident delayed all space projects as NASA's organization and morale recovered. The accident heightened concern over safety and dependence on the Space Shuttle for Space Station operations, issues that were reflected in subsequent Space Station designs. However, even without the *Challenger* accident, the Space Station program was having problems: the cost and complexity of the project continued to increase, and political support was erratic. During the administration of George H. W. Bush, *Freedom* was redesigned and its managerial structure reworked. While Bush was generally supportive of the Space Station, congressional support was weak, and there were frequent, albeit unsuccessful votes to cancel the Space Station. No hardware was placed in orbit, and the projected launch date continued to slip further into the future.

ALPHA OPTION AND THE INTERNATIONAL SPACE STATION

In 1993 Bill Clinton entered the White House with an agenda of economic development and social reform. While he was supportive of the Space Station during the campaign, Clinton's support was not guaranteed because he was also committed publicly to reducing the federal budget deficit. The new Congress was also giving priority to budget cuts. Public apprehension about the deficit required that both Democrats and Republicans appear to reduce federal spending. In this climate, the Space Station was an easy target for budget cutters. In late June 1993, the House defeated an amendment to terminate the Space Station by one vote, 216–215, a sign of how weak congressional support was.[24] With the transition to a new administration, government spending under intense scrutiny, and the public ambivalent about space, the Space Station was in a policy limbo.

The project's weakness was its lack of a strong political rationale. Although the end of the Cold War had reduced concerns about Russian space activities, cooperation with traditional allies had limited public appeal. The scientific research to be conducted on the Space Station was real, but it was insufficient to justify a multibillion dollar project. In fact, many in the scientific community opposed the Space Station as too expensive. For the Space Station to survive, a new political rationale had to be devised.

President Clinton ultimately backed the Space Station but ordered it redesigned.[25] Working furiously, NASA came up with three models that varied in different degrees from *Freedom*'s design. Clinton approved a design that emphasized Option A, which came to be known as "Alpha." While requiring changes, the Alpha design maintained much of *Freedom*'s hardware and international participation. However, the Alpha design was rapidly overtaken by new diplomatic developments. The end of the Cold War had opened many new opportunities for U.S.-Russian cooperation, and space was a major topic of discussions between the two countries. What emerged was a new Space Station design that essentially merged the Alpha model with Russian components to create a totally new project. Symbolic of this change, the project became known as the International Space Station (ISS), although the name *Freedom* lingered for a time. The name *Alpha* returned in 2000 as the semi-official name of the ISS.[26]

Russian participation had several political ramifications. First, the Space Station was no longer an American project with valuable but ultimately dispensable foreign components. The project was now truly international in scope and management. The ISS would be dominated by two countries rather than one and would be wholly dependent on effective cooperation between those countries. However, the incorporation of Russia added a high-profile, exciting, and much-needed foreign policy rationale. Cooperation between Cold War adversaries also gave the ISS a positive sense of poetic irony.

The primary foreign policy benefit was the integration of Russia into the democratic world and forging a new post–Cold War order. At center stage was arms control. An emergent fear, as Soviet institutions crumbled, was the security of nuclear and other weapon stockpiles. As fifteen new countries rose from the ruins of the Soviet Union, many observers were concerned that military technology or hardware would be sold to proliferators in the developing world or that Russian personnel would sell their skills. In response, the United States pressured Russia to alter its arms exportation policies. One agreement, involving the sale of missile technology to India, particularly concerned the Clinton administration. While this was not an explicit part of the ISS agreements, Russia agreed to modify its contract with India. Significantly, the United States paid Russia $400 million as part of the Shuttle-*Mir* project, the same amount Russia claimed that restructuring the sale to India cost.[27]

There were also technical implications of Russian involvement. The Russians had valuable expertise in space station operations. This experience, earned in the Salyut and Mir projects, was seen by NASA as contributing to the ISS. Russian participation also meant the ISS would have a larger crew and more electrical power than the Alpha option.[28] Although this was not borne out by events, advocates of Russian participation also promised that the overall cost of the Space Station would be reduced and that the facility would reach habitability status far sooner than the Alpha plan.

However, Russian participation was highly controversial. Misgivings were voiced in Congress, even from traditional Space Station supporters. The greatest fear was the potential loss of American aerospace jobs if some Space Station work were to be done abroad. Political instability in Russia raised questions about the strength of its democracy and the country's ability to fulfill its international commitments.[29] Russia's contributions to the ISS were necessary for its operation and as such were classified by NASA as being "critical path" items. Although some members of Congress warned about such dependence on Russia, NASA assured Congress that the monetary and scheduling cost of any possible Russian withdrawal from the project would not severely disrupt the project.[30]

Ultimately, it was the desire to integrate Russia into U.S.-led institutions and the promise of faster deployment that won enough adherents to save the Space Station. Linking the Space Station to better relations with Russia was the best political solution for a project that had lost its main political rationale. Reborn, the ISS received an additional boost in 1995 when Congress approved multi-year funding for the ISS, fixing the annual budget at $2.1 billion.[31] This placed the project on a firmer financial footing and gave the ISS a stronger political coalition, joining the White House and Congress as well as Republicans and Democrats.

Building the ISS

PRELUDE TO THE SPACE STATION: THE SHUTTLE-*MIR* PROGRAM

With Russia on board, the Space Station began anew with a revised development schedule. Phase I (1995–98) was devoted to integrating American and Russian techniques of conducting space operations.[32] During Phase II an initial station (consisting primarily of American and Russian components) was to be assembled and utilized. Contributions from the other partners would be added during final construction in Phase III, when full utilization of the Space Station would be under way.

Phase I, the Shuttle-Mir program, served several purposes. Its explicit goal was to give American astronauts long-term spaceflight experience using *Mir*, the only space station then in existence. Seven astronauts went to *Mir* on missions that lasted up to six months. Russian cosmonauts flew on American Space Shuttles seven times.[33] Nine Space Shuttle missions docked with *Mir* to exchange crews and deliver supplies. Phase I missions also aimed to work out the managerial and technical hurdles of joint operations between countries, using technologies and techniques separately developed over thirty years.

Unfortunately, there were many such hurdles. *Mir* was an aging and treacherous facility. A number of technical problems during Phase I were capped by "two life-threatening emergencies" that imperiled *Mir* and its crew.[34] One accident, a collision with a robot supply ship seriously damaged one module of *Mir*. An even more serious situation, an on-board fire started by faulty life-support equipment, placed the entire Shuttle-Mir program in question. It was charged by many critics of cooperation with Russia, including James Sensenbrenner (R-WI), then the powerful chair of the House Science Committee, that NASA was risking American lives on *Mir*.[35] These incidents raised questions about the safety not only of *Mir* but also of the entire plan to cooperate with Russia. Although NASA sets safety standards for the ISS, Russian performance on safety has not always been acceptable to NASA or to Congress. The accidents heightened these fears. Despite the controversy, NASA completed the Shuttle-Mir Phase I program and went ahead with the joint construction of the ISS.

FIRST FLIGHTS, NEW DELAYS

The Shuttle-Mir program completed, the partners began Phase II of the ISS, the initial construction stage. After fourteen years of planning and delays, on November 20, 1998, the first ISS component, *Zarya* (Sunrise), was launched from Russia. Two weeks later, the shuttle *Endeavour* connected *Zarya* to the American *Unity* module. While this was a promising start, the next module, the Russian *Zvezda* (Star) was plagued by delays and was not launched until July 2000. However, the pace of ISS activities stepped up in November 2000 with the first "Expedition" crews living on the Space Station for four-month missions. Since then, numerous segments have been attached to the growing outpost.

The ISS has not, however, escaped the perils of its past. Entirely separate from the delays attributed to Russia were cost overruns that began to exceed the $2.1 billion budget cap. Depending on how one views accounting measures used by NASA, it could be said that NASA began exceeding the $2.1 billion cap in fiscal year 1997.[36] As a result, the total cost of the ISS continued to grow, and an independent review headed by Jay Chabrow in 1998 concluded that the cost of building ISS could be $24.7 billion (rather than the $17.4 billion stated in 1993). The Chabrow report also concluded that assembly could take ten to thirty-eight months longer than NASA anticipated. The completion date has also slipped from 2004 to 2006. Political support for the Space Station is still variable; and in a final irony, as the ISS is being assembled in orbit, calls for its cancellation have never stopped.

Using the Space Station: 2002 and Beyond

With assembly under way, utilization of the ISS is the next phase. The planned uses of the Space Station have changed considerably since it was first proposed in 1984. As noted, the trend has been toward a reduction in the number of different missions and activities to be performed on the Space Station. This has largely been due to budget restrictions and to the smaller station plans that have emerged from redesign exercises. Presently, the primary use of the ISS will be microgravity research, including material processing and the potential manufacture of special materials in space. Such research will include the study of metals, chemicals, and other liquids in controlled gravity environments in the Japanese-American centrifuge module when it is launched. Private companies have been encouraged to explore possible programs of microgravity research on the ISS.

A major element of the Space Station scientific program is biomedical research. This has two major components. The first is the study of humans in space and the effects of long-duration spaceflight. This is vital for future space missions (especially Mars) and could also have ground applications. The second form of biological research involves research on medicines and drugs. Ultra-pure mixtures of drugs could be produced in the centrifuge. The value of the ISS is its permanent place in orbit. Long-term studies could be conducted that would be impossible on the Space Shuttle. Space Station senior scientist Kathryn Clark noted: "Imagine if researchers at the National Institutes of Health were only able to walk into the lab for two weeks a year."[37] However, there is a potential conflict between the presence of both humans and microgravity research. The motions of the crew and the docking/undocking of spacecraft will produce minute motions of the Space Station that will reduce the efficiency of microgravity experiments. Careful scheduling of experiments and docking/undocking of spacecraft will be necessary to avoid disruption of research.

Many additional missions have been proposed and, although not currently planned, could be added at a later date. The ISS is potentially an element of a greatly expanded orbital infrastructure. It could serve as both an assembly point and a base for maintenance of satellites. It could be used as a base for the construction of other large structures that could not be placed in orbit using a single launcher. Structures that have been suggested include solar powered satellites, communication relays, and other space stations. The orbital maneuvering vehicles cancelled early in the program could be revived in the future to support such operations.

The Space Station could be used as an orbiting "garage" with spare parts and equipment necessary for the repair of damaged satellites or the upgrading of existing satellites. Newly launched satellites could be checked out prior to final deployment. All of these activities would presumably increase satellite life span and reduce operating costs. The successful repair of the *Solar Max* satellite by a Space Shuttle crew in 1984 is an example of this procedure. Additional examples of such work include the *Hubble* repair missions and the repair of *Intelsat VIF3* in 1992.

Another possible mission for the future is use of the ISS as a starting-off point for missions to the moon or to Mars. Large transport spacecraft could be assembled near the ISS, and crews could use it for training prior to interplanetary flights. The ISS could also be used as a quarantine zone for crews returning from Mars as a precaution against the introduction of alien organisms to Earth. If missions to the moon or Mars are to be conducted in the next century, the ISS or some future space station will likely be an important, if not essential component of training and flight operations. At present there are no such missions planned, but the existing ISS concept does not rule out using the Space Station in such a role.

Policy Issues

THE ROLE OF THE INTERNATIONAL PARTNERS

The ISS is potentially a way to conduct or facilitate more ambitious activities in space both in and beyond Earth orbit. To be able to take on any additional roles and even to succeed in its current missions, the ISS must continue to survive criticism and bad luck. The perils that have dogged the Space Station project from its birth have yet to be fully overcome, and additional issues continue to shadow the program. Six separate space agencies representing sixteen countries will be involved to some degree in the assembly and use of the ISS. In the best of times, the construction of a structure as large and complex as the ISS would be highly problematic technically, managerially, and politically.

Organizationally, the United States has enjoyed the role of senior and managing partner. Although the participation of Russia has given that country a central role, NASA is responsible for "overall program management and coordination" including safety requirements.[38] Between them, the United States and Russia are providing the vast majority of ISS components and in return receive the greatest percentage of Space Station resources and crew time.

The United States is providing the bulk of the Space Station superstructure and a laboratory module named *Destiny*. Russia is contributing laboratory modules, additional superstructure components, and a module that provided initial attitude control and living quarters. These contributions are essential for the operation of the Space Station and are therefore classified as "critical path" items. It is this essential nature of its contributions that makes Russia so important to the ISS and has given it such a strong influence over the assembly schedule.

In addition to Russia are the original partners who joined the *Freedom* project in the 1980s and whose contributions are smaller but still important for enhancing the value of the ISS. Japan and the ESA are each developing laboratory modules that the United States will launch and attach to the main ISS.[39] Canada is contributing a robotic "arm," similar to the system developed for the Space Shuttle, which will be used to assemble and maintain the Space Station. This item, deployed in 2001, is the only contribution by the original partners that lies in the critical path.[40] NASA has also signed bilateral agreements with Brazil and Italy for additional Space Station components.[41]

The ISS is governed by five agreements signed in 1998 between the participating states and agencies. All of the participants except Brazil are signatories to the Intergovernmental Agreement (IGA), which sets the overall legal framework and management of the ISS. Concurrent with the IGA are four Memoranda of Understanding (MOU) signed by the participating agencies: NASA, ESA, the Russian Aviation and Space Agency (RKA), the Canadian Ministry of State for Science and Technology, and the Government of Japan on behalf of the Science and Technology Agency. The MOU detail the construction and utilization of the ISS and establish the responsibilities of each partner.

Although the share of resources, crew time, and access to facilities has been worked out, the implementation of these agreements may not be free of conflict. Russia has full use of its laboratory modules and other Space Station resources that it provides, although it has already sold some of its research time to the other partners.[42] The European and Japanese laboratories are to be shared with the United States (with a small amount of each reserved for Canada). Crew time and resources for each partner are to be fulfilled "over time," which will require constant negotiation to ensure that all the partners are satisfied that they are receiving their fair share of Space Station benefits. Trading of resources and crew time between the existing partners or additional countries is also possible.

A final issue is management of the Station. The United States enjoys the greatest formal power over managerial decisions; but Russia, because of the size and criticality of its contribution, has a great deal of influence. The other partners have been concerned with maintaining their position vis-à-vis the United States and Russia to avoid being reduced to minor actors. This is not just symbolism. The partners have been unhappy about the unilateral nature of some American policy decisions relating to the ISS. Decisions regarding the redesign and the participation of Russia were initiated with little or no consultation with the international partners, a fact that irritated the other countries.[43] Russia presented the flight of space tourist Dennis Tito to the partners as a fait accompli, a move that undermined the cooperative spirit. If the ISS is to be successful, it must have both genuine partnership between the contributors and strong central management. That tension between control and cooperation will never be fully resolved, but a modus vivendi must be reached and followed faithfully by all the partners, including the United States and Russia.

THE U.S.-RUSSIAN AXIS

Although good relations with the original partners are important for the success of the ISS, the linchpin of the Space Station today is continued amity between the United States and Russia. Because the Russian contribution is on the critical path, Russia is just as essential for the construction of ISS as is the United States. This key role means that the United States would have no easy solution should Russia withdraw from the project.

Russian financial problems have already created scheduling delays. NASA had originally anticipated that Phase II construction would be completed in 2000, but this was quickly obviated by delays, primarily on the Russian side. The postponed deployment of *Zvezda* delayed the entire project. Since this module provides power, crew accommodations, and attitude control, it had to be attached before additional segments could be launched and before the Space Station could support a crew. The delay created opportunity costs because the facility remained empty in orbit longer than planned. NASA also had to develop costly contingency plans in the event that Russia failed to launch *Zvezda.*

Domestically, the Russian delay hurt relations between NASA and Congress. There were concerns that Russia would divert resources needed for the ISS for the maintenance of *Mir* instead. Russia did prove reluctant to part with *Mir,* promising to de-orbit the facility by mid-1999 but maintaining it in orbit until March 2001.[44] There have also been renewed concerns that Russia is not fulfilling its obligations under the Missile Technology Control Regime (MTCR) and may be transferring missile technology it had agreed not to sell.

An additional concern is the alleged difference in how NASA and the RKA define acceptable risk in space. American suspicions, old as the Space Age, that their Soviet rivals had a lower regard for the lives of space crews, did not end with the passing of the Cold War. The series of near tragedies on *Mir* renewed fears about excessive risk taking and a more cavalier attitude toward crew safety by Russian space officials. Critics of Russian participation warn that weak safety standards could threaten the ISS. The GAO reported in March 2000 that although "Russian elements have complied with the majority of space station safety requirements," there are still several key areas of noncompliance that increase the element of risk.[45] Finally, Russia's insistence that tourist Dennis Tito visit the ISS placed new strains on the relationship and revealed a certain frustration within NASA at being subject to its partner's unilateral actions.[46]

Nonspace issues also could undermine the central ISS partnership. If U.S.-Russian relations were to suffer a serious reversal, the ISS project would be in jeopardy. Russian withdrawal from the project would create new delays and financial problems that would likely result in the end of the ISS as currently conceived. U.S.-Russian relations remain volatile as many policy and geopolitical issues divide the two countries. Military actions, for instance, by the United States in Kosovo and by Russia in Chechnya, have strained relations. More closely related to space, American moves to test a missile defense system and attempts by Congress to link ISS cooperation to Russian foreign policy have drawn Russian ire. A major long-term cooling of U.S.-Russian relations could undermine the political stability the program needs. Since the ISS is projected to last ten years, it is impossible to predict how relations between the partners will affect its management and use.

CULTURAL AND SOCIAL ISSUES

Beyond technical and political issues is the human dimension. Long-duration space missions in the past have witnessed various problems of group and individual psychology. Spacecraft are restricted spaces that leave little room for privacy or diversion. When small numbers of people are placed in such an environment, they face numerous psychological pressures. ISS crews may experience interpersonal conflicts that could disrupt working and personal relationships. The presence of individuals from different national, ethnic, and cultural groups poses additional challenges.

Psychological and interpersonal difficulties have flared on several space missions. Interaction between orbiting crews and ground controllers have not always been amicable, especially when crewmembers believe that unreasonable demands or expectations are being pressed upon them. During the so-called *Skylab* rebellion, astronauts' resentment over an excessive work schedule led the crew to take an unplanned day off work.[47] Russian cosmonauts have also felt occasional resentment over orders from ground controllers, straining this vital relationship.

The long-term psychological and physiological effects of spaceflight have been closely studied for years but are still not well understood. The emotional strain of isolation from friends and family is one factor that emerges in long space missions. Russian experience may be illuminating in making plans for the ISS. A diary kept by *Salyut 7* cosmonaut Valentin Lebedev during his seven-month mission reveals separation anxiety and a progressive sense of physical fatigue.[48]

An additional issue arising out of the ISS is the presence of culturally diverse crews. In late 1999, one multinational training exercise in Moscow witnessed serious altercations between trainees from different countries over personal behavior.[49] The likelihood of such incidents in the future is unclear. The presence of multinational crews in the confined space of the ISS may pose some unique challenges for mission success. Most space crews to date have been of a single nationality, with the occasional presence of crewmembers from other countries. Missions with mixed crews, such as aboard the Space Shuttle and the Russian/Soviet guest cosmonaut program, have generally been of relatively short duration. The important exception to this is the Shuttle-Mir program, when American astronauts lived on *Mir* for up to six months with Russian crewmembers. This experience was mixed. The book *Dragonfly,* by journalist Bryan Burrough, recounts cases of psychological stress that strained relationships between crewmembers,[50] although it is difficult to separate problems produced by stressful situations (like the *Mir* fire) and those caused by cultural conflict. However, some of the *Mir* astronauts reported very positive experiences during their flights.

With sixteen countries participating, the ISS will likely always have citizens of two or more countries in each crew. There is a potential for poor communications due to language barriers or reliance on stereotypes. In addition, standards of acceptable behavior (such as rules of social interaction, sexual mores, deference to authority, and personal space needs) differ from culture to culture. Different cultures also have distinct means of identifying and resolving problems. While such diversity could prove advantageous, it could compound personal conflicts if crewmembers resort to stereotypical beliefs or attribute conflicts to nationality rather than personality. Space agencies of different countries reflect national cultures and have unique institutional cultures, another factor that emerged in the Shuttle-*Mir* program.[51] During long missions that last three or more months, it is important that cultural differences do not lead to clashes that undermine crew relations and work. The early missions to the ISS have witnessed amicable relations between crewmembers and no reported cases of psychological problems. The future will show if this happy record continues.

THE ROLE OF PRIVATE INDUSTRY

The ISS will be available for use by both public and private sector organizations. The participation of private corporations is important if NASA is to prove that the ISS is an engine of scientific and technological progress. It has been U.S. policy since the 1980s to encourage private firms to use the Space Station for commercial development. The general trend away from state management and toward the privatization of government services contributed to this policy. It has been suggested that private firms could lease or buy one or more sections of the ISS from the government or contribute additional research modules. While these suggestions have not been clearly spelled out, former NASA administrator Dan Goldin stated that 30 percent of the U.S. portion of the Space Station would be available to private firms and that the entire station could be transferred to private management after five to ten years of government operation.[52]

Transferring all or part of the ISS to private operators would have two advantages for NASA. The primary benefit would be the freeing up of budgetary resources for new projects. Dan Goldin described privatization as freeing NASA to do more interesting work: "Our hope is to turn the keys of the Station over to an entrepreneur, if the private sector sees opportunity. The government would just become one of many tenants and users of the station. The entrepreneurs could make money as we wave good-bye to low-Earth orbit to explore the far frontier."[53] In theory, privatization would allow NASA to focus on research and development but not operate programs after they prove profitable.

Politically, the use of the ISS by a large number of corporate actors would help to legitimize NASA's claim that space expenditures have broad economic benefits. Commercial research might also produce some of the medical and technological advances promised by NASA. The Space Station literature produced by NASA often speaks of creating "a whole new industry based on space operations."[54] Flawless operations may make the ISS a technical success, but it will also be judged for its scientific accomplishments. Private sector interest in the ISS (as measured by use of the facility) will be vital in determining the success of the project and its chances for long-term operation.

However, transfer of ownership or exclusive rights of sections of the Space Station to the private sector could affect agreements with the international partners. One scenario, in which the United States transfers all or part of its laboratory module to private industry, effects agreements signed with the partners. Canada in particular could be affected by decisions relating to the U.S. lab because it has a right to use a portion (2.3%) of the U.S. lab module and would need to be consulted to ensure that its interests are protected. Any privatization scheme involving the management or use of the ISS will require consultation and perhaps the approval of the participating countries. This would be a decision that NASA or the U.S. government could not make on its own, nor should it attempt to do so. Past unilateral decisions by the United States strained relations with the other countries and threatened the Space Station partnership. Any privatization plans should be carried out in conjunction with the partners, even if that requires additional high-level negotiations.

SPACE TOURISM: BOON OR BANE?

One commercial activity originally not envisioned for the Space Station was tourism. The flight of Dennis Tito in April-May 2001 made this once fanciful dream a reality, though it remains unclear when additional tourists will visit space. Tito's flight placed strains on the ISS partnership because NASA and the other partners strongly opposed the flight and Russia's unilateral actions. They eventually relented since there was no way to bar Tito from the ISS short of a complete breach with Russia. Tito also signed an agreement that protected NASA against legal action in case of an accident.[55] The flight was successful, and Tito became, for a short time, a space celebrity and champion for space tourism. The flight itself garnered considerable media attention, renewing interest in various space tourism concepts. If any of these proposals are developed, in a few decades space tourism may become an exotic "adventure" holiday for a select few. However, the number of possible space tourists is likely to be extremely small, given the high cost and the physical demands of spaceflight.

At present there are no crew-rated spacecraft operated by private industry and only a few by governments. NASA is unlikely for political reasons to ever offer commercial flights, especially with memories of *Challenger* and Christa McAuliffe so deeply engrained in the agency's culture. However, the RKA faces severe budgetary restrictions and apparently sees tourism as a potential source of revenue. While private ventures would not necessarily gain access to the ISS, Russia does have access and has shown its willingness to market that access.

If Russia begins to regularly send paying visitors to the Space Station, three policy issues suggest themselves. The most important is safety, both to the ISS and to the tourists themselves. The process of filtering and training prospective tourists is vital, but it may be undermined by the profit motive. Tito reportedly paid $20 million for his "ticket," and the RKA may face pressures to lower standards for training or health. The death of a private citizen associated with the ISS (however tenuously) could damage the entire project's reputation and political support. An accident that kills a space tourist could undermine public support for citizens in space for years to come.

A second issue is the potential disruption of Space Station research or flight opportunities for professional astronauts. This depends largely on the frequency of such flights, which are unlikely ever to be very high. ISS crewmembers have limited time to conduct research because much of their time is involved in Space Station assembly and maintenance. Research time will be restricted further if the crew of the ISS is limited to three by cancellation of the Habitation Module.[56] Flight opportunities will become scarce, especially for Canadian, European, and Japanese nationals. Allowing paying amateurs opportunities denied to those who have spent years in training will be bad for morale and possibly for recruitment.

A third issue is potentially beneficial for the ISS: increased visibility. The problem faced by the ISS, like *Skylab* before it, is the lack of public awareness of its activities. Science aboard a space station lacks the drama of a Moonwalk or a close-up view of distant planets. Occasional space tourism might generate positive publicity for spaceflight, making it more accessible to the average person. Space tourism could therefore boost the visibility of the ISS worldwide. In celebrity-centered modern cultures, public interest follows media and personal stories. For these reasons, a limited program of tourism, with proper safeguards, could prove beneficial for the ISS.

Tito's flight may ultimately become only a footnote to the ISS story, however. Although a private citizen has used his own money to buy a trip into space, there is not likely to be a surge of followers. Space tourism, on the ISS or in some other facility, is not likely to be significant for some time to come. Whether it proves to be a boon or a bane to the ISS or spaceflight in general cannot yet be determined.

MILITARY USES OF THE SPACE STATION

During the early years of the Space Station project, national security activities were included among its functions. NASA was not specific about these activities, but the agency had hoped to win the Department of Defense (DOD) support for the Space Station. The Pentagon had supported the Space Shuttle, and although the result was not ideal for the military, NASA had sought to continue the partnership. However, the DOD was hostile to the Space Station, wanting NASA to focus its attention on the Space Shuttle. Even before Reagan initiated the program, the DOD made clear that it anticipated no national security uses for a Space Station.[57] On the eve of Reagan's State of the Union Address in 1984, Defense Secretary Caspar Weinberger reiterated that position.[58] Weinberger feared that NASA would be distracted from the more militarily important Space Shuttle and that a Space Station would drain money from defense programs. Nonetheless, DOD officials made it clear they were keeping their options open for the future.

However, proposed military use of the Space Station was highly controversial in many quarters. Many in DOD saw the Space Station as a rival for funds and a potential source of technology transfer to the partner countries. The scientific community was broadly opposed to any military use of the Space Station. The international partners' position was also negative. Recognizing the political liability of military use of the Space Station, NASA back-pedaled somewhat, suggesting that DOD might deploy its *own* space station.[59]

The problem was one of both policy and politics. According to the IGA, all activities on the Space Station had to conform to the "peaceful uses of space" principle explicated in the 1967 Outer Space Treaty and subsequent multilateral agreements governing the use of space. The term "peaceful use" is open-ended enough not to preclude various military uses of space, including reconnaissance and communications. The ISS however, involved countries with very different interpretations of the "peaceful use" clause.

Several military missions could in principle be performed on board a space station, including orbital reconnaissance of foreign countries, battlefield management during military operations, and maintenance of military space infrastructure.[60] However, the Space Station is not the ideal platform for these functions because of its lack of maneuverability and its vulnerability to attack. More plausible was the use of the Space Station as a base to test elements of ballistic missile defense (BMD) technology, then called the Strategic Defense Initiative (SDI).

In 1987 the Pentagon suggested that it might actually have some interest in the Space Station. Weinberger suggested in a letter to Secretary of State George Schultz that the national security use of the Space Station should take precedence over international cooperation and that the U.S. role had to be predominant.[61] The partner reaction was over-whelmingly hostile, briefly threatening the international partnership and the Space Station project itself. A DOD report in March 1988 out-lined in vague, noncommittal terms the potential defense applications of space stations, and the issue gradually faded away. It is possible that the DOD was more interested in undermining the project's political support in Europe and among scientists than in actually using the Space Station. Ultimately, the role of DOD was not significant due to a relative lack of interest by the military in using the Space Station and to the absence of a clear, necessary mission to be performed on it.[62]

However, the U.S. military still reserved a right to use the Space Station should it wish to. The DOD closely monitored all international negotiations relating to the Space Station to ensure that right. The final agreement between the partners governing military uses was based on the nationality of the lab modules. The U.S. military could use the U.S. laboratory based on the American definition of "peaceful use." ESA and Japan could veto any American use of their laboratories inconsistent with their own definition of "peaceful use."[63] Russia had the same rights in the lab modules it supplied as the United States had in its own lab.[64]

The U.S. military has not shown any interest in the Space Station since the late 1980s. However, the use of the Space Station for "peace-ful purposes" is guaranteed to the partners, and the United States in-terprets that phrase to include activities by the U.S. military. In the un-likely event that the United States does seek to use the Space Station for weapons testing, especially for activities related to missile defense, it could cause ill feeling among the partners, including Russia. Although ESA and Japan can veto DOD use of their labs, this would cause ten-sion as well. However, such a move would be a radical departure from existing policy and is probably unlikely. Military activities in space also remain cheaper and more covert if done by robotic satellites.

CREW SAFETY

Crew safety remains a critical policy issue. Spaceflight remains dan-gerous, and time in orbit and during launch is inherently risky. The scheduling and scale of Space Station construction are intense by any standard, enhancing the risk. Assembly of the ISS will require multiple launches, many of which will employ the Space Shuttle.[65] While the Space Shuttle has regained its reputation for safety, memories of the *Challenger* accident remain. In addition, Space Shuttle launches to the ISS will have very short launch windows due to the high orbital inclination of the Space Station.[66] This could recreate some of the time pressures that contributed to the fateful *Challenger* launch decision. In response to safety concerns, NASA and its contractors have hired hundreds of additional workers to handle the more demanding flight schedule.[67]

Beyond a launch accident, there will also be significant risk involved in Space Station assembly and use. A threat to crew safety arises from the number and duration of EVAs that astronauts will be required to perform. Such work will be necessary for the assembly and maintenance of ISS infrastructure. The current assembly plan calls for more than 1,700 hours of EVAs, a number that far exceeds past experience.[68] If the ISS begins to include some construction activities, there would be a further increase in the number and length of EVAs. The large number of extended space walks increases the risk of an accident, radiation exposure, or collision with orbital debris. The Space Station itself is also vulnerable to the tons of human-made debris in Earth orbit as well as meteors.[69]

THE NEXT STEP AFTER THE "NEXT LOGICAL STEP"

The final policy issue relating to the ISS is the next step. Where does this investment of time and money lead? Many ISS activities are presented as steps to Mars, a return to the moon, or a greater degree of commercial activity in space. Will the ISS be upgraded, with new or replacement components added as needed? Will a follow-up Space Station be built? The IGA describes the ISS as having "an evolutionary character" but does not guarantee the Station's future.[70]

The scheduled life expectancy of spacecraft is not fixed. Space facilities often exceed their design capabilities and function much longer than originally expected, provided their value and efficiency has been proven. A case in point is the *Hubble Space Telescope,* which has proven so valuable and so successful that there is a strong consensus that it should be maintained as long as possible, and when that is no longer possible, should be replaced by an even better facility. The Space Shuttle will likely be used longer than is presently planned. Many automatic space probes have outlived their expected life spans by years. Despite its troubles, even *Mir* exceeded its planned five-year mission. The same opportunity exists for the ISS to operate indefinitely by replacing worn out segments or adding on new modules. Eventually, an entirely new facility might emerge from an evolutionary process of upgrading and replacement.

There is also the possibility that new space stations may be constructed in addition to the ISS or as successors to it. There are currently no plans in NASA to build a successor to the ISS, but other actors may pursue this option. If the ISS proves economically viable, private interests may attempt occupied or crew-tended space facilities. Some of the ISS partners (especially ESA and Japan) might use the experience gained in the project and initiate their own space stations. China has expressed interest in building its own space station after it begins human spaceflights. Future space stations could guarantee the permanent occupation of space about which so many space advocates have dreamed.

The answer to the question of longevity depends on the perceived success of the ISS. This is less dependent on the technical success of the ISS construction than on its utilization program, which is scheduled to begin during the assembly phase and continue at least until 2012. Research on the ISS will be expensive, and much of it will be arcane and beyond the understanding of the public. The presentation of this work to the public is vital if the ISS is to be seen as a success. Publics and leaders alike must be convinced that the ISS is worth the vast expenditure of funds. The history of the Apollo program demonstrates that technical success alone cannot guarantee a project's survival. Even a large, expensive infrastructure may be abandoned if the public and political leaders lose interest. That is the ultimate challenge for the ISS.

Future Scenarios

THE OPTIMISTIC SCENARIO:
"EVERYTHING GOES ACCORDING TO PLAN"

Many things must go right for the ISS to succeed, and as in other endeavors, success is a politically defined concept. An optimistic scenario assumes that the current ISS program goes forward essentially as planned and that the facility is completed more or less on schedule. For the ISS to succeed over the long run, the international partnerships, especially the central U.S.-Russian relationship, must remain stable. The Space Station's domestic political support must continue to be stable enough to ensure that budgets do not fluctuate greatly. Participation of private firms as research users of the Space Station will be needed to enhance its credibility as a public good, especially if private firms generate marketable goods or processes using the ISS. Whatever benefits accrue from the ISS must be highly visible to the public if the project is to be judged successful. Finally, the ISS must operate safely and without accidents for the expected ten-year-plus life span.

If these conditions occur, new opportunities will present themselves. Additional modules or even a new successor Space Station may be proposed to continue the ISS past its planned lifetime. More ambitious space missions, such as flights to Mars or to the moon are additional possibilities that may arise from a successful decade of ISS operations. Additional countries may join the project as junior partners (on the model of Brazil) or as Space Station users.[71] The ISS could become a model for cooperative ventures in space and on Earth.

THE PESSIMISTIC SCENARIO: "THINGS GO WRONG"

The optimistic scenario is dependent on the proper working of people, machines, and institutions as well as on a certain degree of good fortune. However, things may not go according to plan. Minor difficulties are to be expected in any large-scale technological system. That the Space Station has survived this long is a tribute to those who have fought for it since 1984. Realistically, minor difficulties and delays will occur, but these are not likely to derail the ISS any more than the delay of *Zvezda*. While domestic political support has been uneven, the Space Station has proven to be too big to cancel. Cancellation will be even more difficult now that crew operations have begun. The power of "sunk costs" is very great, especially if some progress is visible and the international partnerships hold together. The money and time spent on the project should help to insulate the Space Station from outright cancellation. The very fact of several billion dollars of hardware in orbit serves as a powerful argument against cancellation. However, the Space Station is not immune to cancellation. Several plausible events could disrupt the ISS schedule and undermine its political support.

The United States is central, and the ISS cannot exist without political and budgetary support from the White House and Congress. Political change in the United States could derail the project. The economic downturn at the time of writing, combined with the September 11 terrorist attack, is changing priorities and could produce demands for government budget cuts, leading to a delay or scaling down of the Space Station. This scenario is not unprecedented: the Space Station narrowly escaped cancellation under such conditions in 1993. Historically, NASA has never received all the funding it has sought. Budgets will continue to fluctuate depending on domestic economic conditions, the perception of economic return, and how many benefits accrue to the United States.

Russia is the other country essential for the survival of the ISS, and its participation is also not guaranteed. Domestic political change in Russia or a souring of U.S.-Russian relations could cause the country to withdraw from the project. Russia's economy remains weak, and although the Russian space program still has prestige value for its leaders, this may not be enough to ensure its budgetary stability. If Russia attempts to withdraw before the Space Station is fully assembled, this could lead to cancellation or politically damaging delays to the project. However, a falling out with Russia over a major policy dispute could also cause a rebound in American nationalistic support for "our" Space Station.

If the political coalition holds together, the complexity of the project could still be its undoing. Equally damaging to the ISS would be an accident that involves the loss of life. The numerous Space Shuttle flights and EVAs required to build the ISS present many opportunities for such a tragedy. An accident that kills astronauts could lead to a public perception that the ISS is too risky (like *Mir*). A catastrophic Space Shuttle accident would at a minimum force a prolonged grounding of the fleet and at worst could terminate the entire U.S. human spaceflight program. An in-orbit accident could also end the project. Alternatively, a series of smaller accidents or mission failures occurring in close proximity could produce the same effect. Public debates may even question the value and ethics of sending people into space. Risk aversion is very high in Western societies, especially the United States, as the public reaction to the *Challenger* accident and American combat deaths in recent military interventions demonstrate.

Depending on the degree of damage, life lost, and the political fallout from such an accident, the Space Station could be delayed for several years. Additional uncertainty over the completion or survival of the Space Station would tend to limit private sector investment. Budgets and management practices would likely be under greater scrutiny, and political support could weaken. The effect of a Space Station accident on future missions will depend on the context of the situation. Should the United States be experiencing a severe economic recession or other domestic problems, there may be sentiment to cancel the Space Station. If deaths included "civilian" astronauts or tourists, there would be a greater pressure to scale back or eliminate human spaceflight. This is not surprising; many took the death of the teacher-in-space much harder than the deaths of the "professional" astronauts in the *Challenger* crew. The public reaction would also depend on the degree to which the Space Station is completed and whether it had been judged a success to date.

If the ISS is cancelled or is seen as a failure, any follow-on station or more ambitious missions will be far less likely. The ISS, whether or not it serves as a base for further exploration, will be a test case for any moon-Mars expeditions. Opponents of large-scale space projects will correctly argue the United States cannot attempt a mission to Mars or a moon base if it cannot successfully construct a less-complex and less-expensive space station in low-Earth orbit. Because such ventures will almost certainly be international in nature, failure of the multinational ISS would also undermine the chances for a Mars mission.

The optimistic scenario assumes that everything goes more or less as planned and that the ISS is able to live up to its expectations. Although optimistic scenarios often prove unrealistic, the ISS should begin to produce real scientific, if not economic returns within a decade. At the same time, it should be noted that spaceflight remains a dangerous and uncertain activity. The pessimistic scenario is based on unpredictable events and accidents. The ultimate success of the ISS depends on many factors—political, managerial, and technical. The Space Station must be judged to be *both* a technical and a political success. For better or worse, the future of human spaceflight (in and beyond Earth orbit) will hinge on the ability of Space Station supporters to convince publics and leaders alike that the ISS has proven the worth of sending people into space.

Conclusion

The saga of the Space Station provides many lessons. Viewed negatively, the Space Station story to date is disappointing, an example of how *not* to run a huge technological program. Viewed more positively, the ISS is now a reality. It may be judged a success in that the large, multinational coalition of actors behind it has held together despite political, economic, and technical pressures. Practically, the ISS will likely be the primary human spaceflight activity that the United States and its partners will pursue for at least the next decade.

The project's past suggests that large space projects face difficulties that may make them politically difficult, regardless of their rationales. For ten years, the Space Station existed on paper only, and the scientific and social benefits it promised were elusive. Now that the ISS is partially in orbit, the next challenge is to bring the project to completion. The long, high-risk process of assembling the ISS will be vital in shaping the public perception of its value. If that process is undermined by accidents, technical failures, cost overruns, or a persistent Russian failure to live up to its commitments, the ISS may be the last (as well as first) of its kind. This project may foretell the things to come. Voyages to Mars, a

return to the moon—indeed, the entire endeavor of human spaceflight—
may very well depend on the success the International Space Station.

NOTES

The author wishes to thank W. Henry Lambright and Agnes Gereben Schaefer
for comments on earlier versions of this chapter. The opinions expressed here
are, of course, those of the author alone.

1. Vernon van Dyke, *Pride and Power: The Rationale of the Space Age* (Urbana:
   University of Illinois Press, 1964).
2. In this chapter, Space Station, when capitalized, refers to the project begun
   in 1984 and continuing today as the ISS. Generic references to other projects
   or proposed facilities will be in lower case.
3. NASA, "Space Station: Presentation to the National Research Council's Committee on Space Station," Slide OSS-5192 5/1/87 (Washington, DC: NASA
   Historical Collection, 1987). This slide, setting forth the "Reasons Why" the
   Space Station was important, has appeared in many other NASA presenta-
   tions and publications.
4. An excellent analysis of the beginning of the Space Station project is Howard
   McCurdy, *The Space Station Decision: Incremental Politics and Technological Change* (Baltimore: Johns Hopkins University Press, 1990). Other valuable accounts of various periods in the Space Station's history may be found
   in the following: Hans Mark, *The Space Station: A Personal Journey* (Durham, NC: Duke University Press, 1987); John Logsdon, *Together in Orbit: The
   Origins of International Cooperation in Space Station Freedom,* Monograph
   in Aerospace History #11 (Washington, DC: NASA History Division, 1991);
   John Madison and Howard E. McCurdy, "Spending Without Results: Lessons
   from the Space Station Program," *Space Policy* 15 (1999): 213–21; and Marcia
   Smith, *CRS Issues Brief: Space Stations* (Washington, DC: Congressional Research Service, 3 November 2000).
5. Craig Covault, "President Orders Start on Space Station," *Aviation Week and
   Space Technology,* 30 January 1984, 16–19.
6. Madison and McCurdy, "Spending Without Results," 213.
7. NASA, *International Space Station Fact Book* (Washington, DC: NASA, October 2000), 3. On-Line: www.spaceflight.nasa.gov.
8. General Accounting Office, *Space Station: Estimated Total U.S. Funding Requirements* (Washington, DC: GAO, 1995), 2. The GAO estimate is higher in
   part because it includes money spent on the Freedom project prior to 1994,
   which the NASA estimates exclude.
9. Smith, *CRS Issues Brief,* 1; NASA, *ISS Fact Book,* 3.
10. NASA, *International Space Station Assembly Sequence: Revision F* (August
    2000). On-Line: www.spaceflight.nasa.gov/station/assembly/flights/chron.
    html.
11. Ronald Reagan, "Address Before a Joint Session of the Congress on the State

of the Union," in *Public Papers of the President: Ronald Reagan. 1984*, vol. 1, 1 January–29 June 1984 (Washington, DC: U.S. Government Printing Office, 1986), 90; NASA, *International Space Station Fact Book*. On-Line: www. station.nasa.gov, 1998, 3; Franklin Martin and Terence Finn, *Space Station: Leadership for the Future* (Washington, DC: NASA, 1987), 8.

12. The full partners in the ISS project are Canada, Japan, Russia, the United States and eleven members of the European Space Agency (Belgium, Denmark, France, Germany, Great Britain, Italy, the Netherlands, Norway, Spain, Sweden and Switzerland). Brazil is participating through a bilateral agreement with the United States.

13. The first reference to an orbiting space station was in the 1869 novella, "The Brick Moon," by Edward Everett Hale. Space stations also play a major role in the speculations of space pioneers Konstantin Tsiolkovsky, Hermann Noordung, and Hermann Oberth. For discussions of the history of the space station idea, see John Logsdon, "Space Stations: A Historical Perspective," in *Space Station: Policy, Planning, and Utilization: Proceedings of the AIAA/NASA Symposium on the Space Station, Arlington, Virginia, July 18–20, 1983* (New York: AIAA, 1983), 14–22. See also T. A. Heppenheimer, *The Space Shuttle Decision: NASA's Search for a Reusable Space Vehicle* (Washington, DC: NASA History Office, 1999), 6–11.

14. For some of von Braun's writings on space exploration, see John Logsdon, et. al., eds., *Exploring the Unknown: Selected Documents in the History of the U.S. Civil Space Program*, vol. 1, *Organizing for Exploration* (Washington, DC: NASA, 1995), 176–94, 195–200. See also Howard McCurdy, *Space and the American Imagination* (Washington, DC: Smithsonian Institution, 1997).

15. Heppenheimer, *Space Shuttle Decision*, 245–89, details the negotiations between NASA and the Nixon White House during the period of the Space Shuttle decision.

16. During his Senate nomination hearing, NASA administrator James Beggs suggested that the development of a space station should be "the next step" for the U.S. space program. The phrase, "the Next Logical Step," began appearing in NASA publications and speeches soon after, and this became the semiofficial slogan of the project. See U.S. Congress, Senate Committee on Commerce, Science, and Transportation, *Nominations-NASA* (Washington, DC: U.S. Government Printing Office, 1981), 22.

17. Mark, *The Space Station*, 131.

18. NASA, "Revised Talking Points for the Space Station Presentation to the President and Cabinet Council" (Washington, DC: NASA Historical Collection, 30 November 1983); NASA, "Presentation on Space Station" (Washington, DC: NASA Historical Collection, 1 December 1983).

19. Reagan, "Address," 90.

20. "Station Decision Overrode Strong Opposition," *Aviation Week and Space Technology*, 30 January 1984, 16.

21. Interview with James Beggs, 22 July 1999.

22. Mark, *Space Station*, 154, 156–61.

23. The 1988 Intergovernmental Agreement was signed by the United States, Canada, Japan, and nine ESA members (Belgium, Denmark, France, Great Britain, Italy, the Netherlands, Norway, Spain, and West Germany).

24. James Asker, "NASA's Space Station Dodges Another Bullet," *Aviation Week and Space Technology,* 28 June 1993, 23–24.

25. "Clinton Orders New Design For Space Station," *Aviation Week and Space Technology,* 22 February 1993, 20–21.

26. William Harwood, "Crew of 'Alpha' Males Moves into Space Station," *Washington Post,* 3 November 2000, A2. The Expedition One crew requested that the name *Alpha* be used as the Space Station's call sign during their four-month mission. The media regularly began referring to the ISS as *Alpha,* though NASA still refrains from doing so.

27. Smith, *CRS Issues Brief,* 10.

28. Government Accounting Office, *Space Station: Impact of the Expanded Russian Role on Funding and Research* (Washington, DC: GAO, 1994), 10.

29. James Asker, "U.S./Russian Station Plan Raises Doubts in Congress," *Aviation Week and Space Technology,* 11 October 1993, 25. See also U.S. Congress, House of Representatives. Committee on Science, Space, and Technology, Subcommittee on Space, *United States-Russian Cooperation in the Space Station Program: Parts I and II* (Washington, DC: U.S. Government Printing Office, 1994), 24–25, 111–12.

30. James Asker, "NASA Fights Budget Cuts, Defends Russia on Station," *Aviation Week and Space Technology,* 23 May 1994, 56–57.

31. James Asker, "House Panel Approves Multiyear Station Funding," *Aviation Week and Space Technology,* 12 June 1995, 46.

32. Phase II involves building a primarily U.S.-Russian core station. Phase III adds the European, Japanese, and Canadian components.

33. Smith, *CRS Issues Brief,* 6.

34. Ibid.

35. F. James Sensenbrenner, "Mir Press Conference," 18 September 1997, 2. On-Line: www.house.gov/science/sensenbrenner_9-18.html.

36. Smith, *CRS Issues Brief,* 7.

37. Kathryn Clarke, "Profile" (interview with Brian Berger), *Space News,* 22 May 2000, 22.

38. *Agreement Among the Government of Canada, Governments of Member States of the European Space Agency, the Government of Japan, the Government of the Russian Federation, and the Government of the United States of America Concerning Cooperation on the Civil International Space Station.* Signed in Washington, January 29, 1998, Article 7.2; hereafter cited as *1998 IGA.*

39. Japan and ESA have secured the right to use their own launch vehicles to transport supplies to the Space Station, although U.S. and Russian spacecraft will be the primary vehicles to build and service the ISS.

40. Canada's contribution is so important to the success of the Space Station that the 1998 IGA requires Canada to transfer all hardware and plans to the United States should Canada ever choose to withdraw from the project (*1998 IGA*, Article 28.3a).

41. Although participating in the ISS, Brazil did not sign the IGA and is not considered a full partner. Italy's agreement with the United States is in addition to its participation through ESA. A set of three MOU governing the early development phase were signed between the United States and the original partners in 1985. A second set of MOU and an IGA governing detailed development and utilization were signed in 1988 by the same partners. These earlier agreements were superceded by the 1998 agreements (*1998 IGA*, Article 25.4).

42. "Russian Space Agency Makes Sales," *New York Times*, 5 October 1998. On-Line: www.nytimes.com.

43. Craig Covault, "Columbus at Risk in Station Plan," *Aviation Week and Space Technology*, 29 November 1993, 22–24.

44. CNN, "Russia Again Pledges to Retire Mir Next Summer," 17 September 1998. On-Line: www.cnn.com; Simon Saradzhyan, "Revival of Mir Sparks Concern About ISS Commitments," *Space News*, 17 April 2000, 26; Warren E. Leary, "Proud Russia Keeps Mir Aloft," *New York Times*, 23 May 2000, 1; "Mir Space Station Is No More," *New York Times*, 23 May 2001. On-Line: www.nytimes.com.

45. Allen Li, "Space Station: Russian Compliance with Safety Requirements, Testimony Before the Subcommittee on Space and Aeronautics, Committee on Science, House of Representatives" (Washington, DC: General Accounting Office, 16 March 2000), 1.

46. Deborah Zabarenko, "NASA Chief Says Tito Sparked 'Symmetry of Mistrust' with Russia," Reuters News Agency at www.space.com, 29 May 2001.

47. Mary Conners, Albert Harrison, and Faren Akins, *Living Aloft: Human Requirements for Extended Spaceflight* (Washington, DC: NASA Scientific and Technical Information Branch, 1985), 290. Also see Henry S. F. Cooper, *A House in Space* (New York: Bantam, 1976).

48. Valentin Lebedev, *Diary of a Cosmonaut: 211 Days in Space* (New York: Bantam, 1990).

49. Simon Saradhyan and Jen Tracy, "Tensions in Station Mock-Up Spur Call for Cultural Training," *Space News*, 10 April 2000, 16, 52.

50. Bryan Burrough, *Dragonfly: NASA and the Crisis Aboard Mir* (New York: Harper Collins, 1998).

51. NASA Office of Inspector General, "Untitled Memorandum from the Office of Inspector General to F. James Sensenbrenner" (Washington, DC: NASA Headquarters, Revised Version, 1997), 8–10.

52. CNN, "NASA Considers Turning Over Space Station to Private Enterprise," 25 September 1999. On-Line: www.cnn.com.

53. Quoted in ibid., 1.

54. NASA, *The Economic Effects of a Space Station: Preliminary Results* (Washington, DC: NASA, 1983), 2.

55. CNN, "Report: NASA Agrees to Let Tourist Go into Space, April 20, 2001." On-Line: www.cnn.com. The partners approved Tito's flight as an exemption to normal crew selection procedures. See NASA, "International Space Station Partnership Grants Flight Exemption for Dennis Tito" (Washington, DC: NASA, 24 April 2001).

56. The Habitation Module may not be built for budgetary reasons, although the United States is discussing with Italy the possibility of its building a similar unit (CNN, "U.S., Italy Teaming Up on Alpha Living Quarters," 19 April 2001. On-Line: www.cnn.com).

57. "Letter From Paul Thayer, Deputy Secretary of Defense, to James Beggs, Administrator, NASA, August 11, 1983" (Washington, DC: NASA Historical Collection, 1983).

58. "Letter From Caspar Weinberger to James Beggs, January 16, 1984" (Washington, DC: NASA Historical Collection, 1984).

59. Such a suggestion was made by NASA Deputy Administrator Dale Myers in 1987. See Dale Myers, "Excerpts From Remarks Prepared For Delivery: Air Force Association National Symposium, Colorado Springs, Colorado" (Washington, DC: NASA Historical Collection, 1987).

60. U.S. Department of Defense, *Potential Department of Defense Use of the Permanently Manned Space Station* (Washington, DC: NASA Historical Collection, 1 March 1988).

61. "Letter From Caspar Weinberger to George Schultz, April 7, 1987" (Washington, DC: NASA Historical Collection).

62. Department of Defense, *Potential Department of Defense Use* .

63. *1998 IGA,* Article 9.3b.

64. Interview with Lynn Cline, 9 July 1999. Cline is the Deputy Associate Administrator for External Affairs at NASA and a participant in the international negotiations.

65. Some crewmembers will travel to the ISS aboard Russian *Soyuz* spacecraft. There will also be automated supply and logistics flights by Russian, and possibly European and Japanese, spacecraft.

66. Government Accounting Office, *Space Station,* 9.

67. Warren Leary, "Launching of Shuttle Will Inaugurate Push to Complete an Outpost in Space," *New York Times,* 7 September 2000, 2. On-Line: www.nytimes.com.

68. Smith, *CRS Issues Brief,* 7.

69. Aerospace Safety Advisory Panel, *Annual Report* (Washington, DC: NASA, 1994), 17–19.

70. *1998 IGA,* Article 1.4.

71. An informal proposal by China to join the ISS was rebuffed by the U.S., but

other countries could join the project in the future. Israel and Ukraine are two proposed candidates. Former NASA Administrator Goldin is on the record as recommending that other countries join the ISS. See Dan Goldin, "The Challenge of Space Exploration in a New Era," *Space Times* (January-February 1995): 7–9.

5　High Impacts

Asteroidal Utilization, Collision Avoidance,
and the Outer Space Regime

Daniel H. Deudney

P OLITICS, far more than nature, abhors a vacuum. Not surprisingly, the extension of human activities into Earth orbital space during the second half of the twentieth century was accompanied by the creation of an elaborate political regime.[1] The physical environment of orbital space is unlike any on Earth, but the political order in space is an ancillary to the sovereign state system, paralleling the extraterritorial regimes governing the high seas and Antarctica. A basic principle of this regime, codified in the Outer Space Treaty of 1967, is that states may not extend sovereign control over celestial bodies. As with the high seas, the outer space regime regulates uses of a communal resource that is subject to many diverse and occasionally conflicting demands. This chapter explores the implications of human utilization of asteroidal bodies for the space enterprise and the outer space regime. Two main arguments are advanced.

First, there are strong reasons to believe that human utilization of asteroidal bodies, long advocated by space visionaries, is soon likely to commence, probably on an extensive scale and possibly very rapidly. The most probable catalyst for major space activities directed at the asteroids is avoidance of a collision of such a body with the Earth. As more asteroids are discovered and their orbits are calculated, it is only a matter of time before a collision is anticipated or a highly visible (and perhaps destructive) collision occurs. Once this happens, I hypothesize that major public resources will be allocated to the further scientific investigation of asteroids and to the development and demonstration of techniques to manipulate asteroidal orbits. Earth security will become a major, possibly a central purpose of the space enterprise.

Second, asteroidal diversion for Earth security will have far-reaching implications for the evolution of the outer space regime. It is widely recognized that asteroids pose a fundamental problem for the existing outer space regime: as asteroids come into practical human use, their current treatment as a communal resource will be untenable. The outer space regime will require modification, and political conflicts over alternative arrangements could be severe. A range of alternative space regime designs has been discussed, ranging along a spectrum from complete *partition* (sovereign state or corporate appropriation), to completely *public* (international development authority). The current view on regime selection, particularly in the United States, is strongly toward the partition end of the spectrum.

In contrast, I argue that the most likely scenario for asteroidal utilization—collision avoidance—strongly points toward the selection of a regime design somewhere between the current arrangement, which could be called *communal,* and a purely public one. As humanity mobilizes the political energy necessary to apply the physical energy to nudge asteroidal bodies into different trajectories, the outer space regime will also be pushed in a more communal and public direction.

Asteroids are often viewed as "islands in space." Conventional wisdom anticipates states appropriating them like the "spice islands" were appropriated by early European explorers. In contrast, I argue that a more appropriate analogy is Antarctica, a vast, distant, and inhospitable island of rock and ice that has been cooperatively demilitarized and largely devoted to science. But unlike in Antarctica, diverting asteroids will be a major step in the creation of a more general "Earth security" or "planetary security" system, along with avoiding nuclear war and environmental destruction.

My argument unfolds in three main steps. The first part summarizes and surveys the four main scenarios for asteroidal utilization that have been extensively conceptualized. The second part assesses possible triggers—political and nonpolitical—for the activation of these scenarios. The third part describes alternative regimes for the asteroids and assesses the political impact of collision avoidance.

Asteroidal Utilization Scenarios

Interest in asteroids has grown rapidly in the last two decades in the wake of the new scientific consensus that such objects periodically collide with the Earth, wreaking great destruction. The decisive breakthrough was the realization, beginning in 1980, that the abrupt mass extinction of the dinosaurs approximately 65 million years ago was the result of a collision with a celestial body and that earlier collisions are likely causes of other major mass extinctions punctuating the record of life on Earth.[2]

Asteroidal bodies, or planetoids, were first discovered in the nineteenth century, primarily in the main asteroid belt between Mars and Jupiter. Subsequent observation in this century has discovered a class of objects whose orbital paths take them across the orbit of the Earth, and these are collectively known as Apollo objects. Searching for these bodies has not been a high priority for professional astronomers, and many are being discovered by amateur astronomers.

Scientists have come to understand that asteroidal collisions have played a major role in shaping the development of life.[3] However, it is only over the last several decades, the period of the space age, that modern natural science has recognized these facts. In part because of the assumptions of gradualism in geology and paleontology, scientists did not look for evidence of catastrophic collisions and were very reluctant to accept the evidence that was available.[4] Barriers between geology, biology, and astronomy also discouraged investigation of phenomena that crossed disciplinary lines in such major ways. Advocates of the idea that the Earth had been struck violently by celestial objects were generally treated as fringe and unscientific.[5]

Results from preliminary exploration of the Earth's moon in the 1960s and 1970s decisively demonstrated that extensive lunar cratering was the result of celestial bombardment, not vulcanism. Examination of the Earth from orbital satellites revealed a large number of formations that were sites of ancient collisions. Spectacular visual confirmation was provided by the breakup of the comet Shoemaker-Levy 9 and its collision with Jupiter in 1994.[6]

The second wave of the intellectual revolution, in paleontology, occurred in the 1980s and 1990s as decisive evidence began to accumulate for the hypothesis that the cretaceous era (the last period in which dinosaurs existed) was abruptly ended by an immense asteroidal collision, now confidently sited on the Gulf Coast of the Yucatan Peninsula. A crucial initial piece of evidence was the anomalous high levels of the metallic element iridium in the rock layers, which indicated extraterrestrial origins because it was known that asteroidal bodies had much higher levels of this element than were present in Earth's crust.[7] By the late 1990s the dominant general narrative of life on Earth included a pivotal role for major collisions in triggering the five great extinctions that punctuate the geological fossil record of earlier life forms.[8] Some scientists now also advance plausible arguments that primitive life, and/or many of the molecular precursors to life, arrived on Earth via asteroidal or comet bombardments.[9]

As the significance and number of near-Earth objects have become better understood, a variety of scenarios for the utilization of these bodies have been advanced. From the earliest visions of space development, schemes for asteroidal utilization have been present, but until recently they have been overshadowed by nearer-term near-space applications (rockets, satellites, shuttles, and stations), and, in the longer-term scenarios, by the grand and semiofficial "von Braun Paradigm" of planetary exploration and colonization.[10] Despite this relative marginality, scenarios of increasing sophistication and plausibility have been developed by advocates holding very different visions of space development and its value.

Four scenarios have sufficient plausibility and extensive articulation to warrant serious assessment: scientific investigation, collision avoidance, commercial exploitation, and military employment. The main features of each of the four scenarios will be described, and in the next section, factors effecting their activation will be assessed.

SCENARIO I: SCIENTIFIC INVESTIGATION

The first scenario for human use of asteroids is for scientific purposes. All human space activity outside the immediate vicinity of Earth has been for purposes of gathering scientific knowledge. Scientific interest in asteroidal bodies has several dimensions. First, important questions concern the composition and origin of these bodies. If, as is generally assumed, asteroids are the remnants of materials left over from the formation of the solar system, their primordiality can shed light on the evolution of the solar system. Second, study of asteroidal bodies is important for the burgeoning field of astrobiology, which seeks to understand the conditions in which life has emerged in the universe. Study of the chemical composition of nonmetallic and nonrock bodies can shed light on the abundance of molecular precursors to life.

Despite these important questions, scientific investigation of asteroidal bodies has not received major governmental support compared to the resources allocated for human spaceflight (*Apollo,* the Space Shuttle, and the Space Station); interplanetary probes of the larger bodies (Luna, Mars, Venus, and the outer planets); and space-based deep-space astronomy. With the major exception of the manned space program, these resource allocations reflect the priorities of the scientific community, which has privileged astronomy over planetary science, and planetary science over asteroidal science.

Despite these historic asymmetries, NASA's programmatic shift to launching more numerous smaller probes more frequently ("faster, better, cheaper") has provided an opening for asteroidal scientific missions, most notably the recently successful Near Earth Asteroid Rendezvous (NEAR), which has successfully placed a small probe into orbit around the Earth-approaching asteroid Eros.[11] Inadequate resources have been devoted to the scientifically mundane but potentially vital practical task of thoroughly scanning the sky to detect and locate a higher percentage of the estimated population of Earth-approaching asteroidal bodies.

SCENARIO II: COLLISION AVOIDANCE

As evidence has accumulated about previous celestial collisions, substantial efforts have been devoted to understanding the prospects for future violent encounters and to envisioning schemes to avoid them. Popular awareness of these threats has been enhanced by a stream of popular books, television documentaries, and science fiction movies. Efforts to systematically map the population of near-Earth objects (NEOs) have grown, and have begun to attract some government support. Extensive and sophisticated analyses of risks have been developed. Several substantial studies and workshops have analyzed the technical dimensions of diverting asteroidal bodies.[12] Congressional hearings have examined the topic, and international discussion in the United Nations and elsewhere has ensued.[13]

What are the security risks of celestial bombardment? While the probability of a major collision in the near future is low, it has also become clear that smaller objects strike the atmosphere with much greater frequency than previously assumed.[14] An explosion at the remote Tungusta site in Siberia in 1908 is estimated to have been equivalent to 10 megatons of TNT. A substantial number of explosions in the range of kilotons of TNT equivalent have been recorded in the upper atmosphere by satellites designed to monitor for nuclear explosions in the atmosphere and near space. It remains only a matter of time before such an explosion occurs on or over a more populated area. Risk analyses developed by astronomers Clark Chapman and David Morrison indicate that the average individual's likelihood of being killed by an asteroidal collision is greater than the likelihood of dying in a nuclear power plant accident.[15] Many billions of dollars have been spent avoiding nuclear accidents, but virtually nothing has been spent avoiding an asteroidal collision.

Given these real dangers, an extensive scientific and technological literature on diversion scenarios has emerged. In one of the earliest studies, a group of MIT students developed a scenario for using *Apollo*-era heavy launch vehicles to deliver nuclear explosives to the asteroid Icarus in order to alter its trajectory.[16] However, the use of nuclear explosions runs the risk of fragmentation rather than diversion. Alternatively, humans could land on an asteroid and construct an electromagnetic gun (a large slingshot-like mechanism), to propel pieces of the body in sufficient mass, in appropriate directions, and with sufficient velocities so that the asteroid's orbit would be altered so as to avert collision with the Earth.[17] In assessing the prospects for successful diversion, four factors are important: the size of the object (for example, the Hale-Bopp comet was 250 miles in diameter); its composition; the time between discovery of collision course and actual collision; and the extent to which diversion capabilities have been prepared in advance.

SCENARIO III: RESOURCE EXPLOITATION

Another cluster of scenarios entail the use of asteroidal resources for space construction and development. During the 1970s and early 1980s when mineral resource scarcities were being experienced and anticipated, visionaries in the space community developed elaborate schemes for the industrial exploitation and colonization of asteroidal bodies. Some envisioned the mining of asteroids for precious metals that would be brought back to Earth.[18] Others envisioned using asteroidal materials to construct giant solar energy collectors in the vicinity of the Earth that would beam massive quantities of energy through the atmosphere to extensive networks of microwave receivers.[19] In the grandest visions of this period, massive space cities would be fabricated out of asteroidal material and populated by teeming masses of humans.[20] Several major U.S. government studies assessed their feasibility and consequences, but no significant public resources were allocated to their realization. As fears of acute mineral and energy scarcity have receded, the attraction of these scenarios has also declined.

Scenarios for utilizing asteroidal materials for space development have not disappeared but have taken a more modest, more practical, and nearer-term direction in the last decade. Consonant with the general emphasis on space commercialization, a number of vigorous private sector ventures are underway to visit and eventually exploit NEOs. Entrepreneurs hope to mine asteroids for metal and to extract water and other volatiles from them. The crucial enabling factor in these plans is the anticipation that the cost of launching a pound into orbit will fall by approximately a factor of ten as new launch technologies come on-line in the first decade of the twenty-first century.

SCENARIO IV: MILITARY EMPLOYMENT

The history of space technology development has been intimately intertwined with the pursuit of enhanced military capability. Despite the relative lull in Great Power strategic competition in the 1990s, states continue to be keenly sensitive to military technological change and its potential for altering their relative power positions. Not surprisingly, several scenarios for military utilization of asteroids have been developed.

In one of the first major analyses, Robert Salkeld advocated basing nuclear weapons and nuclear command and control facilities on asteroids.[21] Writing in the late 1960s when fear of "first strike" capabilities animated much strategic military concern, Salkeld reasoned that asteroid-based nuclear capabilities would provide a robustly secure "second-strike" capability. Having witnessed bomber bases and then fixed missile bases become vulnerable to preemptive attack, Salkeld argued that sea-based capabilities also could be subject to some technological revolution, perhaps rapidly and asymmetrically. In contrast, the distances involved in deep-space basing would ensure that a nuclear-armed state would always have at least a "long trigger" retaliatory capability. Although Salkeld was a U.S. Air Force officer, his proposals found little official support. High confidence in the continued ability of ballistic missile submarines to avoid tracking and detection grew as submarines became quieter and were equipped with longer-range missiles, and as antisubmarine warfare detection capabilities grew more sophisticated. These trends, along with the development of land-mobile ICBMs, meant that the nuclear superpowers did not perceive second-strike capability to be in fundamental jeopardy.

A more recent scenario for the military use of asteroids emerged in the 1980s as part of the enhanced interest by the United States in developing anti-ballistic missile (ABM) systems. Asteroids are of potential use in the development of a space-based ABM capability because they are seen as a source of cheap shielding material. The Achilles heel of a space-based ABM system is the vulnerability of its satellite platforms to attack either from enemy satellite platforms or from ground-based weapons. Assuming two states each deployed roughly similar space-based ABM capabilities, a large military advantage would accrue to the state that struck first to cripple or destroy the other side's capabilities. The solution to this vulnerability would be to add shielding to satellite battle-stations. Even assuming the development of cheaper and heavier lift capabilities to move material from Earth's surface, some analysts have argued that it would be cheaper to acquire bulk material for shielding from near-Earth asteroids.[22] To realize this possibility, large quantities of material would have to be moved from asteroids to low-Earth orbits.

Technological Feasibility of Utilization Scenarios

The overall technological feasibility of these scenarios varies. Scientific investigation can be carried out most readily. Search and mapping employs ground-based telescopes that exist in great number. Fly-by and landing probes are considerably more expensive, but these capabilities have already been demonstrated, and continuing advances in component technologies are likely to further lower their costs and increase their capabilities and reliability. Diversion scenarios appear technologically feasible in principle but would be much more expensive. Diversion scenarios would entail transporting heavier payloads, and probably humans as well, over great distances in the inner solar system. The realization of diversion scenarios thus depends in significant measure upon advances in general space infrastructure of launch vehicles and human spaceflight capabilities.

The overall technological feasibility of commercial development scenarios also appears high in principle, although generalizations are hazardous since so many different commercial development scenarios, ranging from the modest to the grandiose, have been advanced. Mining asteroidal bodies for precious metals would depend on the general capabilities of the space infrastructure as well as on the development of more specific material-processing capabilities. While the more modest versions of commercial development scenarios do not appear to have any currently apparent technological "show stoppers," cost and profit estimates must be viewed as highly speculative. Finally, the overall technological feasibility of the military utilization scenario must in principle also be judged high, although its costs are likely to be substantially greater than the other scenarios due to the sheer volumes of material that would be moved. Activating the military scenario would entail activating the other three scenarios as well, since the resource base would need to be mapped and assayed, orbital manipulation technologies would need to be developed, and materials processing would be needed to support the expanded space infrastructure and shielding fabrication.

Triggers of Scenario Activation

Assuming that these scenarios are all broadly feasible technologically, which of them are likely to be pursued? In broad terms, all four utilization scenarios are dependent on the allocation of additional financial and organizational resources. But what factors are likely to trigger the authoritative allocation of sufficient resources and support to activate these scenarios? In addressing this question, it is useful to divide activating factors into two classes—political and nonpolitical—and to consider their potential roles in each of the four scenarios.

TRIGGERS OF SCIENTIFIC INVESTIGATION

Scientific investigation is the cheapest and most technologically feasible scenario.[23] Unlike the other three, it is currently proceeding, albeit at a leisurely pace. It is incrementally advancing because of the commitment of amateur astronomers, a network of university-based researchers, and occasional NASA missions. Therefore, it is appropriate to speak, not of the activation of the scenario, but of its acceleration. Acceleration of the scientific investigation scenario would occur if three factors change.

First, the allocation of space science and astronomy resources by NASA and National Science Foundation (NSF) is largely a product of priorities determined by the scientific community. Therefore, a change in priorities by the scientific community could substantially accelerate scientific investigation.

A second factor that could accelerate the activation of the scientific investigation scenario is a change in the priorities of the activist issue networks that seek to shape the allocation of public resources.[24] Despite the extensive recent work by political scientists on nongovernmental actors, activists, and issue networks, the space issue area has not received much attention.[25] The overall priorities of the citizen space lobby are diverse, but asteroidal investigation does not loom large in their agenda. Emerging in the late 1970s in the wake of the post-Apollo reductions in spending, much of the initial energy of the space activist community was devoted to advocating grandiose space colonization and industrialization schemes that were patently utopian. In the 1980s activist energy was heterogeneous and often divided, with some advocating expanded military space activities, while others opposed it. The agenda of space commercialization also absorbed significant energies and, in combination with other important factors, registered significant policy impact. Other activists supported the human spaceflight program, planetary scientific exploration, environmental monitoring, and international cooperation. Only recently has there emerged small advocacy networks concerned primarily with advancing asteroidal investigations. Given that the resources that need to be allocated are relatively modest in comparison with other space activities, it is reasonable to assume that the existing and emerging activist energies in this direction could yield incremental acceleration of asteroidal investigation. A concerted effort on the part of all the space activist and advocacy community could trigger the full realization of the asteroidal investigation scenario. Also, given the small numbers of individuals involved, the potential for a very small number of individuals to make a decisive difference is great.

Third, and perhaps most important, the scientific investigation scenario could be activated decisively by either the discovery of a near-Earth object on collision course with the Earth or the occurrence of a highly visible collision. An interesting phenomenon of the last few years has been the number of objects that are, upon first discovery, thought to be colliders or near-missers, and the manner in which the media has covered these stories.[26] As more and more objects are discovered and the resolution of search telescopes improves, one must conclude that it is only a matter of time until a collider is mapped. Also, given the frequency of collision with smaller objects, their large population, and the difficulties of locating them, one must also conclude that it is only a matter of time until another collision, either an air or ground explosion, occurs.

Once a collider has been either definitively mapped or a collision occurs, I hypothesize that the "asteroid policy issue," and indeed the entire space enterprise, will be quickly and radically transformed. The larger the physical impact, the larger the political impact. Should a collision occur with loss of life and property, particularly in the United States or in one of its close allies, the debate will shift immediately from one of "how little is too much?" in asteroidal investigation spending, to one of "who is to blame for not anticipating and fixing this problem?" In terms of the overall space enterprise, such an event is likely to be a catalyst much like the launch of *Sputnik* in 1957[27] and is likely to evoke a major reorientation and reinvigoration of national and international space efforts. Acquisition of knowledge of asteroids may thus be appropriately thought of as akin to the mapping of earthquake faults, and asteroidal collision thought of as an "earthquake from the sky."

TRIGGERS OF COLLISION AVOIDANCE SCENARIOS

The most likely triggers of collision avoidance scenarios significantly overlap with those at play in the activation of accelerated scientific investigation. It is possible, but not probable, that activists and advocates of collision avoidance could generate enough support for a demonstration of asteroidal manipulation capabilities in the absence of knowledge of an impending collision or experience of a recent collision. Also, if either the military scenario or an ambitious version of commercial development were triggered, the development of techniques for orbital manipulation for military and commercial purposes would in effect constitute a demonstration of collision avoidance capability.

By far the most probable trigger for the activation of the collision avoidance scenario would be the discovery of a potential Earth collider or the experience of an actual collision. Indeed, once such knowledge were obtained, the scientific investigation and the collision avoidance scenarios would largely cease to be distinct and would become two phases or components of one scenario: scientific investigation would be oriented toward providing information for collision avoidance; and effective collision avoidance would require enhanced scientific investigation. Given these similarities and links, I hypothesize that it is simply a matter of time until the collision avoidance scenario is activated.

TRIGGERS OF COMMERCIAL DEVELOPMENT SCENARIOS

Commercial development is heterogeneous and is widely seen as the scenario least dependent on a large public commitment of resources. This may not be an accurate assumption, however. Three different possible triggering factors can be identified.

First, many advocates of commercial development scenarios emphasize that the cost of access to space plays a decisive role in the feasibility of commercial asteroidal development. Since an order of magnitude decrease in the cost of launching a pound into orbit is only likely with a significant public investment, the commercial development scenario hinges significantly on public priorities and investments. Thus, a major advance in space infrastructure development could significantly activate commercial development. The pattern of space commercialization since the 1950s is that heavy government activity accompanied by contracts to private ventures gradually evolves into independently viable commercial ventures only after technologies have matured and markets have been established.

Second, commercial development may also be stimulated by the mapping and assaying activities of scientific investigation. Third, as knowledge of the asteroids and their composition increases, there is a reasonable chance that a body composed of valuable material will be discovered. Such a discovery could have catalytic effects much like the discovery of a few flakes of gold at Sutter's Mill in California in 1848. Thus, there is a reasonable chance that, as scientific investigation proceeds or is accelerated, sooner or later a "gold mine in the sky" will be discovered.

TRIGGERS OF MILITARY EMPLOYMENT SCENARIOS

Whereas the first three scenarios are most likely to be triggered by the introduction of new knowledge, the military employment scenario is most likely to be triggered by renewed interstate political rivalries. Expert assessment of prospects for pacific relations in the decades ahead is sharply divided. Some hold that the "long peace" of the last half-century is structurally rooted and deeply robust, the product of nuclear deterrence; growing interdependence; the growth of international norms, regimes, and organizations; and the expansion of liberalism, democracy, and capitalism. With equal conviction others argue that conflicts of interest between major states are inherent in anarchic state systems and that it is just a matter of time until major new rivalries emerge. The 1990s was a period of relative harmony among the Great Powers, and the relative power of the United States and its allies is unmatched in modern history.

There are gathering clouds of conflict on the horizon. Recent years have seen the decay of the nonproliferation regime and the spread of weapons of mass destruction and ballistic missile technologies to so-called "rogue states." These developments have stimulated and reinvigorated American interest in the deployment of at least a modest anti-ballistic missile capability.[28] A crucial watershed will be the relationship between these efforts and the ABM Treaty of 1970, which severely circumscribes the testing and deployment of such technologies. If the United States unilaterally abrogates this treaty commitment, as President George Bush said would occur, and begins deployment of limited ABM capabilities, other nuclear states, most notably Russia and China, are likely to respond (if the predictions of balance of power theory are any guide) with increased deployments of offensive ballistic missiles. This would end the restraints of the SALT and START Treaties on offensive weapons, in which case the United States is likely to respond with the commitment to a fuller ABM capability, including a substantial space-based component.[29]

The rate and implications of such developments will also be greatly shaped by the more general strategic and political relations among the Great Powers. If relations are deteriorating for other reasons (most notably China-Taiwan conflict and reassertion of Russian imperial ambitions), the pace of the reappearance of strategic arms competition is likely to be accelerated. Conversely, if more general political relations remain good or improve, these strategic military developments are likely to be slowed and possibly halted or reversed. In assessing the overall probability of this political scenario, it is worth remembering that less than twenty years ago the United States and the Soviet Union were in a vigorous strategic and political competition. In sum, there is a plausible, if not yet probable scenario for the political triggering of an ambitious ABM deployment, within which military employment of asteroidal material might be pursued.

OVERALL PATTERNS OF ACTIVATION TRIGGERS

Given these diverse observations, what general patterns can be observed? First and most striking is the potentially enormous impact of newly acquired knowledge as triggers for the activation of asteroidal utilization scenarios. Aside from the military case, the most powerful likely triggers are nonpolitical rather than political. The slow accretion of knowledge about asteroids resulting from the currently slow-paced scientific investigation has explosive potentials to trigger acceleration of the investigation scenario and the rapid activation of the collision avoidance and commercial development scenarios. A change in scientific priorities could accelerate scientific investigation, and a change in broader political priorities could trigger activation of collision avoidance and commercial development scenarios. But far more likely is that such acceleration and activation would result from the politically exogenous acquisition of knowledge about an impending collision or experience of a recent collision, or discovery of a valuable asteroidal resource.

Political Consequences of Asteroidal Diversion

Space activities occur in a physical but not a political vacuum. The existing communal outer space regime has emerged through interaction of state interest, the space environment, and space technology but is widely viewed as outmoded for governing asteroids. So what direction will the regime take? Focused on commercial development and possible military employment, many space advocates support the partition of asteroidal bodies and oppose a space regime based on public principles. However, if the collision avoidance scenario is activated first, the outer space regime is likely to be diverted in very different directions, and much conventional wisdom is on a collision course with reality.

The argument proceeds in four steps. First, I overview the relationship between the territorial state system and extraterritorial regimes. Second, I describe the main features of the existing outer space regime. Third, I survey alternative designs for the governance of the asteroids. Fourth, I describe emerging conflicts over asteroids and assess the interests and relative power of the conflicting parties. Finally, I assess the impact of asteroidal diversion on the outer space regime.

THE STATE SYSTEM AND EXTRATERRITORIAL REGIMES

For at least the last five centuries, the territorial sovereign state system has been the dominant mode of political organization on Earth. At the core of this approach to political order is the demarcation and division of political space into segmented compartments that are mutually recognized as politically independent and self-governing, or "sovereign." [30] States are territorial entities with delineated borders, and authority is highly fragmented, with each state claiming political autonomy. In this order, common goods are relatively rare and are difficult to achieve. But rising levels of interaction and interdependence have created common problems and have slowly but surely evoked international governance arrangements to provide rudimentary restraints on large-scale violence, the management of the international economy, and the regulation of environmental externalities. [31]

However, from its very beginnings in early modern Europe, the sovereign state system has been forced to deal with fluid extraterritorial realms (most notably the high seas, atmosphere, and outer space), which resist segmentation. [32] These spaces have been ordered by evolving and distinct subsystems of governance, which political scientists refer to as "regimes." [33] Regimes are loose governance arrangements that (1) are sector specific, (2) are usually multilateral, (3) usually involve specialized technologies and expert communities, and (4) involve a set of rules, norms, and principles. Regimes are cooperative enterprises that crystallize into persisting institutions and sometimes require substantial organizational capacities. Regimes entail treaties, some of which become constitution-like for particular issue areas and spatial domains; but they generally lack sanctions against violation. However important regimes may be to the governance of particular issue areas and extraterritorial spaces, they are ultimately annexes and adjuncts to the territorial state system. As such, they are ultimately dependent on state power and interest.

Alternative political regimes for spatial governance can be organized in three ways: *partition, communal,* and *public.*[34] Partition arrangements allocate ownership of an asset to some particular owner or ruler. All territorial space on Earth has been partitioned, with the important exception of Antarctica. In communal arrangements an asset is treated as common property, open to the use of all but the possession of no one. Finally, in public arrangements a resource or place is also the property of all but is governed by a public organ acting on behalf of all. Communal property is frequently subject to depletion, crowding, and collision. Much of the international law of the high seas and of outer space has basically evolved as responses to these problems within a communal framework.

THE OUTER SPACE REGIME

As human activities have expanded into outer space over the last several decades, an outer space regime has emerged and been codified in internationally accepted treaties.[35] Overall, outer space is governed communally. It has four main features, each of which is likely to be significantly affected by asteroidal utilization.

First, the outer space regime allows free passage. This principle emerged first in practice and then was codified in the Outer Space Treaty of 1967. The establishment of the free passage principle was due to a combination of space "geography" and technology, and state interests. The Soviet Union, the first state to launch an orbiting satellite, had much to lose from a free passage regime because this would permit other states to observe activities within the Soviet Union that were otherwise hidden. Because satellite orbits must pass over many countries in a short period of time, the partition of orbital space into spheres or zones (most simply accomplished through the vertical extension of national sovereign air space into orbital space) would have foreclosed the use of outer space.

Second, the current outer space regime as codified in the Outer Space Treaty of 1967 prohibits the appropriation of celestial bodies by sovereign states. At the time this treaty was negotiated, the Soviet Union and the United States were in a "race" to reach the moon. Because neither state could be sure who would win, both had an interest in preventing the possible appropriation of the moon by the other. During the 1970s, as part of the general New International Economic Order (NIEO) and "Common Heritage of Mankind" agenda of developing states, an additional agreement, the Moon Treaty, was negotiated, which explicitly applied the newer language of the Common Heritage to the moon.[36] This treaty was seen both by Third World advocates and by First World opponents[37] as a step toward transforming the regime from a communal to a public arrangement. This would eventually entail the creation of an international organization to regulate lunar activities and to guarantee that less-developed states benefit from lunar exploitation. Although numerous developing nations ratified the Moon Treaty, the leading space-faring states did not, thus aborting the beginnings of a public regime for celestial bodies.

Third, the outer space regime has developed measures to deal with crowding and degradation. Despite the vast physical size of Earth orbital space, crowding issues have emerged, and the nature of this crowding has been determined by the interplay between the physical environment of space and space technology. Two relatively minor cases of crowding have thus far emerged as significant: in geosynchronous Earth orbit (GEO) and in space pollution, specifically the creation of debris from satellites and rockets that can damage other satellites and that poses a danger to human activities in space.

A fourth important feature of the space regime is the partial regulation of military capabilities.[38] The first and still most important space security activity has been the military use of space by the nuclear-armed states, particularly the United States and Russia. The placement of nuclear weapons in orbit has been banned (in the Outer Space Treaty); states have agreed not to base and test anti-ballistic missile intercept capabilities (the ABM Treaty); and states have agreed not to test nuclear weapons in space (the Limited Test Ban Treaty). This arms control regime is more substantial than that for the high seas, but it falls short of the Antarctic model: states may not *station* weapons of mass destruction in space, but they may *transit* orbital space, and this is what ICBMs do for much of their trajectories. Banning transit of weapons of mass destruction would be, given the current nuclear-state arsenals, a major alteration. States also have deployed a large number of military communication, reconnaissance, and other support service satellites into orbital space.

ALTERNATIVE REGIMES FOR THE ASTEROIDS

A range of regime alternatives are potentially applicable to asteroidal governance. Given all the different features and thus the possible combinations, the full set of alternatives is immense, but the possibilities can be simplified to manageable proportions by arranging them along the spectrum stretching from public through communal to partition. A pure public arrangement would entail the establishment of an Asteroidal Development Authority with sole authority to own and develop asteroids. The governance of this organization would be configured somehow to represent, and its revenues somehow distributed to benefit, the entire international community. At the other end of the spectrum, a pure partition would entail the unadorned extension of state sovereignty to different asteroids. States would somehow assert claims over asteroids, and once the initial allocation was completed, they would have sole authority over their respective "space islands."

In between these two pure types are a wide range of possibilities for the modification of the existing communal regime. Moving from the pure public arrangement, modifications could include permits, licenses, leases, sales, and taxes on private development of particular asteroids. Governance of the Authority could be configured more like international organizations such as the International Monetary Fund rather than like the UN General Assembly, and revenues could be retained for further development or allocated to some specific goals. Moving from the partition model, modifications could include more equitable mechanisms for the initial allocation of sites and bodies, sets of restraints and responsibilities to accompany possession rights, and an ancillary international regulatory body.

POLITICAL CONFLICTS OVER ASTEROIDAL GOVERNANCE

As the prospect of asteroidal utilization has become increasingly credible, an extensive discussion and debate over modification of the principles of the regime has begun. Extensive analyses and viewpoints have been set forth in space policy journals, law reviews, and Internet sites. Moving beyond the expert community, this topic was extensively discussed and debated at the Third Outer Space Conference held in Vienna in 1999.

At first glance, the fault lines of disagreement in these discussions and debate parallel to some extent those that occurred during the negotiations of the Law of the Sea Treaty that stretched from the middle

1960s through the early 1980s. On one side, the wealthier states with the potential capability to access and exploit asteroids have argued that some system of property rights should be established in order to encourage asteroidal development, in effect replacing the existing communal regime with some version of a partition. They argue that asteroids are not suitable for common pool resource treatment and are like islands in the ocean. They oppose the creation of an international organization with significant regulatory or developmental authorities, arguing that such organizations are often corrupt, inefficient, and slow-moving. They also reject any notion that the allocation of frontier resources should be skewed to remedy historical patterns of inequity and dispossession.

On the other side, poorer states argue that the communal principles should be altered in favor of some sort of public arrangement.[39] They point out that the allocation of this common property on the basis of "squatters' rights" would severely disadvantage them because they lack the capabilities to access and develop these bodies. They also point out that the mineral resources of asteroids would compete with their exports and further diminish their relative share of global wealth. Poorer states tend to approach this issue with vivid memories of injustice and dispossession. They view this domain as an opportunity to rectify historical grievances but fear its disposition will replicate the abuses and inequities that they blame for their current misfortunes.

Despite these similarities, there are three differences between the debates over the Law of the Sea Treaty and the current debates over asteroidal governance. First, the overall ideological intensity of the poorer states has diminished since the 1970s. The Third World stance in the Law of the Sea debates was part of a more general, ambitious, and controversial New International Economic Order (NIEO) agenda. The collapse of this program, the decline of statist economic orientations, and the spread of neoliberal economic policies have combined to create a very different general political context for these debates.

Second, there has been a substantial ideological and political shift in the developed countries in the same direction as in the less-developed countries, away from support for statist and governmental activities. International organizations, while supported by large majorities of the general public, are anathema to the dominant economic and political elites. Private American space activities have risen sharply, and dynamic private sector actors are ideologically and politically mobilized for further private space development. The Outer Space Treaty was negotiated by a Democratic administration with a strong belief in the importance and efficacy of international organizations. If the recent rejections of treaties to reduce global warming, create an international criminal court, and control biological weapons are any indication, any scheme to strengthen or create an international organization would find a hostile reception in the United States Senate.[40]

Third, the leverage position of the developing world is weaker in this area than in the formulation of the Law of the Sea Treaty. In the Law of the Sea debates, developing states had something the developed North wanted: a guarantee of continued "innocent passage" through coastal waters and straits.[41] In contrast, in negotiating an asteroidal regime, developing states have nothing of comparable importance wanted by the wealthier spacefaring states. The share of world space activities and capabilities in the hands of the developed nations, and particularly the United States, has always been much higher than in the area of maritime affairs. While some diffusion of space capability has occurred (particularly toward Europe), this has been more than compensated by the sharp decline in Russian space capability and activity from that of the Soviet period. These asymmetries are compounded by the relative growth in the economic and military power of the developed countries, particularly the United States.

COLLISION AVOIDANCE AND THE OUTER SPACE REGIME

The various factors discussed above suggest that a partition regime is the wave of the future for asteroidal governance. But, there are other circumstances that point toward the selection of a modified communal or public regime design. The power and interest analysis discussed above fails to consider which of the scenarios for asteroidal utilization is first triggered. Much of the contemporary debate tends to assume that commercial (or military) scenarios will occur first. If this happens, then there is indeed a strong presumption in favor of a partition regime design. Assuming, on the basis of my earlier analysis, that collision avoidance is most likely to be pursued first, I argue that a public regime alternative is much more likely to emerge.[42] Four reasons support this conclusion.

First, the benefits from asteroidal diversion are a public good, and no one country is likely to want to underwrite the cost of such an enterprise on its own. Because a large collision would have global effects and because it would probably be difficult to predict the site of a smaller collision accurately, asteroidal diversion can be classified as a genuine global or planetary public good. Given this, even the most powerful and wealthy states would have a great incentive to pursue multilateral solutions in order to attract contributions from as many other states as possible.

Second, the unilateral pursuit of collision avoidance is likely to raise suspicions from other states. Because important technologies with potential military application would be involved, no major country would want its rivals or potential rivals to develop such capability unilaterally. Also, the possible use of nuclear explosives in diversion would require compromise of the denuclearization of space, and major states would want to be certain that such activities were not being used as clandestine nuclear testing programs. Finally, the many nonnuclear states would resist any employment of nuclear explosives in space except under genuine international partnership for fear that the already fragile global nuclear arms control regime would be compromised.

Third, the configuration of the existing manned space infrastructure, particularly the International Space Station project, also points toward a more public approach. Any significant diversion of asteroids in the near to medium term would almost certainly rely heavily on this expensive infrastructure. With an estimated life-cycle cost in the neighborhood of $100 billion dollars, the space station is too expensive to be readily duplicated.

Finally, in thinking about asteroidal regime formation, the Antarctic model may be applicable in important ways.[43] The "island in space" metaphor for asteroids has perhaps carried with it the implication that asteroids are similar to the "spice islands" that the early modern Europeans accessed and quickly appropriated.[44] But a better insular analogy from the oceans may be the big cold ice and rock island of Antarctica. For the foreseeable future, asteroids are likely to remain places that are costly, difficult, and dangerous to visit. But unlike Antarctica, the rock and ice islands in the sky will again fall upon us, and our interaction with them is likely to be shaped primarily by this possibility and its avoidance.

Conclusions and Implications

This exploration of scenarios for the utilization of asteroids has addressed three questions. First, in a brief synthetic summary of the existing literature, possible scenarios have been described: What uses are possible? Second, these scenarios have been evaluated as dependent variables: Which factors, political and nonpolitical, are most likely to activate different scenarios? Third, collision avoidance has been evaluated as an independent variable: What will be the impact of asteroidal diversion on the outer space regime?

In contrast to conventional wisdom, two main arguments have been advanced. First, the most probable catalyst for major space activities directed at the asteroids is collision avoidance. As more asteroids are discovered and their orbits calculated, it is only a matter of time before a collision is anticipated authoritatively, or a highly visible (and perhaps destructive) collision occurs. Once this happens, major public resources are likely to be allocated to the further scientific investigation of asteroids and to the development, demonstration, and employment of techniques to manipulate asteroidal orbits. Second, asteroidal diversion will have far-reaching implications for the evolution of the outer space regime. In contrast to the widespread view in American policy circles that the communal outer space regime should give way to a partition for commercial or military uses, collision avoidance is likely to push the regime in a more public direction.

Five implications follow from these arguments. First, increased investment in asteroidal discovery and mapping could have an immense leverage effect on the entire space enterprise. More than any other area of space expenditure, asteroidal discovery and mapping has the potential to radically stimulate further public investment in space.

Second, the entire current set of space policies and priorities can be thought of as being subject to massive exogenous shock, in the form of the discovery of a collider or experience of a collision, that will rapidly and radically alter policy. Furthermore, this shock is likely to occur sooner or later no matter what we now do. The entire space enterprise is sitting on an active earthquake fault, and it is just a matter of time until a "shake-up" occurs.

Third, it is appropriate to reconceptualize how we view the knowledge acquired from asteroidal scientific investigations. This knowledge is now in the same category as knowledge about celestial bodies that are immensely distant spatially and temporally. Such knowledge is sought to answer the most fundamental scientific questions of when and how the universe and life began. While the cultural, philosophical, and theological implications of such knowledge are huge, their practical material importance is low. In contrast, knowledge about the specific location of near-Earth objects has tertiary scientific importance but potentially great practical importance. Humans will never travel to other galaxies and may only travel to neighboring stars in centuries ahead. The Earth is the only known abode of life in the universe, and humanity's fate for the foreseeable future is inextricably linked to Earth. The Earth has and will be subject to collision damage ranging from the locally to the globally catastrophic. Thus, it is appropriate to think of asteroidal investigations as analogous to the activities of the United States Geological Survey or the National Weather Service, since what is at stake is the mapping of potential natural threats to the human habitat.

Fourth, historical patterns of allocating public space resources are cast in a rather embarrassing light. The search for a catalytic activator of public support for enlarged space activities has been something of a Holy Grail in the space advocacy community since its earliest inception in the 1920s. How can governments be persuaded to allocate the large resources necessary to develop the ability to access and develop space? Beginning with the German Rocket Society's enticement of the Wehrmacht,[45] and extending through the 1950s and 1960s with Cold War military and prestige competition ("the race to the moon"), to the International Space Station as a political effort, the major steps in space development have occurred, not because the general political system is committed to space exploration and development for its own sake, but rather because space development is seen as a means to achieve military or political goals that have nothing intrinsically to do with space. In asteroidal investigations, the solution to this perennial problem is, and has long been, at hand.

Finally, the space enterprise will be fundamentally transformed by focusing on collision avoidance. The space program will become part of "planetary defense" and an "Earth security" program. Collision avoidance will join the avoidance of nuclear war and environmental destruction as parts of a planetary security system.

NOTES

Ronald Diebert, Henry Lambright, John Logsdon, Agnes Gereben Schaefer, and M. J. Peterson offered valuable comments on earlier versions of this chapter.

1. *Regimes* are loose subsystems of governance that involve specialized technologies and require special rules, norms, and principles. Regimes are discussed at length later in this chapter.

2. William J. Broad, "Newfound Crater Could Explain Worst Mass Extinction," *New York Times,* 25 April 2000, C1.

3. For a synthesis of the new perspective, see Derek Ager, *The New Catastrophism: The Importance of Rare Events in Geological History* (New York: Cambridge University Press, 1993).

4. For the hegemonic assumption of gradualism and its consequences, see Stephen Jay Gould, "Toward the Vindication of Punctuational Change," in *Catastrophes in Earth History*, ed. W. A. Berggren and J. A. Van Couvering (Princeton: Princeton University Press, 1984), 9–34. For the new catastrophism as a paradigm shift, see William Glen, *The Mass Extinction Debates: How Science Works in a Crisis* (Stanford: Stanford University Press, 1994).

5. The most notable advocate, Immanuel Velikovsky, *Worlds in Collision* (New York: Macmillan, 1950), made excessive claims that helped discredit catastrophism. For critiques, see D. Goldsmith, ed., *Scientists Confront Velikovsky* (Ithaca: Cornell University Press, 1977), and Clark R. Chapman and David Morrison, "Catastrophism Gone Wild: The Case of Immanuel Velikovsky," *Cosmic Catastrophes* (New York: Plenum, 1989), 185–96.

6. Gerrit L. Vershuur, "The Great Comet Crash of 1994" and "The Aftermath," chaps. 14 and 15 in *Impact! The Threat of Comets and Asteroids* (New York: Oxford University Press, 1996), 169–90.

7. John S. Lewis, *Rain of Iron and Ice: The Very Real Threat of Comet and Asteroid Bombardment* (Reading, MA: Addison-Wesley, 1996).

8. Going back even earlier, there is strong support for the view that the earth's ocean and atmosphere were constituted by celestial bombardment of lighter elements (augmented by continuous outgasing from the solid Earth) that would not have been present on the largely rock and metallic Earth as it first coalesced and cooled. See J. R. Spencer and J. Mitton, eds., *The Great Comet Crash* (New York: Cambridge University Press, 1995).

9. P. J. Thomas, C. F. Chyba, and C. P. McKay, eds., *Comets and the Evolution of Life* (New York: Springer, 1997).

10. Duane A. Day, "Paradigm Lost," *Space Policy*, 19 August 1995, 153–59.

11. For NEAR and its findings, see Warren E. Leary, "Taking a Close Look at Earth's Strange Neighbors," *New York Times*, 11 April 2000, C1.

12. G. Canavan, J. Solem and D. G. Rather, eds., *Proceedings of the Near-Earth-Object Interception Workshop* (Los Alamos Publication, LANL 12476-C, 89–110, 1993); and Tom Gehrels, ed., *Hazards Due to Comets and Asteroids* (Tucson: University of Arizona Press, 1994).

13. U.S. House of Representatives Subcommittee on Science, Space and Technology, *The Threat of Large Earth-Orbit-Crossing Asteroids*, 103rd Congress, 1st session, 1993.

14. For accessible syntheses of recent knowledge, see Duncan Steel, *Rogue Asteroids and Doomsday Comets* (New York: Wiley, 1995); Verschuur, *Impact! The Threat of Comets and Asteroids;* John and Mary Gribben, *Fire on Earth* (New York: St. Martin's, 1997); and John Erickson, *Target Earth! Asteroidal Collisions Past and Future* (New York: McGraw Hill, 1991).

15. Clark Chapman and David Morrison, "Threat from the Skies: Will a Comet Strike?" *Cosmic Catastrophes* (New York: Plenum, 1989), 275–87; and "Impacts on the Earth by Asteroids and Comets: Assessing the Hazard," *Nature* 367 (1994): 33–40.

16. Louis A. Kleiman, ed., *Project Icarus* (Cambridge: MIT Press, 1968).

17. H. J. Melosh, I. V. Nemchimov, and Yu. I. Zetzer, "Non-Nuclear Strategies for Deflecting Comets and Asteroids," in *Hazards Due to Comets and Asteroids*, ed. T. Gehrels (Tucson: University of Arizona Press, 1994), 1111–34.

18. John S. Lewis, *Mining the Sky: Untold Riches from the Asteroids, Comets, and Planets* (Reading, MA: Addison-Wesley, 1996); Brian O'Leary, *The Fertile Stars* (New York: Everest House, 1981).

19. For detailed description and evaluation, see Office of Technology Assessment, *Solar Power Satellites* (Washington, DC: Government Printing Office, 1981).

20. Gerard O'Neill, *The High Frontier* (Garden City, NY: Anchor/Doubleday, 1982).

21. Robert Salkeld, *War and Space* (Englewood Cliffs, NJ: Prentice Hall, 1970).

22. C. Meinel, "Near-Earth Asteroids: Potential Bonanza for Ambitious Military Space Projects," *Defense Science 2003+* (February-March 1985). For the most theoretically ambitious defense of large-scale space weaponization as a path to planetary dominance, see Everett C. Dolman, *Astropolitik: Classical Geopolitics in the Space Age* (London: Frank Cass, 2001).

23. David Morrison, "An International Program to Protect the Earth from Impact Catastrophe: First Steps," *Acta Astronautica* 30 (1993): 11–16.

24. For analyses of space advocacy and its impacts, see William Bainbridge, *The Spaceflight Revolution* (New York: Wiley, 1976); Michael A. G. Michaud, *Reaching for the High Frontier: The American Pro-Space Movement, 1972–84* (New York: Praeger, 1986); Howard E. McCurdy, *Space and the American Imagination* (Washington, DC: Smithsonian Institution Press, 1997).

25. The relevant universe of political science concepts and literature, particularly concerning transnational relations, epistemic communities, and advocacy networks is enormous. For a recently developed framework with particular applicability to space, see Margaret Keck and Kathryn Sikkink, *Activists Beyond Borders: Advocacy Networks in International Politics* (Ithaca: Cornell University Press, 1998).

26. For example, see Warren Leary, "Big Asteroid Passes Near Earth Unseen in a Rare Close Call," *New York Times*, 20 April 1989; Malcolm W. Browne, "Fireball Over Greenland Sends Scientist on Hunt for a Meteor," *New York Times*, 19 December 1997, A17; Malcolm W. Browne, "Asteroid Is Expected to Make a Pass Close to Earth in 2028," *New York Times*, 21 March 1998, A1; and "After Asteroid Episode, Scientist Agree to Agree," *New York Times*, 20 March 1998, A19.

27. For a vivid picture of this shock and its political effects, see Walter A. McDougall, . . . *The Heavens and the Earth: A Political History of the Space Age* (New York: Basic Books, 1985).

28. For arguments in favor of a limited national missile defense, see James M. Lindsay and Michael E. Ohanlan, *Defending America: The Case for Limited National Missile Defense* (Washington, DC: Brookings Institution, 2001).

29. For a critique of large-scale space-based weapons deployment linked to a geopolitical (contextual material) analysis of the orbital environment, see Daniel Deudney, *Whole Earth Security: A Geopolitics of Peace* (Washington, DC: Worldwatch, 1983).

30. An immense literature has developed on these points. For a useful recent synthesis, see Alexander B. Murphy, "The Sovereign State System as Political-Territorial Ideal: Historical and Contemporary Considerations," in *State Sovereignty as Social Construct,* ed. Beirsteker and Weber (New York: Cambridge University Press, 1996), 81–120.

31. Included in the large literature about international cooperation, see Elinor Ostrom, *Governing the Commons: The Evolution of Institutions for Collective Action* (New York: Cambridge University Press, 1990); and Oran Young, *International Cooperation* (Ithaca: Cornell University Press, 1989)

32. For analysis of extraterritorial regimes, see Marvin Soroos, "The International Commons: A Historical Perspective," *Environmental Review* 12 (1) (Spring 1988): 1–22; Seyom Brown, Nina W. Cornell, Larry L. Fabian, and Edith Brown Weiss, *Regimes of the Ocean, Outer Space and Weather* (Washington, DC: Brookings Institution, 1977); and Mark Zacker, "The Development of Regimes for Nonterrestrial Spaces," in *Multilateralism Matters,* ed. John Gerard Ruggie (New York: Columbia University Press, 1993).

33. An immense theoretical, empirical and policy literature on regimes exists. Key theoretical statements are Stephen D. Krasner, ed., *International Regimes* (Ithaca: Cornell University Press, 1982); and Andreas Hasenclever, Peter Mayer, and Volker Rittberger, *Theories of International Regimes* (New York: Cambridge University Press, 1997).

34. In more technical terms from Roman Law, widely used in subsequent international law and political science, these three alternatives are termed *res privata, res communis,* and *res publica.*

35. For a useful recent synthesis and overview of the space regime, see Ralph G. Steinhardt, "Outer Space," in *The United Nations and International Law,* ed. Christopher Joyner, (New York: Cambridge University Press, 1997), 336–61.

36. *Agreement Governing the Activities of States on the Moon and Other Celestial Bodies* (Washington, DC: Government Printing Office, 1980).

37. For the developed state criticisms, see Art Dula, "Free Enterprise and the Proposed Moon Treaty," *Houston Journal of International Law* 3 (21) (1980); Nancy Griffin, "Americans and the Moon Treaty," *Journal of Law and Commerce* 46 (Spring 1981): 729–63; and T. Twibel, "Space Law: Legal Restraints on Commercialization and Development of Outer Space," *University of Missouri at Kansas City Law Review* 65 (Spring 1997): 589–97.

38. For an overview, see Philip D. O'Neill, Jr., "The Development of International Law Governing the Military Use of Outer Space," in *National Interests and the Military Use of Space,* ed. William J. Durch (Cambridge, MA: Ballinger, 1984).

39. Nandasiri Jasentuliyana, "International Space Law and Cooperation and the Mining of Asteroids," *Annals of Air and Space Law* 15 (1990): 343–357.
40. Charles William Maynes, "America's Folding Commitment to the World," in *Global Focus: U.S. Foreign Policy at the Turn of the Millenium,* ed. M. Honey and T. Barry (New York: St. Martin's, 2000): 85–106
41. For the importance of this factor, see Mark W. Janis, *Naval Power and the Law of the Sea* (Lexington, MA: Lexington Books, 1976).
42. For an earlier statement on the political effects of large-scale cooperative space activities, including asteroidal diversion, see Daniel Deudney, "Forging Missiles into Spaceships," *World Policy Journal* (Spring 1985): 271–303.
43. For the influence analogies have played in space regime formation, see M. J. Peterson, "The Use of Analogies in Developing Outer Space Law," *International Organization* 51 (2) (Spring 1997): 245–74. For features of the Antarctic regime, see Philip W. Quigg, *A Pole Apart: The Emerging Issue of Antarctica* (New York: New Press, 1983).
44. Dandridge Cole and Donald W. Cox, *Islands in Space: The Challenge of the Planetoids* (Philadelphia, PA: Chilton Books, 1964).
45. Michael J. Neufeld, *The Rocket and the Reich: Peenemuende and the Coming of the Ballistic Missile Era* (New York: Free Press, 1995).

6   The Quest for Mars

W. Henry Lambright and Debora L. VanNijnatten

T HE EARLY twenty-first century stands as a watershed between
the space program that was and the space program that will be.
The past is highlighted by Apollo and by Neil Armstrong's epochal "one
small step for [a] man . . . one giant leap for mankind." The future that
could be is human spaceflight to Mars. As the moon highlights NASA's
twentieth-century past, Mars stands as a symbol for what can come in
the twenty-first century. It is an exciting and inspirational goal by which
advocates can organize action and mobilize political support. For them
the question is less *whether* an expedition to Mars will come than *when,
how,* and *why.*

Through unmanned flights and related technological development,
NASA is already moving today toward human spaceflight to Mars, but
the process is halting and fragmented. There was an earlier decision to
send humans to Mars, but it lacked commitment. Whether the next decision will be sustained remains to be seen. Critical to doing so will be
the creation of a coalition of support as substantial as the goal is large.
If that coalition can be maintained, the decision to go to Mars will lead,
not to a brief moment of glory as with Apollo, but eventually to a permanent presence on the Red Planet. In this chapter, we review the history
of the quest for Mars and speculate about its future.

The von Braun Vision and Apollo Discontinuity

Mars has been a destiny in literature and in the media for a long time.
Turning science fiction into reality has required technological vision.
The man who supplied that vision and created what some have called a
paradigm for human space exploration was Wernher von Braun.

In the early 1950s, von Braun, already famous as the man behind
Hitler's *V-2* missile, then with the U.S. Army, and later with NASA, out-

lined a technological trajectory for human spaceflight that culminated in Mars.[1] First, unmanned satellites capable of orbiting the Earth had to be developed. Second would come Earth orbital flights by humans. Third, it would be necessary to develop a reusable spacecraft for travel to and from Earth orbit. Fourth, a permanently inhabited space station would be needed as a place both to observe Earth and to serve as a way station for launching expeditions beyond Earth orbit. Fifth, human exploration of the moon would commence. And sixth, finally, would be an expedition to Mars.

Politics, in the form of Cold War competition, led in the 1960s to a discontinuity in the von Braun paradigm. The United States leaped ahead to the moon sooner than projected. Moreover, once Apollo ended, the question was whether NASA would continue on to Mars—or go back to some of the earlier steps in von Braun's strategy.

Stepping Back: Nixon

The first policy decision concerning a manned Mars program was a rejection.[2] It came not long after Apollo's triumph in 1969. In that year, advocates of a Mars program, including von Braun, saw their vision incorporated into a planning process for post-Apollo.

Vice President Spiro Agnew chaired a Space Task Group that offered President Richard M. Nixon a choice of three long-range objectives: (1) a comprehensive program consisting of a manned Mars expedition, a space station orbiting the moon, and another station in Earth orbit that would be serviced by a shuttle vehicle; (2) an intermediate program costing less but including a Mars mission; and (3) an Earth-orbiting station and a vehicle to shuttle back and forth between the station and Earth.[3]

The Nixon White House rejected the Mars mission completely. The political climate was against following up Apollo with a similar program of monumental scope. There were budget problems, a war in Vietnam, and civil strife at home. Space was no longer a national priority. The conditions that made Apollo possible in the 1960s were not present in the new decade. For NASA, the policy problem was not how to go to Mars but how to keep the human spaceflight program alive. In 1972 Nixon chose the minimal manned space program: the Space Shuttle, a transportation system to low-Earth orbit. The last manned flight to the moon took place that year. The huge technological capability created for Apollo in the 1960s, such as the *Saturn* rocket, atrophied and was eventually abandoned. Apollo's policy goal was to win a race with the Soviet Union to the moon, and that goal was achieved.

The heroic years of NASA were followed in the 1970s by less-spectacular actions in a very different decade. NASA may have wanted to go to Mars, but political leaders and the general public had other priorities. When von Braun died in 1977, his original step-by-step paradigm continued, but NASA was back at an earlier point in the trajectory than it had been in 1969.

Keeping the Dream Alive: Advocacy Groups

Nixon took Mars off the presidential space agenda. Most of NASA's resources were poured into development of the Space Shuttle, but Mars remained on the NASA agenda as an unmanned science mission. In the mid-1960s, NASA had sent the *Mariner* spacecraft to Mars, and the first photograph was taken in 1965. Images revealed a barren world. That impression, along with other NASA priorities, had placed even robotic missions on the back burner for years. It was not until the *Viking* probes to Mars, which arrived on Mars in 1976, that the Red Planet got a serious and detailed reexamination.[4] With two orbiters and two landers, *Viking* surveyed the planet with the announced aim of determining the presence or absence of life. The answer seemed to be no life, although that determination was not conclusive. *Viking's* apparently negative result returned Mars to the recesses of NASA's concerns. Enthusiasm for Mars in government was at a low ebb.

However, there was a group of graduate students and faculty in astrophysics at the University of Colorado who were not totally discouraged by the failure of *Viking* to find life. Instead, they discussed the possibility of bringing Mars "back to life" through human settlement. Over the next two years ad hoc discussions became more serious. The group of about twenty called themselves the "Mars Underground," a fitting appellation, given the lack of official interest in Mars in Washington.[5]

In 1978, a seminar was initiated at the University of Colorado, organized by members of the Mars Underground. In 1980, Chris McKay and others associated with the Mars Underground attended a meeting of the American Astronautical Society (AAS) in Washington and met Leonard David, a writer who had arranged student conferences at AAS meetings in the past. David encouraged the students to organize a national conference around their question of how to bring life to Mars.

The group held the first "Case for Mars" conference in late April 1981 in Boulder, with approximately one hundred people attending. Three years later, a second Mars conference took place, featuring Thomas Paine, former NASA administrator and visionary in space policy. In

1985, President Ronald Reagan appointed Paine to head a blue-ribbon National Commission on Space to look beyond the Space Station, which Reagan had recently decided to build. The Paine Commission recommended establishing a human outpost on Mars as a thirty-year NASA goal.[6]

These external events helped Mars advocates within NASA, a relatively weak and "underground" group themselves. However, the potential momentum for Mars was blunted by the *Challenger* disaster of 1986. While NASA sought to recover from the technological and political fallout of *Challenger,* advocacy continued outside the agency. A third national conference on Mars was held in Boulder, Colorado, this time with Carl Sagan giving the keynote address. One thousand people attended the conference, which was publicized by the international media.[7] Among those who attended was Robert Zubrin, a Martin-Marietta engineer, who would soon become a leader among Mars enthusiasts.

In the wake of *Challenger,* NASA asked Sally Ride, the first female astronaut, to study the future of NASA. Her report, issued in 1987, recommended Mars as one of the four NASA missions.[8] The recommendation came at a time when the Soviet Union was itself proposing a possible Mars program. In January 1989, President Ronald Reagan declared it the long-range goal of the nation to "expand human presence and activity beyond Earth orbit into the solar system."[9] Ever so slowly, the work of outside advocates, events, and presidential rhetoric were converging to make Mars a legitimate topic for conversation within government. It was back on the White House agenda.

The Bush Decision

With the coming of George H. W. Bush to the presidency, Mars advocates got what they wanted, a clear presidential endorsement. In 1989, on the twentieth anniversary of the first landing on the moon, Bush proposed "a long-range, continuing commitment . . . first . . . for the 1990s . . . *Space Station Freedom* . . . next—for the new century—back to the moon . . . back to stay. And then . . . a manned mission to Mars."[10]

Bush did not give any timetable (in the sense that Kennedy gave a deadline for Apollo) or budget. He gave a goal and said he would have the National Space Council determine what it would take to fulfill the mission. The congressional and public reaction was flat, however. George Johnson, writing in the *New York Times,* expressed the prevailing view that the call for a Moon-Mars goal "sometime next century struck many people as abstract and unconvincing."[11]

The next adjective that came to be applied to the Bush decision was "too expensive." The initial NASA study of how to implement the Bush decision said it could take thirty years and cost $450 billion or more.[12] The cost estimate had the effect of virtually killing congressional support for a Mars program at birth. This was a time of growing budget deficits, and in 1990 Bush and Congress reached an agreement that put caps on expenditure increases. The Bush decision was out of synch with the times, which were downsizing where many government programs were concerned.

However, when Zubrin, moving to the fore as an outside-government advocate, spoke at the Fourth Case for Mars Conference in Colorado, he presented the option of a much less expensive program that eliminated the moon as an interim step as well as the development of much expensive hardware. His idea, called "Mars Direct," would take ten years and cost about $20 billion.[13] Zubrin's ideas attracted considerable media attention and stimulated a NASA "Semi- direct" plan at $55 billion.[14] The Mars Underground was becoming a Mars movement, and Zubrin was emerging as its chief spokesman.

Implementing the Space Exploration Initiative (SEI)

For the first time, there was a presidentially legitimated program for sending humans to Mars, established by NASA following the president's decision as the Space Exploration Initiative (SEI). The presidential decision, however, was weak. President Bush did not push SEI, and Congress was indifferent at best, with some very powerful opponents of the program. Even NASA, as an organization, looked askance at SEI.[15] NASA had many more immediate problems with manned space, such as the Space Shuttle and Space Station. Financially constrained, it suffered another political and technological setback when the Hubble Space Telescope, launched in 1990, produced blurred pictures and later had to be repaired. The Bush administration convened a blue ribbon group, chaired by Norman Augustine, chairman and CEO of Martin Marietta, to consider NASA's manifold troubles and pose a possible future course.[16]

The Augustine committee divided NASA's missions into two: Mission to Earth and Mission from Earth. With respect to Mission from Earth, the group was clear that a space program without human spaceflight was unthinkable. But what was to be its goal? The committee declared that Bush was right about Mars. This was the "magnet." Justifying Mars had to be done "largely on the basis of intangibles—the desire to explore, to learn about one's surroundings, to challenge the unknown and to find what is to be found." To get to Mars would require many steps along the way, such as "unmanned visits" and "returning for extended periods to the moon in order to refine our hardware and procedures and to develop the skills and technologies required for long-term planetary living." One of these steps was the Space Station, which was "essential as a life sciences laboratory, for there is simply no Earthbound substitute."[17]

However, the Augustine Committee did not state a timetable or budget for Mars. It said NASA should follow an "availability of funding" strategy. Other priorities were not to be sacrificed. Exactly what that meant was unclear. The panel did call for substantially increasing the NASA budget over the 1990s, a condition that would provide more flexibility to NASA. "Availability of funds" and "go as you [can] pay"—the Augustine formula—was a fine idea as long as funds were available. However, this was not to be, for the Cold War was ending and NASA had to adjust to a new political and economic environment in the 1990s.[18]

In June 1990, Congressman Robert Walker (R-PA) told an aerospace conference on the Space Exploration Initiative that Congress had just voted down SEI funding. As explanation, he said that NASA management, led at the time by Administrator Richard Truly, had told Congress that if NASA got what it wanted for the Space Shuttle and Space Station programs, Congress was welcome to vote however it pleased on funds for SEI.[19] Whether or not NASA leadership really felt that way, it was generally perceived in Washington that SEI was not a program Truly favored.

The White House appointed a panel under former Apollo astronaut Gen. Thomas Stafford to try to find a new architecture for SEI in place of the $450 billion, 30-year program design NASA's initial study produced. The Stafford committee heard from Zubrin and others. Its May 1991 report ignored Mars Direct and called for a program using multiple spacecraft and nuclear propulsion. It did not state a budget.[20]

In the fall of 1991, one of the Stafford committee members, Michael Griffin, was appointed Associate Administrator for Exploration within NASA and director of SEI, a program still looking for support. Meanwhile, NASA Administrator Truly and the National Space Council had increasing differences, in part relating to the priority of SEI. In March 1992, President Bush replaced Truly with Daniel Goldin, an aerospace executive and known advocate of a Mars program.

At his confirmation hearings in late March, Goldin testified that "humans are destined to explore space." In written testimony for the hearings, he declared, "I have long been an enthusiast for sending humans to explore Mars. In the current environment, we need to concentrate on the small precursor missions and enabling technologies in the near term in order to be ready to exploit the exploration of space when the funding envelope opens."[21]

Goldin: Recasting the Vision

Goldin inherited an SEI program bereft of money. NASA had requested $32 million to get SEI underway and wound up with virtually nothing from Congress.[22] He spoke with Sagan, a Mars enthusiast, who advised him that the only way to get congressional support was to reduce the magnitude from the huge amount NASA had calculated originally to $50 billion, and from thirty years to fifteen years. Also, perhaps funding could come from Europe, Japan, and other nations, helping the United States to finance the program. Goldin found that Congress simply felt NASA had too much on its plate and that SEI was not credible in the current funding environment.[23]

Nevertheless, the Bush administration wanted SEI, and Goldin tried to get funding for the SEI program in what turned out to be Bush's last budget. In January 1993 Bill Clinton became president and eliminated all the funds Bush had proposed for SEI. In April the SEI office was closed. Goldin, who was retained by Clinton, explained that NASA was not giving up on Mars, just "taking a pause."[24] In fact, Goldin was finding it would be a major test of his ability just to retain the Space Station, which was under attack from within both the Clinton administration and Congress. By the end of 1993 the Space Station was saved, but it was clear that both the president and Congress were in no mood to discuss a manned Mars program. The only Mars decision the new administration had made was one of termination, a decision with which Congress concurred.

Unmanned Expeditions to Mars—Faster, Better, Cheaper

During 1993 the first robotic U.S. expedition to Mars since *Viking*, the $1 billion *Mars Observer*, arrived at Mars.[25] However, something went wrong and contact was lost.

Rather than lamenting the disaster, Goldin used the loss as an opportunity for change. As he saw it, the existing NASA approach, which was to design large-scale spacecraft and pack them with as many experiments as possible, was flawed. Such spacecraft cost too much, took too long to build, and if anything went wrong, constituted huge losses. Why not take advantage of the microelectronics revolution, asked Goldin, and build more spacecraft that were smaller and less expensive, and launch them more frequently?

Goldin rammed through a change in program philosophy that influenced space science and Earth observation missions dramatically. "Faster, better, cheaper" became Goldin's mantra, repeated over and over again. It allowed for keeping programs operating even as he downsized personnel and lived with a steady state or even declining budget. Mars missions were replanned and redesigned in accord with the faster, better, cheaper philosophy.

Manned Mars planning—the remnant of SEI—was located, at least initially, in a small study office of NASA's Space Science Division. Goldin said he was concentrating on getting the Space Station up but added, "My deepest dream is that in my lifetime I will some way be responsible for a mission to Mars. It would be the next noble thing we could do as a society." The last noble action, he believed, had been Apollo.[26]

In 1996 a team of NASA and university scientists claimed that a meteorite found in Antarctica, which was originally from Mars, contained fossilized remains of ancient Martian bacteria. Goldin informed the White House of the stunning news. However, once publicized, the claims were disputed by other scientists, and before long the unresolved debate quelled enthusiasm surrounding the meteorite. Far more important as the spur to public and governmental interest in Mars was an event in 1997.

Pathfinder, the successor to the 1993 *Mars Observer,* landed on Mars on July 4th, 1997. Its tiny roving vehicle, Sojourner, explored Mars' mid-latitude geology. Millions of people were able to see the Martian landscape on their television screens and follow events on NASA's Web site. *Pathfinder,* which cost approximately $250 million, seemed to vindicate Goldin's "faster, better, cheaper" strategy.[27] More significantly, it showed a latent public fascination with Mars that could be kindled by real-time images. NASA made it known that it would be scheduling unmanned trips to Mars every twenty-six months, when Earth and Mars were most closely aligned. While no one said it officially, the implication was that the robotic flights were precursors to a manned journey—perhaps by 2019, the fiftieth anniversary of the moon landing. NASA's strategic plan stated the possibility of human flights to planetary and other bodies by 2010–23.[28]

Of course, all this was dependent on getting the Space Station built and having the unmanned probes of Mars go well. The Space Station was in fact being delayed due in part to Russian failure to deliver on promises made earlier. NASA would have to provide resources to help the Russians at a time when its own resources were stressed to the limit.

There were reports that some in NASA regarded talk of Mars as diversion of attention from more immediate needs. A leak to the media in 1998 stated that NASA was terminating all exploratory research connected with returning to the moon and going on to Mars. Quelling an incipient furor, Goldin himself reversed that decision. Later that year, at a memorial service for Alan Shepard, America's first man in space, Goldin declared, "Alan, America *will* go to Mars."[29]

Zubrin and His Allies

Meanwhile, external advocacy for Mars continued to grow. In 1996 Zubrin had published *The Case for Mars,* a book that presented his vision of how to go to Mars, live on Mars, and eventually transform Mars into a planet for human habitation. The book helped spark interest in Mars throughout the world. In 1998 Zubrin joined with others, including former SEI director Michael Griffin, who was no longer with NASA, in launching the Mars Society, an international organization dedicated to furthering Mars settlement by public and private means. The founding convention took place in August 1998 in Boulder, Colorado, with 700 attendees and attracted international media attention.[30]

A Setback

NASA's Mars planning and outside advocacy tended to be optimistic —assuming success in each of the many steps along the way to Mars. Unfortunately, reality showed that setbacks were part of the process of technological development. In 1999 two "faster, better, cheaper" Mars probes arrived only to be "lost in space." A *Mars Climate Orbiter* malfunctioned due to human error in navigation. Soon afterward, the *Mars Polar Lander* was also lost due to technical problems. Goldin's management strategy was criticized in Congress and the media as being responsible for these losses. NASA investigated the matter and restructured the program.[31] The principal step in the program, a mission to return to Earth a sample of Mars soil, was postponed from 2005 to some time after 2010.

Getting a Mars Decision

While the twentieth century ended with the Mars unmanned program under reevaluation, there is no question that the twenty-first century will see more robotic probes to Mars. The most difficult question is what will move Mars from vision to reality in terms of human spaceflight? What could trigger a decision by the United States, perhaps in alliance with other nations, that would have unprecedented funding, technological, organizational and political requirements?

TRIGGERS

Historically, *competition* has been a driver. This was most true of Apollo. A front of the Cold War, Apollo was propelled by nationalism, pride, prestige, and belief that preeminence in space meant preeminence in national security and victory in the battle for people's minds. Spurred by the Gagarin flight that placed the USSR first in manned space, Kennedy harnessed space technology to a political goal: to achieve and demonstrate the superiority of the U.S. political-economic system over that of the Soviet Union. For a time after the 1961 decision, Kennedy probed cooperation as a possible goal with the Soviet Union, but that effort proved fruitless, and competition held as the dominant motivator for a decade. A political goal, linked to national interest in winning a technological race, was the driver.

Competition was a factor in succeeding presidential decisions—Space Shuttle, Space Station, and the aborted Space Exploration Initiative (SEI). As long as there was a Cold War, competition mattered—and the pride and prestige that went with it—in the human spaceflight efforts of NASA.

Without the Cold War, the competitive threat from another space power has today become minimal. It cannot be ruled out as a motivator in the future, however. Russia could rise again and revert to its former stance as a competitor. China is likely to become a great power in the twenty-first century. Especially if its ruling regime remains authoritarian, it could use space to assert its role on the world stage. A space race is possible, especially if some resource valuable for Earth is found on Mars.

Cooperation among nations has risen gradually as a second possible motivator for future space decision making. Apollo was strictly a national effort. The Space Shuttle involved some international cooperation. The Space Station entails substantially more cooperation, enough to have been christened the International Space Station by the Clinton administration. In an address about Mars, NASA Administrator Goldin suggested that a human space project to Mars would unite nations of the world as never before and be a stimulus for peace. "The most important reason for missions to the moon and Mars, I believe, is the *political* evolution of humankind," Goldin declared.[32]

A third potential driver is sense of *destiny.* It is the "frontier spirit," an instinctive drive to explore that is built into people. Zubrin talks about "national rebirth" and how "people feel the need for the continued existence of an open frontier." His view is that the stimulus originates in the nature of humanity rather than in the leadership of government. People go into space because they must. It is built into their genes.[33] Cooperation and destiny are variations of an opportunity theme, one political and the other psychological.

Another trigger that some advocates have mentioned is *threat.* However, rather than being connected with competition, this threat is one to the planet as a whole. Sagan has articulated the nature of this planetary threat.[34] He wrote of a potential natural catastrophe from outside Earth in the form of a collision with an asteroid. Such events have occurred in the past and will in the future. Deudney, in chapter 5 of this volume, makes the same point. In addition, Sagan saw Earth threatened by manmade disaster in the form of global climate change. The plausibility of these planetary disasters' stimulating humanity to settle elsewhere in the solar system, particularly Mars, is questionable in the short run. Planetary security could be a long-term stimulus, however.

A fifth possible catalyst is strong *evidence of life* now or in the past. A good part of NASA's space science program is aimed at this goal, and Chyba discusses aspects of the search in chapter 7 of this volume. An organization attempting to establish contact—Search for Extraterrestrial Intelligence (SETI)—scans the heavens in hope of receiving communication from another planet in the universe. What if there were credible evidence of intelligent life outside Earth? That would change priorities in space immediately and profoundly.

CONSTITUENCY

Whatever the trigger, it will be incumbent upon Mars advocates to build an ever-enlarging coalition of support for the decision to go to Mars. The advocacy coalition is relatively small now and is predominantly U.S.-based, but it could grow and widen across nations. To get a decision to go to Mars, the coalition will have to grow and involve government, industry, the scientific community, the media, and the general public. Creating such a coalition requires policy entrepreneurs. Who will play that role?

In Apollo's case, it was the president, but Apollo represented that

rare national decision when a president could embody a national consensus born of crisis. His was a single voice that spoke for the country as
a whole—if only for a brief time. In SEI, Bush tried to play that role. He
spoke primarily for himself and a small coterie of White House planners.
The Space Shuttle and Space Station were largely bureaucracy-driven
and gained presidential declaration but little presidential push behind
the decision. The constituencies in industry, Congress, and the general
public were never particularly extensive.

Because there was relative national consensus behind Apollo at the
start, decision making could be strategic. The end was made clear, along
with timing and cost. Decisions about how to reach the goal became subject to rational calculations about means and ends. Short-term tactics
could be directly related to long-term ends. Budgets could be realistic
because there was broad support for the goal. Competition lent a sense
of urgency and deadline forcing.

But where there is no crisis, the consensus for decision must be built.
This is incremental politics. In such politics, the policy goals are short
term and relatively small. Means easily become disconnected from ends
because ends are vague or tentative. Means are themselves objects of
controversy, and budgets tend to be unrealistic, lest cost make a large
goal even less acceptable. Policy process proceeds, not in a straight line,
but in disjointed pieces. There are many detours and fragmented actions. Whereas strategic decision making is propelled by strong leadership and control, incremental decision making often begs the question
of who is in charge.

Apollo was the most strategic decision in U.S. human spaceflight history. The Bush SEI decision proved strategic only in form; it points up
the limits of presidential decision making in space. Behind the president
there must be a broad and deep coalition of support if a program is to be
sustainable. Given the cost of a Mars program and the precedent of the
International Space Station, it is likely that Mars will require international coalition building. Apollo was a purely national project; the Space
Shuttle was national with international partners; and the Space Station
was a national program with even more international partners, including Russia, the former competitor. In this Space Station program, U.S.
control was diluted from what it had been in previous efforts. There is no
reason to believe that the trend toward internationalizing space project
decisions will not continue. The problem for Mars advocates is not only
to enlist government support in the United States and abroad but also to
build grassroots support in the public.

Ideally, the private business sector would be helping to drive the process, not just as contractors but also as potential joint funders. As Pace and others in this volume show, the role of the private sector in space is growing. However, if the return on investment from near-Earth tourism and space manufacturing is distant, that for Mars exploration is much further still. Moreover, the risks involving human life are huge. The private sector can be part of a Mars coalition, and some wealthy executives may provide funds out of conviction or for public relations purposes;[35] however, the business sector is unlikely to lead in a Mars program absent a perceived profit.

At present the most vocal policy entrepreneurs behind Mars are a disparate band in the public—the Mars Society and similar groups. NASA itself is hampered in playing a visible advocacy role until the Space Station is completed. The Clinton administration enunciated a space policy in 1996 that said as much.[36] However, NASA's present problem may be an advantage, in that it gives proponents time to build a grassroots movement that was not present when Bush made his 1989 pronouncement. With a base of support, and the Space Station's development finished, circumstances could precipitate governmental decision making. Decisions are strong or weak depending on the political support base on which they rest, and Mars requires a considerable constituency, given competing demands for public resources.

Implementating the Decision

If humanity is to go to Mars, there will have to be a major policy decision, given the organization and resource demands. However, even more complicated than getting a decision will be carrying it out. Implementing a Mars decision will involve a vast long-term coordination effort, far more ambitious than the Space Station. Given its relative resources, the United States will most likely be the lead nation, and NASA will be the responsible agency within the United States. A Mars endeavor can be best conceived as a multinational technical project, the largest in history, in which talent, money, and decisions are shared. All of this will make for enormous complexity and unprecedented management challenges. However, lessons—positive and negative—will undoubtedly have been learned from the Space Station.

In the 1960s, NASA was literally re-created for Apollo into a large research and development agency capable of managing a far-flung government, industry, and university team—in essence driving a national coalition. In the 1990s, NASA was consciously reinvented again, this time reducing its size in an effort to bring new economies and efficiencies in the interest of "better, faster, cheaper" space projects. On the assumption that especially bold programs require high-capacity agencies to manage them, the Mars program will almost certainly necessitate a third reinvention. NASA will likely be leader of a coalition that is unprecedented in size, involving both international partners and the private sector. Mars will require a twenty-first-century version of a "large-scale approach" to management. Faster, better, cheaper does not seem adequate to what is involved.

If NASA is to lead in a Mars program, it will have to divest itself of ongoing operational responsibilities for the Space Shuttle and the Space Station, the better to concentrate on the pioneering research and development required of a Mars mission. As Leib points out in chapter 4, maintaining and using the Space Station will be absorbing tasks for many years. However, they do not necessarily have to be tasks performed and paid for by NASA.

Fulfilling a Mars decision will require political and managerial skills of the highest order. The priority of a program can go up or down with an election, the economy, or a technological setback. It is critical that the management team buffer technical decisions from political interference even as political support is sought. The leaders of NASA and its institutional allies must hold to the goal in spite of shifting winds. There is no avoiding the conclusion that an organization that is weak politically cannot take humans to Mars.

THREE ROUTES TO MARS

Implementation can vary in speed. There can be small or large steps. How quickly to go depends on technology and politics. It also depends on the costs spacefaring nations and the public constituency underlying them are willing to bear and the risks they choose to endure.

There are three tracks to Mars that appear in the writings of present advocates: fast, mid-range, and gradual. The *fast track* is provided in the writings of Sagan and (especially) Zubrin. Zubrin calls his plan "Mars Direct." This approach omits the moon as an intermediary step. Zubrin calls the moon a "siren song,"[37] an unnecessary diversion. His rationale is if you want to go to Mars, go to Mars! He argues that the moon is so different from Mars that it would not provide a learning experience any better than Antarctica—or Wyoming, for that matter. Sagan agrees: "A lunar base wouldn't be a detour on the road to Mars, but a trap. We would use up [financial] resources and indefinitely delay going to Mars. Mars is much more exciting."[38]

Zubrin and other "fast trackers" espouse a "live off the land" philosophy. Instead of taking a huge amount of supplies and creating infrastructures along the way, they would fly to Mars as fast as possible and convert resources on Mars to facilitate living there and returning to Earth. Mars Direct, according to Zubrin, could be achieved with minimal new technology within ten years at a cost from $20 to $30 billion.[39]

The *mid-track* is seen in the Augustine and Stafford reports. They call for the moon as an interim step. They emphasize the moon is 250,000 miles away, a three-day journey achieved before. Men and women sent there can presumably return relatively easily if something goes wrong. Mars is 35 million miles from Earth when most proximate. The distance increases to 230 million miles when Earth and Mars are on opposite sides of the sun. That distance and the extra requirements it places on human beings and machines argue for more time, learning, and technological development, using the moon as a stepping stone.[40]

The *gradual track* has been proposed by Wesley Huntress, former Associate Administrator for Space Science at NASA and president of the American Astronautical Society. It provides an interim program for humans in space beyond the Space Station if the nation is not politically ready for the decision to go to Mars. That rationale is linked closely to space science. He lists three grand challenges in space science where human spaceflight is relevant:

> First, to read the history and destiny of the solar system. How did it come to be, what is its fate and what does its origin and evolution imply for other planetary systems? Second, to look for evidence of life elsewhere in the solar system—at Mars, at Europa, wherever in the history of the solar system there has been liquid water; [and] third, to image and study planets around other stars. Ultimately, to find Earth-like planets in other planetary systems.

"The ultimate destination [for human exploration remains] the surface of Mars," he declares, "but the capability to accomplish that mission is developed and tested over time in less risky missions along a natural evolutionary technological pathway. It is not a Mars-or-bust program."[41]

What is the role of humans in accomplishing the space science goals? One is that they can ferry equipment from the Space Station to deeper space where they could build a large space telescope facility. Lagrangian points in space—where the gravity of Earth and the moon balance —allow for stable, relatively unattended equipment and are ideal for observation. However, they are more distant in space than the Space Station's low-Earth orbit. Hence, NASA could develop new capability to go beyond the Space Station to operate further out.

From astronomical operations at Lagrangian points, human beings could move progressively to more difficult tasks in space such as exploring asteroids. Thus, Huntress recommends going back to the moon for reasons of science as well as a spur to develop additional human spaceflight capabilities. Only after these efforts does he propose flight to Mars. Here also he takes a gradualist approach, suggesting that instead of a direct assault, a space station in Mars orbit be built to support operations to and from the surface. All of these steps reduce risk.[42]

ISSUES: DEVELOPING TECHNOLOGY

Each of these tracks has challenges in technological development. The trade-offs are excruciating. Huntress sacrifices speed for scientific payoff but also "buys time" to build support for a Mars decision after the Space Station is built. However, time is money. His plan requires developing a new shuttle to go from the Space Station to Lagrangian points, asteroids, and the moon. He also recommends a new space station around Mars. Choices, particularly those of pace, will be propelled in large part by what kind of trigger stimulates decision. The fastest-paced decisions, because they are more likely to cost more in the short-term and put human lives at greatest risk, will require the most dramatic triggers, the clearest decisions, and the most substantial political support.

Important lessons can be learned from Apollo, the Space Station, and other recent technological projects that can be applied to developing technology for Mars. For example, as Madison and McCurdy note, "Unlike the trip to the moon, which in eight years moved with ever increasing specificity from concept to execution, the Space Station effort for nine years languished in the design phase."[43] During this period approximately $10 billion was spent with little hardware actually being built. This was more than the original projected cost of the entire construction project. Needless to say, the 1984 goal of Reagan to build the Space Station within ten years was missed mightily. The lesson for advocates is to move as quickly as possible through the technology development phase. In this way, proponents can show progress, and opposition has less opportunity to mobilize.

Similarly, NASA is anticipating opposition in connection with an early unmanned mission to Mars—Mars Sample Return. Expecting environmental and health issues to be raised with receipt on Earth of samples, NASA plans to build a containment facility. Although sample return is perhaps a decade away, NASA has enlisted a consultant organization to help plan how to engage the public to deal with perceived risks.

Furthermore, one technology among many that will have to be developed during the implementation period is that of "closed loop ecological life systems." The Augustine panel pointed out that "air and water must be recycled and nourishing food produced within automated closed-cycle support systems." "However," the panel continued, "little is known about constructing reliable biospheres that can be depended upon for continuous automated production of food and organic materials and the removal of toxins and contaminants." Mars will entail long-duration spaceflight of a kind never experienced before. The Augustine panel called closed ecological systems among "the least understood and the most challenging" technologies to be developed in any Mars program.[44]

Another fateful technological development ahead pertains to propulsion. A decision will be made between conventional chemically based fuel or more advanced transportation technologies. The Stafford panel said unequivocally that while a trip to the moon with conventional fuel was possible, a nuclear-powered rocket was the preferred technology in the case of Mars, owing to far greater technical efficiency.[45] It behooves those who favor this technological approach to understand that environmentalists and arms control activists are likely to lobby against nuclear technology as they did against the nuclear-fueled *Cassini* mission. Opposition to means can prevent realization of the end.

ISSUES: THE HUMAN FACTOR

Each of the three routes to Mars will place unprecedented physical and psychological stress on humans. How little is known about such stress is unsettling. In 1991, for example, eight people entered and sealed the airlock on Biosphere 2 in Arizona for a two-year mission. The facility, while controversial and imperfect, did sustain eight humans for the full two years, along with 3,800 species of plants and animals. The crew also was able to produce about 80 percent of its food through intensive agricultural activities and to recycle 100 percent of the human and domestic animal wastes and 100 percent of the water in their environment. Increases in carbon dioxide levels and dropping oxygen levels were a constant threat, however. In addition, some species of plants and animals disappeared, and the biospherians had to struggle to maintain food production in the controlled environment. A number of the biospherians left the facility in a substantially weakened condition.[46]

At one point, a crewmember severed a fingertip in a threshing machine in the Biosphere 2 facility, had to leave it for a brief time to get treated, and then returned. Accidents and health problems in a Mars expedition will have to be treated where they occur. In an expedition to Mars, there will be unique health problems such as dangers from radiation, solar flares, and lack of normal gravity. In preparing for Mars, experience must be accumulated in telemedicine so that procedures can be communicated by experts on Earth to a doctor-astronaut in space and, if the doctor is the victim, to someone else. That a doctor can be a victim in a remote place is pointed up by a recent case where a doctor in Antarctica was diagnosed with possible cancer and could not be readily evacuated due to weather conditions. She had to treat herself as best she could.

Moreover, there are potential psychological traumas. A considerable body of research exists on the behavioral and performance problems associated with long-term isolation in polar locations, especially in Antarctica. Early studies found that Antarctic wintering-over parties experienced such effects as "absent-mindedness" and emotional disturbances.[47] The relatively brief experience of U.S. and Russian astronauts/ cosmonauts on *Mir* suggests that psychological problems can be heightened by cultural differences. There is much speculation and concern about who should ultimately go to Mars in terms of personality, sex, marital status, and so forth. In Biosphere 2, individuals experienced "fits of apathy, listlessness, anger, callous aloofness, and fear."[48]

The Space Station will provide opportunity to learn much about technological and human factors in space. This is one of its chief purposes. However, there are limits to what it can teach, particularly if one of the more direct routes to Mars is selected. The extreme distance of Mars from Earth—35 million miles at its closest—will place singular demands on human endurance and psychology. If conventional chemical rockets are used, it will take 230 days one way and require surface stays of 500 days while the planets realign to expedite a return trip. While nuclear propulsion could provide more flexibility, according to the Stafford panel, explorers are very likely to be away from their home planet for well over two years.[49]

That is a major reason some Mars advocates believe the moon is an essential learning laboratory for technology and man. Establishing a lunar outpost "is needed to learn how to live and work on the surface of an alien planet," said the Augustine panel. "Particularly important will be the testing of habitats; closed ecological life support systems and remote space-rated power plants; learning to process and use indigenous materials; observing the effects of living in extreme heat, cold, and dust in low-gravity fields; and developing reliable systems to provide radiation protection and surface mobility for humans and robots through 300 hour-long days and nights."[50] The moon can provide lessons learned in coping with medical, psychological and socio-cultural problems. Similarly, the approach outlined by Huntress provides opportunities beyond the moon for learning to cope with human factors in deep space, far from home, in preparation for Mars.

ACHIEVING THE FIRST MARS LANDING

Still, when all is said and done, the first expedition to Mars will be a totally new experience. It will be daunting—more so if the fast track is the route, less so if the gradual track is used. An expedition will be preceded by years of unmanned expeditions to survey the planet on select optimal landing sites. The features of Mars are quite different from the moon and Earth. One-third the size of Earth, Mars has a diverse and rugged topography, with a volcano far higher than Mt. Everest and canyons as long as North America is wide. The atmosphere of Mars is mostly carbon dioxide, and there are periodic dust storms. These features require power systems, rover landers, rover vehicles, and habitats especially relevant to Mars.[51]

Landing humans on Mars will be one of the most awesome events in history. It will also be quite controversial. There may be religious groups that will object to the very idea of seeking life beyond Earth. However, the more influential protests are likely to come from environmentalists and scientists because the issue of extraterrestrial life is a double-edged sword. There are those who worry about the possibility of astronauts bringing back to Earth an "Andromeda Strain" that could infect the human species. Others worry that humans will contaminate Mars if there is bacterial life of some form there. Such concerns will have to be taken seriously by advocates of a Mars expedition, and elaborate precautions made. Risks acceptable to advocates will likely not be acceptable to their critics.[52] As noted, long before this issue of contamination is raised in connection with humans, it will have to be resolved with a robotic Mars sample-return mission.

The Distant Future: Settling Mars

The Apollo expeditions to the moon lasted just three years, from 1969 to 1972. Our expectation is that once Mars is visited, the exploration will continue—because, as Sagan suggested, the Red Planet will prove inherently "exciting" in every way.

At first only those specifically trained to be explorers will go. But as resource-conversion techniques improve and biospheres enlarge, more and more people of varying backgrounds will someday go. Scientists will create research bases, much as they did in Antarctica. In the more distant future, people will actually travel to Mars as a place to live. Eventually, the first child will be born—a Martian![53]

As continuing habitation ensues, there will be increased pressures to "terraform" Mars. This is a debate so central to the issue of humans on Mars that it has already begun. Terraforming refers to planetary engineering, a technology development perspective on an extraordinary scale, remaking Mars in a manner fit for humanity.

At the founding meeting of the Mars Society, the single most disputed topic was terraforming. Two competing visions of Mars divided the activists. On the one side were those who saw Mars as the next frontier, much as the New World was a frontier after Columbus or the western United States was a frontier in the nineteenth century. They felt it was man's destiny to conquer and used terms such as "manifest destiny." The other side saw Mars as a pristine, almost sacred place to be protected—a new Eden. As a reporter who covered the meeting noted, "By the end of the debate, a lot of people are really quite cross—a remarkable thing, considering how far off, in both time and space, these martian issues are."[54] Another example at the initial Mars Society meeting was debate over the role of government. What should government do, if anything? How much—or little—government will be enough? Who will govern Mars? Toward whose ends? As the above disputes reveal, humans will transport to Mars issues over which they fight on Earth. The Mars Society meeting showed that while technology may advance rapidly, human nature and attitudes remain the same.

These debates within the activist group not only presage conflict in the future but also divide the activist camp at a time when activists provide energy for keeping Mars on the policy agenda. Any division in the activist group weakens the case for Mars and may delay the decision they want.

Conclusion

In the early twenty-first century, America and the world stand between the manned landing on the moon and a future human spaceflight to Mars. The Bush rhetoric of 1989 aside, there has been no sustained presidential decision to go to Mars; however, it seems likely that once the International Space Station has operated successfully for some period of time, pressures will mount for a decision by the president to announce a new manned mission for NASA.

As the Bush experience with SEI showed, presidential decision making is not enough. The 1989 decision was strategic in form but not in practice. The politics of the time were not ripe for anything other than the most incremental of decisions. What was missing was a broad political constituency to support the goal. Decisions to launch large-scale technological programs require technical and political readiness—a readiness that is not present now.

A constituency is just starting to build. There is a grassroots movement led by the Mars Society, replete with a crusading leader, Robert Zubrin, who writes books and lectures around the country. There are other space associations with a Mars interest. It is thus possible that this grassroots advocacy will grow in years to come.

This will be the case especially if NASA is successful in its robotic flights to Mars. The 1999 loss of Mars probes has slowed down NASA's progress, but once resumed, robotic surveys of the Red Planet have the potential of speeding up unmanned exploration. As scouts, they can discover phenomena that can intrigue the public and focus increasing attention in the direction of Mars. Meanwhile, with the Space Station, astronauts will gather important experience in living and working in space in a multinational setting.

Goldin termed the quest for Mars a marathon, not a sprint.[55] A marathon, while much longer than a sprint, still has a pace and a direction. Getting off to a strong start and maintaining momentum require preparation, persistence, and substantial public entrepreneurship.

Apollo had a constituency born of Cold War competition. NASA managed a national priority in the 1960s, holding approximately 5 percent of the federal budget. If NASA had a similar priority in the 1990s, according to Goldin, its budget would have been $75 billion, rather than the less than $14 billion it averaged.[56]

To go to Mars may not require the crisis-born national priority of

Apollo, a priority that made it an urgent, fast-track program; but it will require a far greater national priority than space now holds—even if "faster, better, cheaper" techniques are brought to bear. However, Mars will still require a large-scale technological and managerial approach, and when human beings are involved, expensive safety measures are essential. Moreover, new technologies will be needed. To get higher priority and attract meaningful political attention that lasts beyond a single decision, the grassroots movement has to grow into a more significant political force. Moreover, advocates must link Mars with politically relevant goals that attract and keep the favor of elected officials not only of the United States but also of its foreign partners.

There will be many motives for going to Mars, including those represented by the new Edenists and the terraformers, but the noblest motive lies in the intangible objective of learning more about humanity's place in the universe. Where did we come from? Where are we going? Are we alone? Moreover, getting to Mars represents a way of pulling nations together in a common, global enterprise that could capture the imagination of the world, contribute to peace, and help an Earth identity to coalesce.

The challenge for Mars advocates is to help technological progress and political opportunity to converge, to take advantage of events, discoveries, and particular personalities in office and turn them into occasions for action. Advocates have little choice today but to proceed incrementally. However, they can think strategically. With Mars as long-term objective, the programs leading to it, such as use of the Space Station as a laboratory for understanding stresses on humans in space and the Mars sample return, are significant efforts in themselves.

It is much easier to envision the technical steps to Mars—such as development of a new launch vehicle, improved biosphere technology, an outpost on the moon, training to deal with psychological effects of isolation, and so on—than to know what will trigger and sustain a sequence of goal-oriented decisions politically. Nevertheless, it seems inevitable that there eventually will be a decision to go, probably a multinational decision. Such a decision will give focus and pace to the overall effort. It will be followed by a host of implementing decisions, some big and some small, about technology, costs, risks, and organization. The process of accomplishment will therefore be uneven and immensely difficult. To use the metaphor of the marathon race, there may be occasions when the speed will slow, then pick up, only to slow again. At every major step, skeptics and dreamers will contest whether to continue. Exploration will compete with a score of more immediately pressing public missions. Yet if Sagan is correct, humanity is a species that "wonders" and, hence, "wanders."[57] The issue, therefore, becomes not whether but when a Mars mission will take place.

NOTES

1. The von Braun approach is discussed in a series of articles in *Colliers* magazine, reported in John M. Logsdon, ed., *Exploring the Unknown: Selected Documents in the History of the U.S. Civil Space Program,* vol. 1 (Washington, DC: NASA, 1995). Planning for Mars has been a long-term affair, as shown by David Portree, *Humans to Mars, Fifty Years of Planning* (Washington, DC: NASA, 2001).

2. For an account of decision making for post-Apollo, see Howard McCurdy, *The Space Station Decision* (Baltimore, MD: Johns Hopkins University Press, 1990).

3. Roger Bilstein, *Orders of Magnitude: A History of the NACA and NASA, 1915–1990* (Washington, DC: NASA, 1989), 108–9.

4. Ibid., 113, 82–83; Richard Kerr, "A Wetter, Younger Mars Emerging," *Science,* 4 August 2000, 714.

5. The story of "Mars Underground" is recounted in Robert Zubrin, *The Case for Mars* (New York: Touchtone, 1996), 70–74.

6. Ibid., 73.

7. Ibid.

8. Bilstein, *Orders of Magnitude,* 139–140.

9. John Noble Wilford, *Mars Beckons* (New York: Knopf, 1990), 154.

10. Michael Collins, *Mission to Mars* (New York: Weidenfeld, 1990), 182.

11. Quoted in ibid., 185.

12. Zubrin, *Case for Mars,* 47, cites $450 billion as a total cost. Estimates vary, depending on what is included.

13. Zubrin uses different estimates, depending on what he includes in the cost of the trip. In chapter 9 of this volume, Howard McCurdy cites Zubrin as calling for a trip costing $6 billion.

14. Zubrin, *Case for Mars,* 3, 64, 68.

15. Brian Burrough, *Dragonfly: NASA and the Crisis Aboard Mir* (New York: Harper Collins, 1998), 240.

16. See Advisory Committee on the Future of the U.S. Space Program, *Report* (Washington, DC: Government Printing Office, 1990).

17. Ibid., 6.

18. Ibid., 8.

19. Zubrin, *Case for Mars,* 274.

20. Thomas Stafford, Synthesis Group, *Report, America at the Threshold: America's Space Exploration Initiative* (Washington, DC: Government Printing Office, 1991).

21. Testimony of Daniel Goldin before U.S. Senate Committee on Commerce, Science and Transportation, 102nd Congress, 2nd Session, March 27, 1992 (Washington, DC: Government Printing Office, 1992), 13, 43.

22. "Face to Face with Daniel Goldin," *Aerospace America* (November 1992): 8.

23. David Morrison, "NASA Honeymoon," *National Journal,* 16 May 1992 1995; Remarks by NASA Administrator Daniel Goldin and Discussion at the 108th Space Studies Board Meeting, 18 November 1992, in NASA History Office files.

24. "NASA Ready to Cut Back," *Washington Times,* 9 April 1993.

25. During the early Space Age, beginning in 1957, the Soviet Union had plans "to beat the United States to Mars." However, a series of unmanned projects that extended intermittently over three decades resulted mainly in failures, especially in contrast to Viking. See V. G. Derminor, *The Difficult Road to Mars: A Brief History of Mars Exploration in the Soviet Union* (Washington, DC: Government Printing Office, 1999), quote on page 1.

26. Marcia Dunn, "Controversial NASA Chief Says, 'I Y'am What I Y'am,'" *News Register* (Wheeling, WV), 17 July 1994.

27. Anne Eisele, "Mars Landing, Mir Woes Captivate World," *Space News,* 8–14 December 1997); "The Payoff Begins for NASA," *Space News,* 30 June 1997.

28. *NASA Strategic Plan, 1998* (Washington, DC: NASA, 1998).

29. Daniel Goldin, Address at Alan Shepard Memorial Service, Johnson Space Center, Houston, TX, August 1, 1998.

30. Robert Zubrin, *Entering Space* (New York: Tarcher-Putnam, 1999), 120–22.

31. Jonathan Lipman, "President Clinton Defends NASA in Light of Presumably Lost Mars Lander," 8 December 1999: www.space.com. Bruce Moomaw, "Can Athena Cut a New Path to Mars," *Space Daily,* 31 July 2000: www.space.com/news/mars2003-000/html.

32. Daniel Goldin, "The Light of a New Age: Space Exploration," address delivered to Association of Space Explorers, Washington, DC, August 24, 1992.

33. Oliver Morton, "For the Love of Mars," *Discover* 20, no. 2 (February 1999): 64–69.

34. Carl Sagan, *Pale Blue Dot: A Vision of the Human Future in Space* (New York: Ballantine, 1999), chap. 21.

35. Microsoft co-founder Paul Allen and former Microsoft chief of technology Nathan Myhruold donated $12.5 million in August 2000 "to help astronomers build the world's largest telescope specifically designed to seek out signals from other civilizations across outer space" ("Paul Allen Funds Search for Space Life, *Akron Beacon Journal,* 3 August 2000).

36. White House, National Space Policy—NSTC-8, 19 September 1996: www.OSTP.gov/NSTC/html/pdd8.html.

37. Zubrin, *Case for Mars,* 135.

38. Quoted in Wilford, *Mars Beckons,* 151.

39. Zubrin, *Case for Mars,* xix, 64.

40. Advisory Committee on the Future of the U.S. Space Program, *Report,* 1990; Stafford, Synthesis Group, *Report,* 1991.

41. Wesley T. Huntress Jr., "Grand Challenges for Space Exploration," *Space Times* 38, no. 3 (May-June, 1999): 4–13.

42. Ibid.

43. J. J. Madison and H. E. McCurdy, "Spending Without Results: Lessons from the Space Station Program," *Space Policy* 15, no. 4 (Nov. 1999): 213.

44. Advisory Committee on the Future of the Space Program, *Report,* 30.

45. Stafford, Synthesis Group, *Report,* 6.

46. "Biosphere 2 Status Report: Creating a Sustainable Agriculture for a Closed System," press release issued by Space Biospheres Ventures, September 1993: www.biospheres.org/sustagr.html.

47. C. S. Mullin, H. Connery, and F. Wouters, "A Psychological-Psychiatric Study of a IGY Station in Antarctica," project report, U.S. Navy, Bureau of Medicine and Surgery, Neuropsychiatric Division, 1958; C. S. Mullin and H. Connery, "Psychological Study of an Antarctic Station," *Armed Forces Medical Journal* 10 (1959): 290–96; C. S. Mullin, "Some Psychological Aspects of Isolated Antarctic Living," *American Journal of Psychiatry* 9 (1960): 362–26; and E. K. E. Gunderson, "Emotional Symptoms in Extremely Isolated Groups," *Archives of General Psychiatry* 9 (1963): 362–68. Other researchers have focused on the attributes of successful leadership of wintering-over expeditions, which is considered crucial; on interpersonal conflict and morale; on the incidence of mental disorders; on personality change; and on the higher levels of adaptability of single vs. married people. It has been argued by some that isolation is not all negative. At least at a limited degree, it can increase a person's ability to focus and sense of personal efficacy. The issue has to do with the limits of people. See P. Suedfeld, "Homo Invictus: The Indomitable Species," *Canadian Psychology* 38, no. 3 (August 1997): 164–73; P. Warshall, "Lessons from Biosphere 2: Ecodesign, Surprises and the Humanity of Gaian Thought," *Whole Earth Review* (Spring 1996).

48. P. Warshall, "Lessons from Biosphere 2," 27.

49. Stafford, Synthesis Group, *Report,* 4.

50. Advisory Committee on the Future of the Space Program, *Report,* 30.

51. Stafford, Synthesis Group, *Report,* 4.

52. The issue of contamination is discussed by Chyba in Chapter 7 of this volume.

53. Daniel Goldin, "Steps to Mars II," Conference Address, Washington, D.C., July 15, 1995.

54. Morton, "For the Love of Mars," 69.

55. Goldin, "Steps to Mars II."

56. Quoted in Brian Berger, "How Far Away is Mars?" *Space News,* 19 July 1999.

57. Sagan, *Pale Blue Dot,* v, xiii.

7   The Search for Extraterrestrial Life

A Core Mission for NASA

Christopher F. Chyba

T HE SEARCH for extraterrestrial life provides a core theme for NASA's scientific research in the twenty-first century and a centerpiece of its program for solar system exploration. The focus of Mars exploration will continue to be the search for extant or extinct life. This search requires understanding Martian conditions relevant to life, especially the history and distribution of liquid water. This goal would be enabled, and public participation enhanced, by putting in place a Mars exploration infrastructure as early as possible. This infrastructure would include a telecommunications satellite network capable of sustaining high data return rates, including live video, and providing global positioning on the Martian surface. Regular video from Mars would bolster a view of humanity as a species that naturally spans the solar system and would have an important impact on the support for both robotic and human exploration.

Space Shuttle missions could play a key role in Mars sample return, retrieving Mars samples from robotic missions that had returned samples to Earth orbit. Such an option might carry scientific and engineering advantages, but its implications for protecting against the possibility of back contamination would need to be carefully assessed. A scientifically and programmatically justifiable fusion of human and robotic spaceflight in the search for life elsewhere could provide a powerful unifying theme to NASA's activities and lead to remarkably high-profile human missions.

Jupiter's moon Europa likely harbors an ocean of liquid water whose volume is twice that of Earth's oceans. Because of this, Europa represents a target for astrobiological investigation of equal importance to Mars. However, dedicated outer planets' satellite-orbiter or lander missions are extremely expensive, and the current structure of the solar system exploration program does not permit a Mars-like commitment to the exploration of Europa (or any other outer solar system moon). Saturn's moon Titan is the other high-priority astrobiology target in the outer solar system, and the arrival of the *Cassini* spacecraft at Saturn in 2004 will move it to the forefront of media attention. If astrobiology is to be a key priority for NASA, a new line may need to be established within the budget of NASA's Office of Space Sciences for a Europa/Titan mission.

Planetary protection issues require substantial further research. Minimizing the possibility of forward microbial contamination of Mars and Europa remains an important challenge. In this context, human exploration of Mars first requires a better examination of the Martian surface for signs of life. Returning Martian samples to Earth for scientific study will require the construction of biologically secure sample-handling facilities. In-flight sterilization is unlikely to reduce these requirements for the first sample-return mission.

NASA has identified the search for life beyond our solar system as a priority. In this light, it is remarkable that the scientific Search for Extraterrestrial Intelligence (SETI) has been altogether absent from the NASA program. SETI is a natural component of any balanced investigation of the origin, evolution, and distribution of life in our galaxy—that is, of astrobiology. There are areas where appropriate private-public partnerships in this field could be of mutual benefit.

There is a natural alliance between planetary exploration and the protection of Earth's environment. Comparative planetology helps us to understand the Earth and therefore the context for Earth's biosphere and our own civilization. Astrobiology helps us to understand the origin and evolution of life itself. Great harm could be done to this alliance were planetary protection issues to be handled with anything other than forthrightness and transparency.

The Rebirth of Exobiology

The twentieth century ended with a remarkable decade of discoveries relevant to the prospects for life elsewhere, and the pace of discovery seems certain to accelerate. Exobiology,[1] nearly moribund after the failure of the *Viking* spacecraft landers to find life on Mars in 1976, has been reborn in just the past ten years, as the following list of remarkable discoveries illustrates.

In the 1990s we learned that other solar systems are common, and indeed we now know of more planets in orbit around other stars than are present in our own solar system. The detections to date have typically, but not exclusively, been of giant extrasolar planets about the size of Jupiter or Saturn, closer to their star than these worlds are in our own system. This is likely due to selection effects; these are the easiest planets to detect.[2] The first sophisticated search for Earth-sized extrasolar worlds has already begun,[3] and we are likely to begin to detect these smaller worlds soon.[4]

We have long known that the elements essential for life are abundant, though not uniformly distributed, throughout the galaxy.[5] It is now also clear that organic molecules, the carbon-containing compounds on which all known life is based (along with liquid water) are common as well. Organic molecules, synthesized abiotically, are present throughout much of our solar system—on planets, on their satellites, and within comets and some asteroids. More than sixty organic molecules have been identified in the interstellar medium, the space between the stars.[6] The idea that organics are to be found throughout the solar system may seem commonplace now, but this view was sometimes bitterly criticized at scientific meetings a mere fifteen years ago.

NASA has announced the discovery from the *Mars Global Surveyor* spacecraft of sites where liquid water has apparently recently flowed at the Martian surface and may continue to exist at or just below the surface today.[7] These sites hold out the prospect for extant near-surface life on Mars. Active liquid water springs or seeps on the Martian surface would, if confirmed, be one of the most exciting results in the history of solar system exploration.

It now also seems likely that our solar system harbors a second ocean of liquid water in addition to the seas of Earth. Liquid water is the sine qua non of life as we know it, but for decades it has seemed possible that within our solar system only Earth had it in abundance in accessible locations. Now it seems very likely, though not quite certain, that Jupiter's moon Europa is home to an ocean of water whose volume is probably about twice that of Earth's.[8] And it is beginning to appear that subsurface oceans may be standard components of large icy satellites in the outer solar system.[9]

The search for life beneath the ice of Europa or the surface of Mars has been made more credible by an important expansion in our understanding of the biosphere of our own planet. In particular, it is now apparent that Earth is host to a deep biosphere of microorganisms whose total biomass rivals that of all life on the surface.[10] This biosphere poses two key questions for the prospects for finding life elsewhere: Could part of the deep biosphere continue to exist even without the copious production of organic matter and oxidants at Earth's surface that is driven by photosynthesis? And, could the *origin* of life occur within the deep biosphere itself, or is access to the abundant energy of sunlight at Earth's surface a requirement for the necessary prebiotic chemistry?

Recent research suggests that at least some component of the terrestrial deep biosphere is independent of the surface. The answer to the question of whether life could originate at depth may be yes as well, but our very incomplete knowledge about the origin of life prevents any firm conclusions from being drawn. A positive answer to the first question makes vestigial deep reservoirs of life seem plausible on Mars, whereas both questions would need to have a positive answer to support the prospects of life on Europa.[11]

Finally, the past decade has seen the start of a systematic survey of the thousand nearest Sun-like stars for intelligent radio transmissions. So far the SETI Institute's privately funded Project Phoenix has examined about half the stars on its target list, scanning billions of frequency channels, 56 million channels at a time, for each.[12] Nothing that satisfies search criteria for an extraterrestrial intelligent signal has been detected, but a thousand stars represent only about one one-hundred-millionth of the stars in our galaxy. Public interest in SETI remains strong, as demonstrated by the three million computer users who have downloaded software from the SETI@home project Web site at the University of California at Berkeley.[13]

A Vision for Astrobiology in This Century

The twenty-first century holds enormous promise for advances in exobiology. Within the next few decades, we will have catalogues of thousands of extrasolar planets and statistically meaningful answers to questions of the prevalence of certain classes of solar systems and of Earth-like worlds. Moreover, we will examine the atmospheres of extrasolar planets spectroscopically and search for the presence of gases that could reveal worlds suitable for life or even hint at life itself. Molecular oxygen (O_2) is a prerequisite for complex multicellular life as we know it on Earth; to this extent we will be able to determine whether Earth-like planets around other stars have atmospheres permissive of that type of life.[14]

NASA maintains an ambitious agenda of Mars exploration in the coming decade, reconceived in response to the loss of the Mars Climate Orbiter (MCO) and Mars Polar Lander (MPL) missions. In 2004, NASA will send two especially capable rovers (each able to traverse more than

100 meters a day) to separate landing sites on Mars, emphasizing the search for evidence of past or present liquid water.[15] The Clinton administration's budget submitted to Congress for fiscal year 2001 recommended substantial growth in the funds provided for Mars exploration—an $80 million increase to an FY 2000 budget of $280 million.[16]

The Mars planetary exploration agenda, revised in reaction to the MCO and MPL failures, will emphasize the key astrobiological objective of a systematic search for near-surface liquid water.[17] The search for such sites and their subsequent exploration should be the near-term focus of a Mars program whose overall goal is the search for life. Other important supporting objectives include the establishment of a communications (and ultimately a global positioning) infrastructure at Mars, regular orbital monitoring, and decisive experiments to determine the nature of the putative surface oxidants that may have mimicked life in the *Viking* biology experiments.[18] (It is remarkable that, a quarter-century after *Viking,* the nature of Mars' surface chemistry has not yet been directly tested.[19]) A longer-range goal is the return of samples to Earth for chemical and biological analysis, perhaps as early as 2012.[20] After a long hiatus following the failure of the *Viking* missions to find unambiguous indications of life on Mars, NASA is returning to Mars in what could be a lasting way. A sustainable return must be comprehensive, building an infrastructure and a knowledge base for long-term, including human, exploration.

Over the next two decades, we will come to know Mars well. The establishment of a Mars exploration infrastructure with high-bandwidth data streams to Earth will make Mars as familiar as are remote locations on Earth such as Mt. Everest or Antarctica.[21] This seems likely to foster a view of ourselves as a species that naturally spans the solar system. We will determine whether liquid water environments at or near the Martian surface (for which we now have evidence[22]) harbor life. We will have explored subsurface aquifers and looked for buried ecosystems. If we discover extant life on Mars, we may quickly determine whether or not it shares an ancestor with life on Earth. (Earth and Mars may have exchanged viable microorganisms within debris thrown into space by big impacts.[23]) If Martian and terrestrial life does share a common ancestor, DNA phylogenetic analysis may allow us to determine the probable world of its origin.

Europa's probable ocean is hidden beneath a layer of ice as much as thirty kilometers thick.[24] Later in this decade (if there are no further delays), NASA plans to launch an orbiter mission to determine with certainty whether this ocean exists and, just as importantly, to pave the way for subsequent surface and subsurface exploration.[25] The first Europa lander, which could launch as part of the first orbiter mission or later as a subsequent mission, may answer the question of whether Europa's ocean contains life. This lander may be able to sample ice that was recently derived from Europa's ocean as water that reached the surface and then froze. Subsequent—and extremely challenging—missions may be able to penetrate the ice layer and explore the ocean directly.

Within the next several decades, if life is abundant throughout Europa's ocean, it may be detected. If Europa's life flourishes only in hydrothermal environments at the base of Europa's 100-km deep ocean, finding signs of it in Europa's surface ice could prove very difficult. We should not minimize the challenge of exploring the floor of this ocean at all, to say nothing of doing so comprehensively. But by the end of the century, we should have made sufficient progress on a variety of fronts that we should begin to feel confident that a negative conclusion for life is more likely than not if such a conclusion need be drawn. Or, spectacularly, we may begin to elucidate an altogether extraterrestrial biology in the coming decades.[26]

With respect to both Mars and Europa, we should feel confident by 2100 in asserting whether life exists on or within either world. The search for fossils of extinct life may prove even more difficult, but here too we should see systematic progress during the coming century. While other worlds in our solar system might also harbor life, Mars and Europa seem to be the strongest candidates, so we are likely to suspect by 2100 that we have a compelling answer to the question of whether life on Earth is alone in our own solar system. If we are fortunate enough to find life at either Mars or Europa, and if this life is of independent origin, we would begin the investigation of a truly extraterrestrial biology. A second independent origin of life in our solar system would be enormously important scientifically and would have a powerful impact on humanity's vision of the prevalence of life in the galaxy.

Coupled with the discovery of thousands of extrasolar planets and the likely—though this remains to be seen—cataloging of numerous Earth-sized worlds, the exploration of a second ocean in the solar system and the extensive and visible exploration of Mars can only bolster the idea that humanity is part of a broader biological universe.[27] This would in turn heighten the public's enthusiasm for human expansion into the solar system, for the first interstellar robotic missions, and for the search for extraterrestrial intelligence.

Should both Mars and Europa prove to be sterile, there could be a backlash against this optimism. That conclusion could probably only be reached with full confidence toward the end of the century, and by that time we are likely—though not certain—to have found numerous examples of Earth-sized planets orbiting other stars. These discoveries would tend to offset the discovery that our own solar system was, apart from the Earth, barren of life. But an absence of Earth-like worlds elsewhere, coupled with a conclusion that life on Earth is alone in our own solar system, would instead lead to pessimism regarding the abundance of life elsewhere.[28]

Over the coming decades the scientific search for extraterrestrial intelligence (SETI) will take advantage of Moore's law (the observed doubling of computer power approximately every 18 months) to expand greatly the rapidity and thoroughness of the search for extraterrestrial artificial radio signals. Only by understanding the many factors that make a world habitable—that determine whether life arises on that world, whether that life gives rise to intelligence, and whether that life develops technology—can the search for electromagnetic signals from extraterrestrial civilizations be given a scientific context. The scientific search for extraterrestrial intelligence does not assume answers to these questions: worlds that can support life may or may not be common; life on such worlds may or may not arise often; that life may or may not develop multicellularity or intelligence frequently; and intelligence may or may not lead to technology. But the scientific investigation of these problems is exciting and inspiring (especially to children and students) and helps humanity place itself in the universe. A continuum of scientific questions extends from the formation of stars and planets to the development of technical civilizations, and the search for extraterrestrial intelligence is a natural component of the scientific investigation of that continuum.[29]

Private funding has now been secured by the SETI Institute for a new radiotelescope, the Allen Telescope Array (ATA), which will permit the survey of a million nearby Sun-like stars at billions of narrow-band frequency channels.[30] The ATA will pioneer techniques for the even more ambitious Square Kilometer Array (SKA). This development strategy has been endorsed by the National Research Council of the U.S. National Academy of Sciences in its latest decadal survey of astronomy in the United States, *Astronomy and Astrophysics in the New Millenium*.[31]

While the SETI@home project will be unable to rival the capabilities of these dedicated searches in many important respects (for example, in the number of channels searched), it nevertheless points the way toward a broad use of distributed computing power that will undoubtedly see important applications in the coming decades, including within astrobiology. The use of the global computational resources of individual citizens to tackle computationally intensive problems of great public interest in itself provides a compelling vision of members of a global society participating in scientific exploration and discovery.

The Robotic Exploration of Mars

NASA has developed a plan for recovering from the loss of the MCO and MPL spacecraft and continuing with an aggressive Mars exploration program.[32] MCO was lost because of an English to metric units conversion error; moreover, the fact that the error went unrecognized throughout the spacecraft's cruise to Mars implies more fundamental management problems than a trivial conversion error.[33] It now appears likely that the MPL spacecraft was lost due to an engineering error that led to a premature shutdown of the spacecraft's descent engine.[34] This inference is based on ground-based testing subsequent to the mission failure; there was no direct telemetry providing data during the spacecraft's descent because a determination had been made that this telemetry was not essential to mission success.[35] This decision, while reasonable from the perspective of a single, extremely resource-limited mission, was clearly unwise from a broader, programmatic perspective.

Under the pressure of further budget challenges, the current Mars exploration strategy could well change again. Regardless of subsequent changes, any successor Mars exploration architecture should learn from the previous mistakes and maintain two important characteristics: programmatic flexibility, and infrastructure for exploration and public participation.

PROGRAMMATIC FLEXIBILITY

The long-term strategy for the exploration of Mars (or an analogous strategy for any other world) should not be overconstrained by a priori programmatic requirements. Prior to the MCO and MPL failures, the Mars surveyor program had been required by NASA to return samples to Earth within the first decade of the twenty-first century and to launch two spacecraft (an orbiter and a lander) to Mars at every launch opportunity (which for Earth-Mars trajectories come every twenty-six months). These constraints may have initially been crucial to selling the program within the administration and Congress to demonstrate that the new program would be ambitious and in the spirit of the "better, faster, cheaper" mantra. But even if Mars exploration pursues an overall exploration strategy whose core goal is the search for extant or extinct life, it should remain free to choose a succession of missions that may fall outside the current programmatic constraints. This should make the program more flexible, better able to respond to new discoveries or additional failures, and more attentive both to establishing infrastructure for a long-term presence and to achieving scientific goals.

Astrobiological investigations should be incorporated into Mars exploration throughout the program and not be relegated to a potentially distant future in which sample return missions are finally realized. The discovery of geologically young sites where liquid water appears to have flowed on the Martian surface[36] emphasizes the extent to which our thinking about how and where to search for indications of life on Mars remains subject to major change while we continue a thorough reconnaissance of the surface.

INFRASTRUCTURE FOR EXPLORATION AND PUBLIC PARTICIPATION

NASA has an opportunity to accelerate the placement of infrastructure at Mars to make its exploration capabilities more robust in a systematic way. This same infrastructure should greatly enhance the public's ability to participate in the exploration. This infrastructure should ultimately include a global telecommunications system, a Global Positioning System, and high data return rates. The Mars exploration infrastructure should have as a high priority the establishment of continuous live video from Mars, with an ultimate goal of returning live video from multiple Martian surface or atmospheric stations.

These capabilities will enable science and facilitate engineering data returns from multiple spacecraft. But perhaps just as importantly, they will allow citizens, including school children, to log onto their computers and select any of a number of dynamic, live video images being returned constantly from Mars. Schools and homes of the future may have large LCD displays hanging on their walls, showing continuous live transmissions from Mars rovers, balloons, or surface stations. The enormous public enthusiasm for the *Mars Pathfinder* Web sites supports the notion that such video would claim a large and enthusiastic audience.[37]

Mars exploration in the 1990s was fueled by renewed interest in the possibility that life may once have existed on that world. After the disappointment of the dual *Viking* landers' failure to find life on the Martian surface in 1976, Mars exploration by the United States endured a hiatus of more than a decade. Then in 1996, preceded by an extraordinary statement from President Clinton at the White House, NASA announced that it had found possible evidence for Martian microbes in the meteorite ALH84001, thought to have arrived on Earth 13,000 years ago, having been ejected from Mars about 16 million years earlier. Although skeptics immediately questioned the persuasiveness of the evidence cited, the announcement galvanized high-level political and public interest.[38] The *Pathfinder* experience showed that this public interest in Mars exploration remains strong.

There are important lessons for any future in situ search for life in the solar system to be learned from the *Viking* spacecrafts' search for life on Mars nearly a quarter-century ago. These lessons are relevant to our upcoming exploration of Europa. I explore them at length in the appendix to this chapter.

Human Spaceflight and Mars Sample Return

Human spaceflight could play an important role in Mars sample return.[39] In this concept, Space Shuttle missions would retrieve Mars samples that had been returned to Earth orbit. (The samples would initially be delivered to a very high-Earth orbit, then lowered to low-Earth orbit using ion propulsion.) Such an option could carry important potential scientific and engineering advantages, for example, in terms of a simplified mission profile at Mars, potentially greater returned sample mass, and far superior thermal control for the sample during its descent through Earth's atmosphere. (Rather than entering the atmosphere after a direct trajectory from Mars, the samples would be returned within the Shuttle cargo bay.) The implications of such a mission profile for guarding against the possibility of back contamination need to be carefully assessed; there seem to be both advantages and disadvantages over a fully robotic return mission.

A scientifically and programmatically justifiable fusion of human and robotic spaceflight in the search for life elsewhere could provide a powerful unifying theme to NASA's activities and lead to remarkably exciting and high-profile human missions. The space agency would be wise to examine legitimate scientific opportunities for creating such a program.

Europa

If the strong circumstantial evidence that Jupiter's moon Europa harbors an ocean of liquid water beneath its ice is correct, then Europa joins

Mars as the most likely location in the solar system to harbor extrater-restrial life.[40] The investigation of this possibility will require a series of missions. At least one orbiter will likely be needed to map the surface thoroughly and to perform the geophysical and remote-sensing obser-vations needed to determine with high confidence that the ocean actu-ally exists and to begin the determination of ice structure. One or more landers would then follow, perhaps melting a small amount of ice at the surface in an attempt to determine the composition of the ocean from which the ice ultimately derives. There will be high public and scientific expectation that the first lander mission will begin the search for life. It will be important to communicate that establishing the chemical and geological context is a critical part of this search (see Appendix).

Ultimately, once the thickness of the ocean's ice cover around Europa is known,[41] a subsequent mission will attempt to melt or drill through the ice and sample or explore the ocean directly. If the prospects for life on Europa prove tantalizing (or more conclusive), sample return missions seem likely, though such missions would be extremely chal-lenging.

If Europa's likely ocean proves to be sterile, that would be a result nearly as remarkable as the discovery of life itself. Such a result would suggest that the origin of life, if not its survival, is more difficult than we might have inferred from the rapidity of life's origin on Earth. In this case, we might still want to investigate Europa sufficiently to understand why it remained sterile. In any case, a program of exploration sufficient to rule out life in or at the bottom of Europa's ocean will likely require decades.

The Space Studies Board of the National Research Council has as-serted that Europa is of such importance that it deserves its own pro-gram of exploration, "with a priority equal to that for the future ex-ploration of Mars." However, this recommendation was qualified: "This equality must, however, be tempered by the uncertainty as to whether liquid water is actually present and [by] the technological challenges posed by the exploration of Europa."[42] There would be a number of im-plications for NASA if this recommendation were to be taken seriously.

Missions to explore Europa are very challenging because of the dif-ficulty of flying direct trajectories to Jupiter and entering orbit around Europa using the launch vehicles currently available in the United States and also because of the extraordinary radiation environment that must be withstood at Europa's location in the Jovian magnetosphere. The U.S. expendable rocket fleet currently has no intermediate launch vehicle appropriate to the mission: the light *Delta* rocket series are insufficient, and the heavy *Titan IV* is unnecessarily large and expensive. Once in orbit, the Europa orbiter spacecraft's lifetime will be limited to about one month before accumulated radiation damage is expected to end the mission, even with radiation-hardened electronics and aluminum shielding of key components.

Originally, the launch of the Europa orbiter had been hoped for as early as late 2003, but problems associated with developing a new high-efficiency and low-mass radioactive power source, and the current absence of an appropriate intermediate launch vehicle in the U.S. rocket inventory delayed this first to early 2006, then to 2008 or even later.[43] In this scenario, the spacecraft would not achieve orbit around Europa until 2011. That is, an entire decade will have passed before we obtain new data from Europa and before we know with complete certainty whether or not Europa harbors an ocean.

This decadal timescale illustrates an important difference between Mars exploration and the exploration of objects in the outer solar system. Flight times to the outer solar system are long. (Three years are required to reach Jupiter by direct trajectory, with about an additional year required to enter orbit around Europa subsequent to achieving Jovian orbit.) In the current program, it could well be that each step in Europa exploration will take a decade or more. In one sense, this might seem a logical scientific program, because it would allow the results of each mission to be fully incorporated into the design of all subsequent missions. But it carries with it impressive delays between successive missions and the programmatic danger of a concomitant waning of public interest. If there were a catastrophic failure of any single mission to Europa, the program of exploration could be set back for more than an entire decade.

If, on the other hand, NASA were to commit to a program of exploration of Europa analogous to that underway for Mars, it could substantially accelerate this timeline. Even for Mars, for which interplanetary flight times are far less, NASA does not delay launching (much less planning) each new mission while awaiting the results of the previous one. (Nor does it do so with comet exploration.) Rather, NASA has determined that the exploration of Mars is a major goal that will require many missions and that multiple missions to achieve various objectives will fly simultaneously or in an interwoven fashion. Confident that it is going to Mars to stay, NASA incorporates new results into the ongoing program as soon as possible but without holding up missions already approaching launch. Programmatically, this arguably less-than-optimal scientific approach (if one took the view, uncommon elsewhere in science, that time delays are scientifically irrelevant) is justified by the fact that Mars is a high-priority objective that we are eager to explore. Yet the delays suffered by waiting to fly each mission to Mars until the results of the previous mission were received would be much less severe than those for Europa because flight times to the Jovian system are so much longer than those for Mars.

In fact, the exploration of Europa is currently at an even greater disadvantage. The sole Europa mission approved fell within the Outer Planets budget line, which also had to accommodate future missions to other outer planets, moons, and small bodies. A mission to the outermost planet Pluto and to Kuiper belt objects is a high priority, and the first Europa lander mission also had to compete with future missions (identified by the planetary science community as of comparable importance) to Saturn's moon Titan, the planet Neptune, and elsewhere.[44] Given this competition with other high-priority planetological objectives, the implementation of a program of Europa exploration that allows launches more than about once each decade would require NASA to establish a separate program line for Europa or a line dedicated to the exploration of Europa and Saturn's moon Titan, another astrobiologically important destination in the outer solar system.

Such a move would only be possible, of course, with support within NASA backed by the Office of Management and Budget and Congress. NASA itself may conclude that flying one spacecraft to Europa every decade is insufficient, given the centrality of astrobiology to NASA's solar system exploration plans. It would seem remarkable for what may be the most astrobiologically important target in the solar system to receive so little attention. At the same time, outer solar system missions involving orbiters or landers are expensive and challenging.

Creating a new budget line would require overcoming some resistance in the solar system exploration community among those not oriented towards astrobiology. But the argument could be made that carving out a separate Europa or Europa/Titan line would free up resources for launches to other important objectives in the Outer Planets budget line. This would only be credible if new money were truly available. At current funding levels, a dedicated program of Europa exploration would require near abandonment of other outer solar system objectives and would engender substantial opposition in the scientific community. There may be a catch-22 here; it may well not be possible to maintain the excitement needed to budget for a new program of Europa exploration in the absence of further exciting results—results that we will not have in hand for nearly a decade, when a spacecraft should finally enter orbit around Europa.

Titan and Other Icy Worlds

The Huygens probe of the *Cassini* spacecraft is scheduled to enter Titan's atmosphere in 2004.[45] Titan is the only moon in the solar system with a substantial atmosphere. Indeed, the organic smog layer in Titan's upper atmosphere prevented the *Voyager* spacecraft from imaging Titan's surface. Titan's atmosphere, like Earth's, is mostly molecular nitrogen with several percent of methane. Calculations of methane's lifetime in the atmosphere suggest that it can only be sustained if Titan is either geologically active (with volcanic outgassing of methane) or if it has seas of liquid methane and ethane on its surface that resupply the methane in the atmosphere just as Earth's surface water ultimately sustains our own clouds. (Titan's surface temperature is about −180° (C). There may be a kind of "hydrological" cycle on Titan in which liquid hydrocarbons rain out, flow through rivers, and collect into seas, only to evaporate once more.[46]

Should even a fraction of these remarkable possibilities be present and be captured by the descent imaging cameras on board the Huygens probe, or should the organic composition of Titan's atmosphere be especially interesting from the point of view of prebiotic chemistry, there will be a spate of public and scientific excitement in Titan as a destination for future missions. Moreover, this enthusiasm will extend over several years as the *Cassini* spacecraft builds up an image of Titan's surface via radar mapping. It may be possible to capture this excitement in the cause of a joint Europa/Titan exploration budget line to be added to the NASA Space Sciences budget. Such a pairing would carry scientific legitimacy because these moons are the two outer solar system worlds of greatest interest for astrobiology (Titan because of its organic chemistry, Europa because of its liquid water). In both cases, the regions of greatest interest are so far hidden from our view (Titan's surface beneath a near-opaque smog layer, Europa's ocean beneath its ice cover), and both represent natural planetary laboratories that will help us fill in gaps in our understanding of planetary evolution and the origin of life.

Europa may not be the only outer solar system world with a subsurface liquid water ocean. One of the strongest lines of evidence for an ocean on Europa comes from the *Galileo* magnetometer experiment, which strongly suggests the presence of a conducting fluid (quantitatively consistent with a salty ocean) beneath Europa's ice. Magnetometer measurements from *Galileo* also suggest that Jupiter's moons Callisto and Ganymede may similarly harbor subsurface oceans,[47] though these oceans could be deeper and less accessible than that of Europa. Subsurface liquid water oceans may be a typical feature of large icy moons throughout the outer solar system, so they may also be present on Ganymede and perhaps on Titan as well. Europa and Titan seem likely to remain the highest-priority worlds for future exploration because of the accessibility of their regions of greatest exobiological interest. However, in the remarkable event that a subsurface biosphere were discovered on Europa, the exploration of the subsurface of the outer solar system's other icy worlds would become a higher priority.

Planetary Protection

The United States is bound by the Outer Space Treaty not to contaminate possible extraterrestrial habitats with terrestrial microorganisms. Article IX states that "parties to the Treaty shall pursue studies of outer space including the moon and other celestial bodies, and conduct exploration of them so as to avoid their harmful contamination and also adverse changes in the environment of the Earth resulting from the introduction of extraterrestrial matter and, where necessary, shall adopt appropriate measures for this purpose."[48] NASA implements this policy, according to a Policy Directive issued by the Administrator, with reference to detailed procedures and guidelines.[49] Advice is regularly sought from both internal and external advisory groups, in particular the Space Studies Board of the National Research Council[50] and the Planetary Protection Task Force, a new advisory panel to NASA's Space Science Advisory Committee (SScAC).[51]

FORWARD CONTAMINATION ISSUES

NASA policy guidance (the NPG) presents the general planetary protection requirements for five categories of robotic missions.[52] These categories range from I to IV for missions to other locations in the solar system that do not involve sample return to Earth. Category V applies to sample return missions. Missions are classified into one or another category depending on mission type (e.g., flyby, orbiter, lander, or probe) and destination;[53] however, category definitions are kept intentionally flexible so that new information can be regularly incorporated. Specific requirements for each planned mission are determined by NASA's Planetary Protection Officer in accordance with the NPG and the most recent scientific advice from internal and external advisory groups. Requirements are lowest for Category I missions (no requirements); these would be missions to bodies such as the Sun or the planet Mercury where there are no prospects for life or prebiotic chemistry. At the other extreme, Category IV missions are landers or probes to destinations of biological interest; these missions must satisfy certain requirements for bioload: the number of spores per square meter of spacecraft surface, and the number of spores within a given cubic centimeter of spacecraft material. Category IV is further subdivided into subcategories A and B, with B corresponding to landers and probes carrying life-detection experiments. These require concomitantly more stringent bioload reduction requirements in order to prevent false positives due to terrestrial microbial contamination. Category V missions must be concerned not only with forward contamination (for which they must meet Category IV requirements) but also with preventing back contamination of Earth. The latter introduces an additional set of major issues that will be discussed in the next section.

The *Viking 1* and *2* Mars landers were baked at about 110° C for 30 and 23 hours, respectively, in order to reduce the bioload of the spacecraft.[54] Prior to baking, they had been cleaned to bioloads below about 300,000 bacterial spores on each lander. The effect of the baking was estimated to have reduced the bioload by about a factor of 10,000 so that something like thirty viable spores are calculated to have remained on the lander at the time of its departure from Earth.[55] The *Viking* biology instruments themselves were subjected to even more stringent heat sterilization.[56]

Bioburden estimates are based on assays for culturable spores rather than on more modern DNA detection techniques. They are therefore likely to underestimate, and perhaps considerably underestimate, the actual bioburden of the spacecraft at launch. The Space Studies Board recommended in 1992 that NASA investigate spacecraft bioload using state-of-the-art life-detection methods;[57] this recommendation should be implemented as a standard component of planetary protection procedures.

Consistent with the 1992 Space Studies Board report, the *Mars Pathfinder* lander and rover were Category IVA missions whose bioburden levels were about the same as the *Viking* prebaking levels, for example, assembled in a class 100,000 clean room (corresponding to a spore surface density of 100,000 per square meter) with heat or chemical sterilization of subcomponents.

I have so far described planetary protection procedures as meeting the United States' legal obligations, as well as addressing the scientific obligation not to jeopardize the investigation of possible extraterrestrial life by introducing false positives. But they are also, I believe, required by an ethical obligation to avoid significantly endangering possible alien biospheres. A key question for the future of Mars exploration is the extent to which bioload reduction will continue to be required. Requirements are unlikely to be relaxed below those now in place until a compelling case is made that Mars harbors no life on its surface and that subsurface niches are difficult to access. Even in this case, missions attempting to sample the deep subsurface would likely continue to have to meet strict bioburden reduction requirements.

Can we already rule out life on the Martian surface? To do so with sufficient confidence to relax planetary protection guidelines for Mars, we would at a minimum have to examine returned Martian samples for signs of life and find none. We would also need to demonstrate explicitly the presence of oxidants in the Martian soil and thereby confidently explain the *Viking* lander results. But even then, there would remain the possibility of vestigial surface habitats for life. The only possible habitats in which Earth-like life would seem to be able to flourish on the Martian surface would be in Yellowstone-like hot springs.

The *Mars Global Surveyor* (MGS) spacecraft has so far failed to find the sort of minerals on the Martian surface that one would expect to find associated with extant or ancient hot springs.[58] But recent dramatic results from the Mars Observer Camera (MOC) on the MGS provides strong evidence for recent ground-water seepage and surface runoff.[59] That is, liquid water environments evidently exist close to the surface; and in the geologically recent past, these have led, in some 120 specific locales so far identified, to water flows on the Martian surface.

Some terrestrial microbes would be able to survive, in the sense of remaining viable, for long periods on the Martian surface,[60] and Martian dust storms would widely distribute any terrestrial microbes brought to Mars—including, perhaps, to sites where liquid water may communicate with the surface. These possibilities require that the planetary protection requirements for Mars remain in place until our knowledge of Mars and its possible environments for life have substantially improved.

Planetary protection requirements are also demanding in the case of

Europa. Europa most likely harbors a liquid water ocean, and on the basis of what is already known, it seems possible that certain terrestrial microorganisms could survive there.[61] Sending a spacecraft into Europa's ocean is an altogether different prospect than landing on the surface of Mars. Europa's surface is much harsher than that of Mars, but any surface mission to Europa or any orbiter that will eventually impact Europa's surface must address the possibility that components of it could be rapidly buried in Europa's ice, protected from the radiation environment, and eventually introduced into Europa's ocean.[62]

Planetary Protection and Human Exploration of Mars

Even if life does not exist at the Martian surface, it is possible that it has retreated to subsurface environments where liquid water is still possible. Directly accessing subsurface aquifers may require drilling hundreds of meters or even kilometers into the Martian surface. Such drilling seems likely to be attempted on Mars within the coming century and could require a human presence in order to be effective.[63] Moreover, field research already underway at the Haughton impact crater on Devon Island in the Canadian Arctic suggests that the hunt for important geological samples may require the adaptability and mobility that humans can bring to exploration.[64] Evidence for recent seepage and surface runoff on Mars is exciting precisely because it suggests that there may be some regions at the Martian surface where liquid water is at least intermittently accessible.[65] Exploration of many of these rugged features is likely to be most comprehensively accomplished with human beings.

Yet if returned Mars samples were to demonstrate the existence of life on Mars or even if extant surface liquid water were to be discovered, the implications for the human exploration of Mars could be profound.[66] Humans shed some 50,000 bacteria per day, and current spacesuits will not prevent this material from reaching the Martian surface.[67] Research, development, and testing of systems to reduce the leakage of human microbes into the Martian environment from spacesuits, through airlocks, and so forth, is needed.

A human presence on Mars (or the presence of a spacecraft with insufficient bioload reduction) could risk the contamination of any Martian hot spring or other surface-water environments. This emphasizes the importance of searching for such possible active environments on the Martian surface. Before humans walk the surface of Mars, we must first better understand the extent of possible surface niches for life. This recommendation again echoes that of the 1992 Space Studies Board report. The presence of such niches would not necessarily preclude human exploration, but they would require that concentrated attention be devoted to human-related planetary protection issues. In this sense, extensive robotic exploration of Mars is an absolutely required predecessor of human exploration.

BACK CONTAMINATION ISSUES

The planetary protection requirements of the first Mars sample return have been carefully studied.[68] Samples returned from Mars must be contained and treated as though potentially hazardous until proven otherwise. No uncontained materials, including spacecraft surfaces that have been exposed to the Martian environment, should be returned to Earth; therefore, the "chain of contact" of the return capsule and the Martian surface must be broken.

Rather than incur the cost of creating biologically secure handling facilities for these samples once returned to Earth, one could instead consider the complete sterilization of the samples while en route to Earth. While some science might thereby be lost, a great amount could still potentially be learned—including with respect to prospects for biology—with sterilized samples, at least if sterilization were by irradiation (possibly gamma irradiation)[69] rather than by heating. However, it would be technically difficult to implement such a protocol in flight. More importantly, the sterilization protocols will likely still need to be validated once the samples reach Earth, and the public will need to be reassured. Moreover, the contact chain of the sample return canister with the Martian surface would still have to be broken. It is unlikely that in-flight sterilization would, in fact, substantially reduce the requirements on the first sample return. Rather than searching for ways to sidestep biologically secure sample retrieval and handling, NASA should continue to meet this challenge head-on with good communication with the public on these issues. Any plan for the Space Shuttle to play a critical role in Mars sample return would need to be carefully assessed in terms of its implications for back contamination.

Beyond the Solar System

NASA has committed itself to searching for life beyond our solar system through the Astronomical Search for Origins theme within the Office of Space Sciences.[70] The first objectives of this program are to search for planets around other stars and then Earth-like planets. But the ultimate goal is to characterize the atmospheres of Earth-like planets as a way of testing whether these worlds are suitable for life or may even display signs of life in their atmospheric composition.

In light of this extrasolar system search for life and the emphasis NASA is placing on astrobiology throughout space sciences,[71] it is remarkable that the scientific Search for Extraterrestrial Intelligence (SETI) has received no attention. Theoretical arguments about the likelihood and abundance of extraterrestrial intelligence are many, contradictory, and interminable in the absence of observational data.[72] But the scientific search for extraterrestrial intelligence has received strong endorsement in each of the past four astronomy and astrophysics decadal reviews of the National Research Council.[73] SETI has also been advocated in a petition published in *Science* magazine signed by a broad range of scientists, including Nobelist biologists and biochemists.[74]

SETI goes virtually unmentioned in NASA's vision of astrobiology because Congress eliminated the SETI High Resolution Microwave Survey (HRMS) from NASA's FY 1994 budget.[75] Since that time the targeted search component (a survey of the thousand nearest Sun- like stars) of the HRMS program has been carried out entirely with private funds by the SETI Institute; other components have not been continued. There has been a feeling among some NASA officials and outside advisors that the scientific search for extraterrestrial intelligence is best left unmentioned within NASA's astrobiology and origins programs lest astrobiology be threatened by association with a project once cancelled by Congress.[76] However, this is now changing as NASA is given strong indications by members of the House of Representatives that the 107th Congress takes the view that SETI should compete on a level playing field with other scientific investigations appropriate to astrobiology.[77]

NASA's *Astrobiology Roadmap* presents three fundamental questions of astrobiology: (1) How does life begin and evolve? (2) Does life exist elsewhere in the universe? and (3) What is life's future on Earth and beyond?[78] In the first decade of the twenty-first century, private donors have sustained scientific research in SETI, but it would not serve science well to foreclose the possibility of government-funded support in an area of fundamental research for reasons that are extrascientific. SETI is a natural component of any balanced look at the origin, evolution, and distribution of life in our galaxy.

There are already areas where SETI could benefit NASA's astrobiology program. One area of possible overlap is in the study of the societal implications of the discovery of extraterrestrial life. The SETI Institute has published research into this question in the context of the discovery of extraterrestrial *intelligent* life;[79] this research is just beginning to be extended to analogous questions of the discovery of less sophisticated forms of life.[80] A second area of potential overlap is more concrete. SETI has already demonstrated a strong private sector interest that could be further capitalized on through private/public partnerships that maximize the government's resources. One possible area where this might manifest itself is in the construction of the Square Kilometer Array (SKA) radiotelescope, as suggested by the most recent National Research Council decadal review.[81] The SKA is an expensive project of great interest to both SETI researchers and other radioastronomers. Representatives of six nations at a meeting of the International Astronomical Union have now signed an agreement to bring the SKA online by the middle of the next decade.[82]

Policy Conclusions

The discussion above can be summarized in a small number of policy recommendations. First, the exploration of Mars should continue to adopt as its core goal the search for extant or extinct life on Mars, emphasizing past and present liquid water environments. Programmatic flexibility should be maximized. It is both scientifically valuable and important for public participation to put into place greater Mars exploration infrastructure as soon as possible. In particular, the creation of a telecommunications network capable of sustaining live video return from Mars should be a high priority. Regular video from Mars could strongly influence the public's view of humanity as a species that naturally spans the solar system, increasing interest in both robotic and human exploration.

Second, Europa likely harbors the second ocean of liquid water in the solar system, and in this context its exploration has an importance comparable to that of Mars. However, the current structure of solar system exploration, struggling to balance important scientific objectives throughout the outer solar system, does not permit a program of Europa exploration that is analogous to that devoted to Mars. If astrobiology is truly to be a key priority for NASA, it will need to establish a new Europa or, more likely, a Europa/Titan mission line within NASA's Office of Space Sciences. This is unlikely to be possible within the existing budget, however.

Third, planetary protection in the context of possible forward contamination of Mars and Europa remains an important issue demanding further technical development. Human exploration of Mars depends on a better understanding of the chemistry of the Martian surface and the prospects for Martian life, especially the existence of surface or near-surface liquid water environments. Returning Mars samples to Earth for scientific study requires the construction of biologically secure sample-handling facilities.

Fourth, the search for extraterrestrial intelligence is a natural component of any balanced investigation of the origin, evolution, and distribution of life in our galaxy—that is, of astrobiology. There are areas where appropriate private/public partnerships in this field could be of mutual benefit.

Finally, a natural alliance exists between planetary exploration and the protection of Earth's natural environment. Comparative planetology helps us to understand the Earth and therefore the context for Earth's biosphere and our own civilization. Astrobiology helps us to understand the origin and evolution of life itself. Certain issues, such as the technically nearly inescapable use of radioisotope thermoelectric generators[83] (RTGs) for much outer solar system exploration, will continue to be a source of tension with some elements of the environmental community, but a rigorous minimization of risk and the clear communication of this objective should ensure public support for such launches. If both sides can avoid careless or inflammatory remarks, the two should be able to proceed as partners. (Kim Stanley Robinson notes the occasional and damaging comment by some space advocates that we must explore space so that after we wreck Earth's environment, we will have somewhere else to go![84]) Careless or angry talk about "manifest destiny" by advocates of Mars exploration could do great damage.[85]

Great harm could also be done to this alliance were planetary protection issues—whether in the context of forward or back contamination—to be handled with anything other than forthrightness and transparency. Currently, public concern over biological contamination from Mars missions ranks well below the public's concern over other environmental and technological risks.[86] Scientifically based planetary protection measures and good communication with the public about them should ensure that this continues to be the case. With the support of the public, the coming decades could be the most extraordinary in the history of space exploration. The discoveries made in the next few decades could, in turn, guarantee enormous public enthusiasm for both robotic and human spaceflight and could engender a sense of our planetary civilization as part of a larger biological universe.

Appendix: Lessons from *Viking* on Mars

The *Viking* biology package consisted of three experiments that searched for life in samples collected from the Martian soil. The experiments established broad criteria for the detection of life based on the assumption that Martian life could be recognized through its metabolism. One of these experiments, the labeled-release (LR) experiment, searched for microbes that would ingest any of a half-dozen simple organic molecules provided by the experiment and then metabolize one or more of them into a carbon-containing gas such as carbon dioxide. The LR experiment gave tantalizing results that in some respects mimicked those expected from life. Indeed, the head of the *Viking* biology team commented that "if information from other experiments on board the two *Viking* landers had not been available, this set of data would almost certainly have been interpreted as presumptive evidence for biology."[87] But a biological interpretation was called into question by the results of other biology experiments and undercut by an instrument not formally part of the biology package, the *Viking* gas chromatograph mass spectrometer (GCMS).

The GCMS searched for organic molecules in the Martian soil that could be released under stepwise heating to temperatures of 500° (C). None were found to the limits of detection of the experiment, the parts-per-million level (for one- and two-carbon-atom compounds) to the parts-per-billion level (for compounds of more than two carbon atoms). Organic compound levels this high had been expected from estimates of micrometeorite infall on Mars. Despite some continuing scientific debate,[88] both the absence of organics and the results of the biology experiments (including the LR experiment) are now widely interpreted as due to the action of organic-destroying oxidants produced in the Martian atmosphere. That is, *Viking* likely discovered the effect of largely unanticipated Martian chemistry rather than Martian biology.[89] However, a direct demonstration that oxidants are abundant in the Martian surface has not yet been made. Because so much of our thinking about biology on Mars rests on this interpretation of the *Viking* results, it is important that such a direct experiment be performed soon.[90]

The de facto use of the GCMS as a life-detection experiment approached the search for life on Mars from a perspective different from that of the biology package experiments. Whereas the latter relied on a metabolic definition of life, the GCMS in effect conducted a search for life based on a biochemical definition. Viewed as a life-detection experiment, the GCMS simply assumed that life elsewhere would, like life on Earth, be based on organic molecules: no organics, no life. (The converse is certainly not true; the mere presence of organics does not imply the presence of life.)

One lesson from the *Viking* experience is therefore the value of searching for life from the perspectives of different possible definitions.[91] A second lesson is the importance of establishing the chemical and geological context for the interpretation of biological experiments. A third is the value of designing life-detection experiments, when possible, to provide useful information even in the case of a negative result.

Perhaps most important, the *Viking* experience suggests that the biochemical definition seems likely to trump appeals to other definitions in a remote-sensing context. In the absence of compelling organic biomarkers, other biologically suggestive experimental results are likely to be distrusted. With the smaller, more strongly payload-constrained missions to Mars and elsewhere that NASA will likely be flying throughout the coming decades, this is an important conclusion.[92]

One possible exception to this general conclusion might come from a microscopic exploration that imaged entities doing something unambiguously alive, such as propelling themselves or reproducing. In such a case, especially in the absence of biochemical information, the importance of excluding the possibility of forward contamination is abundantly clear. The scientific imperative to avoid a false positive—that is, that one not detect organisms that one has carried along on one's own spacecraft—is one example of the critical issue of planetary protection discussed above.

NOTES

1. I take *exobiology* to mean the study of the conditions relevant to the origin of life and the search for (and perhaps eventually, the study of) life elsewhere. The word, awkward in its combination of Greek and Latin roots, dates to a paper by the Nobel prize–winning geneticist Joshua Lederberg (*Science* 132 [1960]: 393–98). The word *astrobiology* is now becoming more commonplace (at least within the United States), because of its adoption by NASA (e.g., in NASA's Astrobiology Institute). European countries are choosing exobiology for their nascent program. Astrobiology has a pedigree about as good as exobiology, having been coined by the astronomer Otto Struve in 1955. It is sometimes claimed that astrobiology is broader than exobiology, embracing evolutionary biology as well as exobiology. However, astrobiology seems to imply that one is studying the biology of stars (*astron* is from the Greek for star) and therefore seems to me a less appropriate combination than its

cousin words *astrophysics* or even *astrochemistry*. The word *cosmobiology* (the biology of the cosmos), originally used by J. D. Bernal in 1952, may be the best choice but is currently seldom used. *Bioastronomy* is used by the International Astronomical Union but is rarely heard outside the formal meetings and proceedings of that body. I treat all these words as synonyms and choose to use *astrobiology* throughout this essay except when a historical point requires a different choice. For a discussion of the history of each of these terms, see S. J. Dick, *The Biological Universe* (New York: Cambridge University Press, 1996).

2. For reviews of extrasolar planet discoveries and technologies, see G. W. Marcy and R. P. Butler, "Detection of Extrasolar Giant Planets," *Annual Review of Astronomy and Astrophysics* 36 (1998): 57–97; and N. Woolf and J. R. Angel, "Astronomical Searches for Earth-like Planets and Signs of Life," *Annual Review of Astronomy and Astrophysics* 36 (1998): 507–37. An up-to-date listing of extrasolar planet discoveries may be found at www.*exoplanets.org/*.

3. L. R. Doyle et al., "Observational Limits on Terrestrial-sized Inner Planets Around the CM Draconis System Using the Photometric Transit Method with a Matched-filter Algorithm," *Astrophysical Journal* 535, no. 1 (2000): 338–49; L. R. Doyle, H. J. Deeg, and T. M. Brown, "Searching for Shadows of Other Earths," *Scientific American* 283, no. 3 (September 2000): 58– 65.

4. A candidate NASA mission that is likely to be the first spacecraft mission to detect extrasolar planets in the terrestrial-planet size range is the Kepler mission, which will use photometric methods to detect the passing of planets in front of their stars; see www.kepler.arc.nasa.gov/. Another potential mission is the Terrestrial Planet Finder (TPF), which, beginning sometime after 2010, might be capable of looking for evidence of life on extrasolar planets by examining these worlds' atmospheres; see www.tpf.jpl.nasa.gov/.

5. Throughout this chapter, I use the word *life* to mean "life as we know it on Earth" unless otherwise specified; that is, life based on the element carbon, on a liquid water solvent, and on using as an energy source either light or chemical disequilibrium. It is both enjoyable and scientifically valuable to speculate about the possibilities of life as we *don't* know it. See, for example, R. Shapiro and G. Feinberg, "Possible Forms of Life in Environments Very Different from the Earth," in *Extraterrestrials: Where Are They?* 2d ed., ed. B. Zuckerman and M. H. Hart (New York: Cambridge University Press, 1995), 165–72, but our understanding here is so limited that no realistic strategy for exploration can yet be based on these speculations. At the same time, in 2004 we will in effect begin to explore an environment conceivably permissive of one such possibility, Titan, where a form of life based on a nonpolar solvent (hydrocarbons) rather than a highly polar solvent (water) could imaginably exist. For a discussion of the requirements for "life as we know it," see C. F. Chyba, D. P. Whitmire, and R. Reynolds, "Planetary Habitability and the Origins of Life," in *Protostars and Planets IV,* ed. V. Mannings, A. P. Boss, and

S. S. Russell (Tucson: University of Arizona Press, 2000), 1365–93. A classic discussion of these points is given by H. F. Blum, *Time's Arrow and Evolution* (New York: Harper, 1955); a more recent examination is that of J. D. Barrow and F. J. Tipler, *The Anthropic Cosmological Principle* (New York: Oxford University Press, 1986).

6. For a review, see. G. Winnewisser, "Interstellar Molecules of Prebiotic Interest," in *Astronomical and Biochemical Origins and the Search for Life in the Universe,* ed. C. B. Cosmovici, S. Bowyer, and D. Werthimer (Bologna, Italy: Editrice Compositori, 1997), 5–22. There is no comparable population of diverse silicon-based molecules observed, suggesting that silicon does not provide a pervasive alternative to carbon-based life.

7. M. C. Malin and K. S. Edgett, "Evidence for Recent Groundwater Seepage and Surface Runoff on Mars," *Science* 288, no. 5475 (30 June 2000): 2330–35.

8. For a review, see R. Pappalardo et al., "Does Europa Have a Subsurface Ocean? Evaluation of the Geological Evidence," *Journal of Geophysical Research* 104, no. 10 (25 October 1999): 24015–55.

9. See, for example, C. Zimmer et al., "Subsurface Oceans on Europa and Callisto: Constraints from *Galileo* Magnetometer Observations," *Icarus* 147 (2000): 329–47; M. G. Kivelson et al., "*Galileo* Magnetometer Measurements: A Stronger Case for a Subsurface Ocean on Europa," *Science* 289, no. 5483 (25 August 2000): 1340–43; and "Solar System's Largest Moon Likely Has a Hidden Ocean," JPL Press Release, 16 December 2000: www.galileo.jpl.nasa.gov/news/release/press001216.html.

10. Surface biomass is dominated by the mass of trees and amounts to about 8×10^{17} g. There is a comparable biomass, mostly microbial, in the Earth's oceans. The best estimate of Earth's subsurface biomass puts it at about 5×10^{17} g, with substantial uncertainty. See W. B. Whitman, D. C. Coleman, and W. J. Wiebe, "Prokaryotes: The Unseen Majority," *Proceedings of the National Academy of Sciences of the USA* 95, no. 12 (9 June 1998): 6578–83.

11. For a review of these topics with appropriate references, see Chyba, Whitmire, and Reynolds, "Planetary Habitability," 1365–93.

12. Project Phoenix looks for signals in the "microwave window," the least noisy region in the galactic electromagnetic background. It scans for narrow-band (1-Hz-wide) signals between 1 GHz and 3 Ghz. No natural source for such narrow-band signals is known. Phoenix's target stars lie within about 150 light years of Earth. Details about Project Phoenix may be found at www.seti-inst.edu.

13. The *SETI@home* project, which is not a project of the SETI Institute, may be accessed at www.setiathome.ssl.berkeley.edu/.

14. See, for example, Woolf and Angel, "Astronomical Searches for Earth-like Planets," 507–37; and www.tpf.jpl.nasa.gov/.

15. J. N. Wilford, "NASA Sending 2 Rovers to Mars in Twin Trips Landing in 2004," *New York Times,* 11 August 2000. See also "Mars Exploration Rovers": www.sse.jpl.nasa.gov/missions/mars_missns/mars-m03.html.

16. See, for example, *American Institute of Physics Bulletin of Science Policy News,* no. 19, 15 February 2000; *www.aip.org/enews.fyi/.* The FY 2001 request for NASA space science as a whole was just over $200 million above the FY 2000 appropriation of $2,193 million. In FY 2000, these increases were accompanied by a substantial increase in earmarks, significantly threatening the flexibility in the overall Space Science program and leading to worrying cuts in research and analysis (R&A), which is critical to reaping the scientific benefits of space exploration and funds much of the training of the next generation of space scientists. Cutting R&A amounts to eating the seed corn.

17. The NASA Mars exploration "follow the water" strategy is described at www.mars.jpl.nasa.gov/follow/.

18. H. P. Klein, "The *Viking* Biological Investigation: General Aspects," *Journal of Geophysical Research* 82, no. 28 (1977): 4677–80; H .P. Klein, "The *Viking* Biological Experiments on Mars," *Icarus* 34, no. 3 (1978): 666–74; G. V. Levin and R. L. Levin, "Liquid Water and Life on Mars," *Proceedings of the SPIE— The International Society for Optical Engineering* 3441 (1998): 30–41; H. P. Klein, "Did *Viking* Discover Life on Mars?" *Origins of Life and Evolution of the Biosphere* 29, no. 6 (1999): 625–31; L. David, "Scientists Say Mars *Viking* Mission Found Life," www.space.com/news/spacehistory/viking_life_0107 28.html.

19. The British-led *Beagle 2* Mars lander will launch in June 2003 and will carry, inter alia, a mass spectrometer that will search for Martian organics and a Mars Atmospheric Oxidant Sensor (MAOS), a solid-state device that will identify and quantify oxidizing species in the Martian atmosphere. See www.beagle2.com/project/index.htm.

20. Current NASA plans call for the first sample return mission to be launched to Mars in 2014, with an earlier 2011 launch date possible. See www.sse.jpl.nasa.gov/missions/mars_missns/mars-srl.html.

21. For a discussion, see P. Shaki, "Options Explored for Receiving Data from Mars," *Space News* (31 May 1999).

22. Malin and Edgett, "Evidence for Recent Groundwater Seepage."

23. Transfer of microbes between planets is sometimes referred to by the quaint historical name of "panspermia." See H. J. Melosh, "Meteorite Origins: Blasting Rocks off Planets," *Nature* 363 (10 June 1993): 498–99; C. Mileikowsky et al., "Natural Transfer of Viable Microbes in Space 1. From Mars to Earth and Earth to Mars," *Icarus* 145 (2000): 391–427.

24. For a review, see R. Pappalardo et al., "Does Europa Have a Subsurface Ocean? Evaluation of the Geological Evidence," *Journal of Geophysical Research* 104, no. 10 (25 October 1999): 24015–55; and C. F. Chyba and C. B. Phillips, "Europa as an Abode of Life," *Origins of Life and Evolution of the Biosphere,* 32 (2002): 47–67.

25. For a description of the Europa Orbiter mission, see www.jpl.nasa.gov/ice_fire/europao.htm.

26. For a discussion of the prospects for life on Europa and the challenges that

will be faced in searching for it, see C. F. Chyba, "Energy for Microbial Life on Europa," *Nature* 403, no. 6768 (27 January 2000): 381–82; *Nature* 406 (2000): 368; C. F. Chyba, "Searching for Life on Europa from a Spacecraft Lander": *www.seti.org/pdf/chyba_lander.pdf;* C. F. Chyba and C. B. Phillips, "Possible Ecosystems and the Search for Life on Europa," *Proceedings of the National Academy of Sciences of the USA* 98, no. 3 (30 January 2001): 801–4; and C. F. Chyba and C. B. Phillips, "Europa as an Abode of Life."

27. I am borrowing the phrase "biological universe" from Steven J. Dick's *The Biological Universe* (New York: Cambridge University Press, 1996).

28. Current attempts to justify such a conclusion are entirely premature. For one such example, see P. D. Ward and D. Brownlee, *Rare Earth: Why Complex Life is Uncommon in the Universe* (New York: Copernicus, 2000), 333. For a reply, see D. Darling, *Life Everywhere: The Maverick Science of Astrobiology* (New York: Basic Books, 2001).

29. I present this argument in detail in my July 12, 2001, testimony before the House Science Committee Subcommittee on Space and Aeronautics. See www.house.gov/science/space/spacehearings.htm.

30. J. N. Wilford, "Institute Gets $12.5 Million to Listen for Faraway Life," *New York Times,* 1 August 2000, D5. The ATA is described at www.seti-inst.edu/science/ata.html, and in accompanying links.

31. Astronomy and Astrophysics Survey Committee, National Research Council, *Astronomy and Astrophysics in the New Millenium* (Washington, DC: National Academy Press, 2000). Chapter 3, section 5.4, "The Search for Extraterrestrial Intelligence," reads in part: "Finding evidence for intelligence elsewhere would have a profound effect upon humanity. Searching for evidence for extraterrestrial life of any form is technically very demanding. . . . This committee, like previous survey committees, believes that the speculative nature of SETI research demands continued development of innovative technologies and approaches, which need not be restricted to radio wavelengths. The privately funded One-Hectare Telescope (1HT) [now named the Allen Telescope Array] which will be the first radio telescope built specifically for SETI research, is a good example of such an innovative approach, and it will pioneer new radio techniques that could be used in the SKA." The full report is available online at www.nap.edu/books/0309070317/html/.

32. The current NASA Mars exploration architecture may be found at www.mars.jpl.nasa.gov/missions/index.html.

33. A. G. Stephenson et al., *Mars Climate Orbiter Mishap Investigation Board Phase I Report,* 10 November 1999: *ftp://ftp.hq.nasa.gov/pub/pao/reports/1999/MCO_report.pdf.* The report identifies as the root cause of the MCO loss as "failure to use metric units in the coding of a ground software file, 'Small Forces,' used in trajectory models." It then lists eight contributing causes: "1. Undetected mismodeling of spacecraft velocity changes; 2. Navigation Team unfamiliar with spacecraft; 3. Trajectory correction maneuver number 5 not performed; 4. System engineering process did not adequately

address transition from development to operations; 5. Inadequate communications between project elements; 6. Inadequate operations Navigation Team staffing; 7. Inadequate training; 8. Verification and validation process did not adequately address ground software."

34. T. Young et al., *Mars Program Independent Assessment Team Summary Report,* 14 March 2000: *www.nasa.gov/newsinfo/mpiat_summary.pdf.*

35. "The litmus test for adding components to the *Mars Polar Lander* was the likelihood of improving the probability of mission success. According to an internal document prepared by . . . [the] project development manager for the Lander program, the transmitter did not meet that test because a downlink during the trip through the martian atmosphere would do nothing to increase the probability of a safe landing." See "NASA's Philosophy Still Works," *Space News,* 20 December 1999: 14.

36. Malin and Edgett, "Evidence for Recent Groundwater Seepage."

37. Sites offering *Pathfinder* updates registered 566 million hits during the first month of the mission. See M. P. Golombek, "Scientific Results of the Mars Pathfinder Mission," *Planetary Report* 19, no. 1 (January/February 1999): 12–17.

38. D. S. McKay et al., "Search for Past Life on Mars: Possible Relic Biogenic Activity in Martian Meteorite ALH84001," *Science* 273 (16 August 1996): 924–30. For a description of the White House and NASA news conferences as well as the initial skeptical reaction of many scientists, see John Noble Wilford, "Replying to Skeptics, NASA Defends Claims about Mars," *New York Times,* 8 August 1996, A1. For this author's viewpoint, see C. F. Chyba, "Life Beyond Mars," *Nature* 382 (15 August 1996): 576–77.

39. See http://mars.jpl.nasa.gov/technology/samplereturn/index.html.

40. See R. T. Reynolds et al., "On the Habitability of Europa," *Icarus* 56 (1983): 246–54; E. J. Gaidos et al., "Life in Ice-covered Oceans," *Science* 284, no 5420 (4 June 1999): 1631–33; T. M. McCollom, "Methanogenesis as a Potential Source of Chemical Energy for Primary Biomass Production by Autotrophic Organisms in Hydrothermal Systems on Europa," *Journal of Geophysical Research* 104 (1999): 30, 729–30, 742; C. F. Chyba, "Energy for Microbial Life on Europa," *Nature* 403, no. 6768 (27 January 2000): 381–82; *Nature* 406 (2000): 368; R. Greenberg et al., "Habitability of Europa's Crust: The Role of Tidal-tectonic Processes," *Journal of Geophysical Research* 105 (2000): 17551–62; E. J. Gaidos and F. Nimmo, "Tectonics and Water on Europa," *Nature* 405, no. 6787 (8 June 2000): 637; C. F. Chyba and C. B. Phillips, "Possible Ecosystems and the Search for Life on Europa," *Proceedings of the National Academy of Sciences of the USA* 98, no. 3 (30 January 2001): 801–4; C. F. Chyba and K. P. Hand, "Life Without Photosynthesis," *Science* 292, no. 5524 (15 June 2001): 2026–27; and Chyba and Phillips, "Europa as an Abode of Life."

41. The presence of an ocean under Europa's crust could be tested in a variety

of ways from a Europa orbiter, including laser altimetric and gravity measurements (see www.jpl.nasa.gov/europaorbiter/; W. B. Moore and G. Schubert, "The Tidal Response of Europa," *Icarus* 147 [2000]: 317–19); direct long-wavelength radar sounding (see C. F. Chyba, S. J. Ostro, and B. C. Edwards, "Radar Detectability of a Subsurface Ocean on Europa," *Icarus* 134 [1998]: 292–302; J. C. Moore, "Models of Radar Absorption in Europan Ice," *Icarus* 147 [2000]: 292–300); or from a Europa Lander via Seismometry (e.g., R. L. Kovach and C. F. Chyba, "Seismic Detectability of a Subsurface Ocean on Europa," *Icarus* 150 [2001]: 279–87).

42. Space Studies Board, *A Science Strategy for the Exploration of Europa* (Washington, DC: National Academy Press, 1999), 3.

43. See L. D. Friedman, "Worldwatch," *Planetary Report* 20, no. 3 (May/June 2000): 18. The schedule called for a Europa orbiter launch in 2008, arrival in the Jovian system in 2010, and the achievement of Europa orbit in 2011. See www.jpl.nasa.gov/europaorbiter/.

44. Exploration of the Solar System Science and Mission Strategy, NASA, December 1999. See http://sse.jpl.nasa.gove/roadmap/pdffiles/Rmap1.pdf.

45. See, for example, www.nssdc.gsfc.nasa.gov/planetary/huygens.html.

46. For an overview, see A. Coustenis and F. Taylor, *Titan: The Earth-Like Moon* (Singapore: World Scientific, 1999).

47. See K. K. Khurana et al., "Induced Magnetic Fields as Evidence for Subsurface Oceans in Europa and Callisto," *Nature* 395, no. 6704 (22 October 1998): 777–80; C. Zimmer et al., "Subsurface Oceans on Europa and Callisto: Constraints from *Galileo* Magnetometer Observations," *Icarus* 147 (2000): 329–47; M. G. Kivelson et al., "*Galileo* Magnetometer Measurements: A Stronger Case for a Subsurface Ocean on Europa," *Science* 289, no. 5483 (25 August 2000): 1340–43; and "Solar System's Largest Moon Likely has a Hidden Ocean," JPL Press Release, 16 December 2000.

48. "Treaty on Principles Governing the Activities of States in the Exploration and Use of Outer Space, Including the Moon and Other Celestial Bodies." *U.S. Treaties and Other International Agreements* 18 (Pt. 3), 2410–98. Entry into force October 10, 1967.

49. D. S. Goldin, NASA Policy Directive NPD 8020.7E; NASA Policy Guidance NPG 8020.12B.

50. The Space Studies Board has completed four major studies on planetary protection issues for NASA over the past decade, all published by the National Academy Press in Washington D.C. These are *Biological Contamination of Mars: Issues and Recommendations* (1992); *Mars Sample Return: Issues and Recommendations* (1997); *Evaluating the Biological Potential in Samples Returned from Planetary Satellites and Small Solar System Bodies: Framework for Decision Making* (1998); and *Preventing the Forward Contamination of Europa* (2000).

51. N. E. Noonan, Report of the Planetary Protection Task Force to the Space Sci-

ence Advisory Committee, October 1999. An overview of planetary protection policy is J. D. Rummel, "NASA's Planetary Protection Program," www.spacebio.net/modules/lu_resource/planetary_protection/.

52. NASA Policy Guidance NPG 8020.12B.

53. Planet/Mission categories are summarized in Appendix E of *Biological Contamination of Mars* (1992); details may be found in NPG 8020.12B.

54. D. L. DeVincenzi, M. S. Race, and H. P. Klein, "Planetary Protection, Sample Return Missions and Mars Exploration: History, Status, and Future Needs," *Journal of Geophysical Research* 103, no. E12 (25 November 1998): 28577–85. This reference provides a historical review of the development of planetary protection protocols.

55. J. D. Rummel, NASA Planetary Protection Officer, personal communication, 3 March 2000.

56. Space Studies Board, *Biological Contamination of Mars* (1992).

57. Ibid., chap. 6.

58. For example, carbonates have not yet been detected. See P. R. Christensen et al., "The Composition of the Martian Surface as Measured by the Mars Global Surveyor Thermal Emission Spectrometer Experiment," *EOS Transactions of the American Geophysical Union* 80, no. 26, P12B-05, 1999; P. R. Christensen et al., "Results from the Mars Global Surveyor Thermal Emission Spectrometer," *Science* 279, no. 5357 (13 March 1998): 1692–97.

59. Malin and Edgett, "Evidence for Recent Groundwater Seepage," 2330–35.

60. R.L. Mancinelli, "Peroxides and the Survivability of Microorganisms on the Surface of Mars," *Advances in Space Research* 9, no. 6 (1989): 191–195.

61. E. J. Gaidos et al., "Life in Ice-covered Oceans," *Science* 284, no. 5420 (4 June 1999): 1631–33; T. M. McCollom, "Methanogenesis as a Potential Source of Chemical Energy for Primary Biomass Production by Autotrophic Organisms in Hydrothermal Systems on Europa," *Journal of Geophysical Research* 104 (1999): 30729–42; C. F. Chyba, "Energy for Microbial life on Europa," *Nature* 403, no. 6768 (27 January 2000): 381–82; *Nature* 406 (2000): 368; R. Greenberg et al., "Habitability of Europa's Crust: The Role of Tidal-tectonic Processes," *Journal of Geophysical Research* 105 (2000): 17551–62; E. J. Gaidos and F. Nimmo, "Tectonics and Water on Europa," *Nature* 405, no. 6787 (8 June 2000): 637; C. F. Chyba and C. B. Phillips, "Possible Ecosystems and the Search for Life on Europa," *Proceedings of the National Academy of Sciences of the USA* 98, no. 3 (3 January 2001): 801–04; C. F. Chyba and K. P. Hand, "Life without Photosynthesis," *Science* 292, no. 5524 (15 June 2001): 2026–27; and Chyba and Phillips, "Europa as an Abode of Life," 47–67.

62. See Space Policy Board, *Preventing the Forward Contamination of Europa* (2000). Discussion of this report may be found in R. Greenberg and B. R. Tufts, "Comment: NRC Report on Preventing Contamination of Europa Falls Short," *Eos Transactions of the American Geophysical Union* 82, no. 26 (2001): 28; L. W. Esposito, "Reply: Report Safeguards Future Studies of Europa," *Eos Transactions of the American Geophysical Union* 82, no.26 (2001):

28; and R. Greenberg and B. R. Tufts, "Infecting Other Worlds," *American Scientist* 89 (July-August 2001): 296-99.

63. See the "Deep Drilling on Mars" Web site (www.ees4.lanl.gov/mars/mars. html) for a summary of the Mars Hydrosphere Drilling Workshop held at Los Alamos National Laboratory on May 12-13, 1998.

64. See remarks by P. Lee in G. Zorpette, "Why Go to Mars?" *Scientific American* 282, no. 3 (March 2000): 40-43.

65. Malin and Edgett, "Evidence for Recent Groundwater Seepage."

66. Liquid water is unstable at most sites on the surface of Mars at ambient Martian temperatures and pressures (B. Lobitz et al., "Use of Spacecraft Data to Derive Regions on Mars Where Liquid Water Would be Stable," *Proceedings of the National Academy of Sciences USA* 98, no. 3 [30 January 2001]: 2132–37). However, water could still be erupted onto the surface from the subsurface and evidently has been throughout Martian history. See, for example, M. H. Carr, *Water on Mars* (Oxford: Oxford University Press, 1995).

67. See J. D. Rummel and M. A. Meyer, "What is Planetary Protection Anyway?" *Planetary Report* 14, no. 4 (July/August 1994): 5. The 50,000 microbes are shed primarily through skin exfoliation; this figure does not include microbes expelled through defecation.

68. Space Studies Board, *Mars Sample Return* (1997); see also J. D. Rummel, "NASA's Planetary Protection Program," www.spacebio.net/modules/lu_resource/planetary_protection/.

69. C. C. Allen et al., "Effects of Sterilizing Doses of Gamma Radiation on Mars Analog Rocks and Minerals," *Journal of Geophysical Research* 104 (1999): 27043-66.

70. Origins: Roadmap for the Office of Space Science Astronomical Search for Origins Theme, 2001. See http://origins.jpl.nasa.gov/library/scienceplan/science01.html.

71. See, for example, NASA Space Science Enterprise Strategic Plan, November 2000. See http://spacescience.nasa.gov/admin/pubs/strategy/2000/sscsp.pdf.

72. For a review of the voluminous literature on this topic, see S. J. Dick, *The Biological Universe* (New York: Cambridge University Press, 1996), chap. 8. My own thoughts on the topic are summarized in C. Chyba, "Some Thoughts on SETI," *Planetary Report* 19, no. 3 (May/June 1999): 6.

73. Most recently, Astronomy and Astrophysics Survey Committee, National Research Council, *Astronomy and Astrophysics in the New Millennium* (Washington, DC: National Academy Press, 2001), chap. 3, "The Search for Extraterrestrial Intelligence," 131-32. Also see *Astronomy and Astrophysics for the 1970s,* Report of the Astronomy Survey Committee, J. L. Greenstein, chair, 1972; *Astronomy and Astrophysics for the 1980s,* Report of the Astronomy Survey Committee, G. B. Field, chair, 1982; The *Decade of Discovery in Astronomy and Astrophysics,* Report of the Astronomy Survey Committee, J. H. Bahcall, chair, 1991 (Washington, DC: National Academy Press). The latter

reads: "Ours is the first generation that can realistically hope to detect signals from another civilization in the Galaxy. The search for extraterrestrial intelligence (SETI) involves, in part, astronomical techniques and is endorsed by the Committee as a significant scientific enterprise. Indeed, the discovery in the last decade of planetary disks, and the continuing discovery of highly complex organic molecules in the interstellar medium, lend even greater scientific support to this enterprise. Discovery of intelligent life beyond the Earth would have profound effects for all humanity" (131–32).

74. These included the Nobelists David Baltimore, Francis Crick, Manfred Eigen, and Linus Pauling as well as Stephen J. Gould, Matthew Meselson, Lewis Thomas, and E. O. Wilson, and physicists such as Stephen Hawking, Martin Rees, and Subrahmanyan Chandrasekhar. See C. Sagan, "Extraterrestrial Intelligence: An International Petition," *Science* 218 (1982): 426.

75. For a history of these events, see S. J. Garber, "Searching for Good Science: The Cancellation of NASA's SETI Program," *Journal of the British Interplanetary Society* 52 (1999): 3–12.

76. See remarks quoted in William Triplett, "Search for Alien Life Reasserts its Credibility," *Nature* 412, no. 6844 (2001): 260.

77. See members' remarks during the House Science Committee Subcommittee on Space and Aeronautics Hearing on Life in the Universe at www.house.gov/science/space/spacehearings.htm.

78. See www.astrobiology.arc.nasa.gov/roadmap/.

79. J. Billingham et al., eds., *Social Implications of the Detection of an Extraterrestrial Civilization* (Mountain View, CA: SETI Press, 1994), 146.

80. M. S. Race, "Societal Issues as Mars Mission Impediments: Planetary Protection and Contamination Concerns," *Advances in Space Research* 15, no. 3 (1995): 285–92; R. O. Randolph, M. S. Race, and C. P. McKay, "Reconsidering the Theological and Ethical Implications of Extraterrestrial Life," *CTNS* [Center for Theology and the Natural Sciences] *Bulletin* 17, no. 3 (Summer 1997): 1–8. One of the primary questions discussed in this article is "What is ethically responsible space exploration?" in the context of the possibility of extraterrestrial life in our solar system.

81. See Astronomy and Astrophysics Survey Committee, *Astronomy and Astrophysics in the New Millennium,* chap. 3, sec. 5.4, "The Search for Extraterrestrial Intelligence."

82. The SKA's design remains to be chosen, and funding has not yet been identified. See "The Sky's the Limit as Radio Telescope Array Is Approved," *Nature* 406, no. 6797 (17 August 2000): 665–66.

83. For a brief discussion of RTGs, see www.jpl.nasa.gov/galileo/messenger/old mess/RTGs.html.

84. K. S. Robinson, "The Green Space Project," *Planetary Report* 18, no. 3 (May/June 1998): 4–5.

85. See the comments quoted in "On to Mars," chap. 25, in J. Achenbach, *Captured by Aliens* (New York: Simon & Schuster, 1999).

86. M. S. Race, "Mars Sample Return and Planetary Protection in a Public Context," *Advances in Space Research* 22, no. 3 (1998): 391–99.

87. H. P. Klein, "The *Viking* Biological Experiments on Mars," *Icarus* 34, no. 3 (1978): 666–74.

88. See, for example, G. V. Levin and R. L. Levin, "Liquid Water and Life on Mars," *Proc. SPIE—The International Society for Optical Engineering* 3441 (1997): 30–41. For a reply, see H. P. Klein, "Did *Viking* Discover Life on Mars?" *Origins of Life and Evolution of the Biosphere* 29, no. 6 (1999): 625–31.

89. For a biologically pessimistic summary of the *Viking* biology results, see N. H. Horowitz, *To Utopia and Back* (New York: W. H. Freeman and Co., 1986).

90. The British-led *Beagle 2* Mars lander will launch in June 2003 and will carry a solid-state device to identify and quantify oxidizing species in the Martian atmosphere. See www.beagle2.com/project/index.htm.

91. Numerous general definitions of life have been proposed; for a fine review, see C. Sagan, "Life," *Encyclopaedia Britannica* (1970); reprinted in *Encyclopaedia Britannica,* 15th ed. (1998), 22:964–81. Virtually all definitions fail for one or another reason. In any case, the definition of greatest utility for current laboratory experiments is likely to be of little use for solar system exploration. See C. F. Chyba and G. D. McDonald, "The Origin of Life in the Solar System: Current Issues," *Annual Review of Earth and Planetary Sciences* 23 (1995): 215–49.

92. See C. F. Chyba and C. B. Phillips, "Possible Ecosystems and the Search for Life on Europa," *Proceedings of the National Academy of Sciences of the USA* 98, no. 3 (30 January 2001): 801–4; and Chyba and Phillips, "Europa as an Abode of Life."

8 Commentary
Creating a New Heritage in Space

John M. Logsdon

T HE LAST forty years of the twentieth century marked the beginning of a great human adventure—the first human forays away from
the near vicinity of Earth's surface. Twelve Americans walked on the
surface of another celestial body. Other remarkable things were accomplished—perhaps most significantly, through communication satellites
the concept of a "global village" became reality. Thus the space heritage
of the twentieth century is certainly profound and will continue to influence perceptions of the desirable state of space affairs well into the
twenty-first century. But the initial global linkup via satellite occurred
in 1969, the same year that Neil Armstrong and Buzz Aldrin became exploratory pioneers. The final two *Apollo* crewmen left the moon's surface in December 1972. Nothing that has happened in space over the
last thirty-plus years matches those accomplishments in global impact
or historical significance.

The heritage of the past, while it cannot be ignored, is not the appropriate base on which to build for the future. For as we look to that future,
I reluctantly agree with noted futurist Sir Arthur C. Clarke, who recently
wrote, "We [do not] have much of a space programme at the moment."[1]
To create a vigorous, productive U.S. space program for the twenty-first
century, an accelerated start on creating a new space heritage is needed.
It is not at all clear that it will be forthcoming.

Of course, there are many spacecraft in use for relaying voice, images,
and data; for observing the Earth to forecast the weather, to monitor
the resources of the planet, and to help preserve strategic stability; for
gathering scientifically valuable data about the solar system and the universe beyond; and for providing precision navigation and timing information to multiple users. Today's world is dependent on space systems

in a variety of ways. Perhaps this is all that can or should be expected as the space sector has matured.

These practical applications of space capability, however, are a far cry from the vivid images of space hotels, tourist cruises to the moon, lunar bases for science and industry, journeys to Mars, large-scale energy production derived from solar powered satellites, and similar exciting but speculative ideas that half a century ago captured the imagination of space enthusiasts. Those visions persist today; the fact that they are not close to becoming reality is the situation Clarke bemoans.[2] Those who try to combine a degree of realism with our enthusiasm about the promises of space need to be frank about how far the current situation in space is from making progress toward these intriguing prospects. As American University professor Howard McCurdy has commented, "The dreams continue, while the gap between reality and expectations remains unresolved."[3] This century's space challenge is closing that gap. It cannot be closed by appeals to the achievements of the past. New rationales, new technologies, and new heroes and heroines are needed.

Indeed, the current U.S. government space program is not even meeting its early, more pragmatic expectations for scientific, economic, societal, and security payoffs. This is the case even though of every dollar the world's governments now spend on space, the U.S. government spends seventy-five cents, and U.S. industry has a leading position in most areas of commercial space activity. The United States is currently the dominant actor in space and should be able to continue its leadership in shaping twenty-first-century space activities. But the purposes to be served by that leading position remain unclear.

In recent years the U.S. government has been marking time in its space affairs: the NASA space budget did not grow during most of the 1990s; and NASA continues to work toward completing a space station program first approved in 1984, using a transportation system begun in 1972 and in operation since 1981. This is far from a fast-moving, forward-looking effort. This static situation reflects the lack of a clear sense of national objectives with respect to space. In the 1960s, U.S. leaders, and indeed the general public, knew why the country was committed to sending people to the moon. There is not a similar agreement on what the United States wants out of today's and tomorrow's government space efforts.

The occasional publicly exciting, scientifically valuable, or commercially successful space accomplishment should not obscure the too-frequent failures of launch vehicles and spacecraft, budget overruns and schedule slippage in major development programs, a human spaceflight program confined to near-Earth orbit for almost three decades now, the unmet promises of many new commercial space applications, the bureaucratic and international rivalries that hamper the global use of space systems for the public good, the still-limited use of space systems to support national security objectives, and the lack of progress in creating and bringing innovative new technologies into widespread use. Unfortunately, this list of disappointing results could go on.

The Roots of the Current Situation

Before directly addressing twenty-first-century space policy challenges, it is necessary to understand how the U.S. space program, once one of the most exciting of national endeavors, has gotten into its current situation. Without such an understanding, a new start will be more difficult.

What is in the most unsatisfactory condition today and faces the most uncertain future is the U.S. government's civilian space program, carried out primarily through the National Aeronautics and Space Administration (NASA). This program will be the focus of most of the rest of this essay.

Other government space programs aimed at intelligence and military objectives also face uncertainties as the nature of future security threats changes and as the appropriate role of space capabilities in meeting those threats is debated. However, there is a "figure of merit" for such debates: Are space capabilities the best among a range of alternatives for meeting various security needs? There is a sense that the answer to that question is increasingly "yes" and that the security uses of space will increase in coming years.

Commercial space activities are also in a far different situation than is NASA. Here the clear metrics of success are market penetration and economic payoffs. As long as space systems provide superior means for carrying out activities for which users are willing to pay a price that includes an acceptable profit, those systems will be developed and used. When other technological means prove superior (for example, fiber optic cables for point-to-point communications, and ground-based systems for mobile communications), commercial space ventures will either not attract needed financing or will fail the test of operating in a competitive market. If commercial space systems can maintain a meaningful market share in the exponentially growing information economy, their profitable future is assured, at least for the foreseeable future.

There once was a similar measure of value associated with the NASA program. On April 20, 1961, in the aftermath of the first human spaceflight by Soviet cosmonaut Yuri Gagarin, President John F. Kennedy asked his advisers to identify a space program "which promises dramatic results in which we could win." A few weeks later the recommendation came back: set the goal of sending Americans to the moon because *"this nation needs to make a positive decision to pursue space projects aimed at enhancing national prestige."*[4] "Dramatic results," "prestige," and "before this decade is out" became the nationally accepted measures against which NASA's activities could be measured. No similar measures exist today.

Although the Apollo Project will go down in the annals of human history as a great accomplishment, its long-term impacts on NASA and the U.S. civilian space program have arguably been on balance negative. While the quest for power and prestige through space achievement may have served the national interest well during the 1960s, it has not been an effective driver of space activities since. NASA's leaders were slow to recognize this reality; just twenty years after *Apollo 11*, NASA was drifting toward irrelevancy.

It is thus possible to trace the sources of the NASA program's uncertain and unsatisfactory condition today all the way back to the Apollo experience. Most fundamentally, Apollo created an image of what the NASA program *ought* to be like, an image that NASA struggled to meet with only limited success for over two decades after the first lunar landing. One of the major goals of former NASA Administrator Dan Goldin in his long tenure at the top of the space agency was to end this long "Apollo hangover" and to get the organization to focus on how to be relevant to twenty-first-century realities. It was not an easy task.

During the Apollo era, NASA focused on the development of large hardware systems for human spaceflight. Apollo involved an almost war-like mobilization of human and financial resources to accomplish a difficult goal on a challenging time schedule. To carry out the program and maintain a substantial level of activity in other areas of space science and applications, NASA created a massive national network of field centers and industrial contractors dedicated to the space program. Spreading Apollo's workload across the country created a strong base of political support for the program in the Congress. Because Apollo had a deadline, brute force engineering often substituted for technological innovation; unproven technologies were used only when there was no alternative. There was little investment in technologies for the future, given the focus on meeting the Apollo schedule deadline. Resources available for robotic programs increased along with the spaceflight budget, leading to proposals for ambitious science and applications missions in the post-Apollo period.

The reality, however, was that Apollo was an anomaly in the short history of U.S. space activities, not a model to be emulated. Yet NASA's leaders in the two decades after Apollo attempted to recreate it to the greatest degree possible, even as the agency's budget shrank to less than one-third of its Apollo peak. They fought successfully to gain presidential approval for two large programs focused on human spaceflight — the Space Shuttle and the Space Station. Those programs were attractive, among other reasons, because they would provide enough work to keep a large portion of NASA's engineering staff and industrial contractor base actively engaged. However, they did not respond to broader national policy objectives in the manner that Apollo did. Robotic science programs grew in size and ambition — for example, the "Great Observatories," Jupiter and Saturn orbiting missions, and the "Mission to Planet Earth." There continued to be only limited investments in technologies for the future, particularly for space propulsion technologies not associated with the Space Shuttle. Though the White House approved the shuttle and station programs, it did not provide continuing strong political support for NASA, and the agency's congressional overseers, with their more limited interests and perspectives, became more influential in controlling NASA's activities than had been the case during Apollo.

When President George H. W. Bush in July 1989 called for "a continuing commitment to manned exploration of the solar system," he found neither the nation nor NASA ready to accept that challenge. Even as it became clear that there was inadequate political will to take on such an expensive, multiyear commitment, the White House was surprised and disappointed by NASA's plan for returning to the moon and undertaking missions to Mars, which were marked by high expense and technological conservatism. After attempting to identify alternative, more innovative approaches to human exploration (going to such bizarre lengths as advertising for new ideas in the *New York Times*) and to convince NASA to reform its management style and programmatic approach, the White

House finally decided that the residual Apollo-era NASA was technologically and managerially at a dead end. A new leader, Dan Goldin, was brought to the agency in 1992 with an explicit mandate for institutional change.

"Reinventing NASA" has proved a daunting challenge for Goldin and his associates. He has moved planning for robotic missions away from a focus on infrequent large missions to a "faster, better, cheaper" approach, with mixed results to date. The NASA and contractor workforce has been downsized, perhaps excessively. But it has been impossible, due primarily to the strength of congressional interests, to make a corresponding reduction in NASA's institutional base; the agency still has the same set of field centers it had at the end of Apollo.

Goldin joined with the White House in attempting to link the floundering Space Station *Freedom* program to high-priority national interests, in this case helping post–Cold War Russia make the transition to democracy while reducing security risks associated with that transition. Russia's difficulties in meeting its commitments to the station have added costs and risks to the program; the broader benefits of involving Russia have yet to be fully assessed. Major responsibilities for operating the Space Shuttle have been assigned to a private-sector contractor, but NASA's recognition that a major Shuttle accident could put its human spaceflight program at risk has set a limit to NASA's disengagement from Space Shuttle operations. All in all, there still remains much to change to make NASA the kind of productive, innovative organization that the country deserves.

An emphasis on creating and using new technology will probably be the most lasting heritage of Dan Goldin's tenure at NASA. He has recognized that NASA had become stuck in the rut of using expensive, risky, and out-of-date technology in too many of its missions; and he has been an articulate advocate for technological (and managerial) innovation. However, the combination of the political and programmatic requirements to continue to operate the costly Space Shuttle program and to complete the expensive development of the International Space Station, when combined with a stagnant NASA budget for a number of years, has limited opportunities for innovation. Yet without such innovation, NASA's reinvention cannot be completed. Thus the agency's future remains uncertain. As the twenty-first century begins, NASA's Apollo heritage has not yet been fully replaced by clear directions for the future.

NASA in the Twenty-First Century:
Challenges and Opportunities

What is required to complete (finally!) NASA's transition to a twenty-first-century organization? The answer is far from simple.

One aspect of the agency's activities, its space science program, actually is already well along in completing that transition. Chyba's chapter in this volume (chapter 7) is a good discussion of some of the exciting scientific and exploratory opportunities that have been identified. NASA is organizing the bulk of its future space science mission planning around the concept of "Origins." Answering questions about the origins, evolution, and destiny of the universe, stars, planets, and life itself is an enterprise meaningful to all people. Planned "Origins" missions incorporate innovative technology and promise scientifically and publicly interesting results. All in all, NASA's science program seems well positioned for the future if current plans can be turned into future realities.

The space science program had a serious setback with the failure of its Mars missions in late 1999. NASA is using these failures as an occasion to rethink both its approach to Mars exploration and how best to implement the "faster, better, cheaper" approach to most space science missions. It will be a challenge for NASA to go beyond the faster, better, cheaper approach and convince the White House and the Congress to provide stable and sustained funding for the more technologically risky, more expensive missions that are at the core of NASA's science plans for the next decade and longer.

NASA's Earth science program (discussed to some extent by Deibert in chapter 3 of this volume) has been making a long transition from its grandiose origins in the 1980s to an effort appropriately sized to its scientific potential in the context of overall U.S. Earth science and global change research planning. Successive reviews of the Earth Observing System (EOS) program have reduced its ambitions, but it remains a complex and expensive undertaking, still to be firmly integrated into a global strategy for Earth observation. As results from Terra, the first major EOS mission, which was launched in December 1999, become available to the scientific community, enthusiasm for NASA's Earth science efforts is likely to increase. While NASA's traditional scientific activities, oriented away from Earth, can be justified in relative isolation from other areas of science, NASA's Earth-oriented scientific activities gain value from being part of a broader scientific effort. Cementing that connection as it carries out currently planned missions and delivers their results to the broader scientific community will be a continuing challenge for NASA.

The most vexing issue for NASA is its future role with respect to humans in space. Almost forty years after the first man went into orbit, human access to space is still limited to a few hundred highly trained astronauts. The International Space Station will finally provide the opportunity to test the belief that there are scientifically and economically valuable things for humans to do during long-duration space missions; however, it will take several decades before the results are fully in.

What about resuming space exploration beyond Earth orbit by human crews? The reality, as illustrated by Lambright and Van Nijnatten in this volume (chapter 6), is that there is no widely accepted or compelling requirement for humans to travel back to the moon, to Mars, or to other distant destinations.

So where does that leave NASA with respect to human spaceflight after getting the International Space Station assembled and in operation? There is no clear answer to that question, and the prospects for major new missions are not promising. According to the current National Space Policy, articulated in 1996, NASA is constrained from spending significant funds on preparations for sending humans beyond Earth orbit until the International Space Station is in operation and producing positive results. It is up to President George W. Bush to decide whether to continue this constraint. Despite attempts by groups such as the Mars Society and the Planetary Society to organize advocacy for exploratory human missions, there is unlikely ever to be widespread public demand that governments undertake such voyages.

If an appropriate transportation system is developed, there could be a large market for public space travel, or space tourism. However, it is unlikely that NASA will have a major role in creating that market (except for helping develop the necessary transportation system, an issue discussed below). With no politically sanctioned exploratory mission on the horizon and the beginnings of a transition to privately financed human flights in sight, NASA could well find its role limited for some years to operating in low-Earth orbit, flying the Space Shuttle and utilizing the International Space Station. This is an outcome NASA's leaders would dearly like to avoid as they seek to restart a program of human exploration sometime in the next decade or so. Realistically, the chances of their being successful, at least in the short to mid term, are not great.

But that could change. NASA is also assigned by national policy the lead government role in developing advanced space transportation capabilities. If it can gain political support for a substantial, continuing effort in this area, NASA could at least temporarily redefine itself as a developer of space infrastructure technology rather than as a pathfinder in human space exploration. The most pressing need in the U.S. space program is lower-cost, more reliable access to space. In particular, access to space is now far too expensive and unreliable to be the basis for widespread, regular human activity in Earth orbit and beyond.

If NASA can take a leading role in developing new space transportation capabilities, it can serve not only its own requirements but possibly also help enable the kind of exciting future for space activities envisioned by Sir Arthur C. Clarke and like-minded visionaries. Clarke, ever the technological optimist, has suggested that "the rocket may play exactly the same role as the balloon [Note: not the airplane!] did in the conquest of air." He suggests that "it is only a matter of time—I trust not more than a few decades—before we have safe and economical space propulsion systems based on new principles of physics which far-sighted engineers and scientists are already discussing."[5] One can only hope that Clarke is correct in his forecast. Greatly improved access to space is the key to a robust future.

Beyond NASA: Longer-Term Prospects

Will the twenty-first century see large-scale activities in Earth orbit and beyond, many involving human presence? If there is no breakthrough in the costs of access to, and operating in, space, the most likely response to this question is in the negative. Of the many visionary activities that have been proposed, few if any are likely at current costs ever to meet the test of comparing economic or political costs with projected benefits. Though this is often not made explicit, it was favorable results from this comparison that provided the stimulus for widespread use of communication satellites or for sending Americans to the moon. If new large-scale ventures fail the cost-benefit test, space will indeed then be seen as just a "place"—a geographic sector within which various economically, scientifically, militarily, and socially useful activities are carried out, but not as a major organizing focus for large-scale human efforts. It is not even clear that the U.S. government will need a major agency dedicated to space work under those conditions.

On the other hand, if NASA's efforts over the next decade in demonstrating the value of humans in orbit and in developing new approaches to space transportation succeed, the future could be quite different. If research and other activities aboard the International Space Station provide economically valuable payoffs, human activity in low-Earth orbit could be commercialized, relieving NASA of the burden of funding such activity. This could potentially free up resources for restarting human exploration of the solar system. While there is limited political and public will for the substantial increase in NASA's budget that would be needed for exploratory missions under current conditions, there does seem to be support for a stable NASA budget in the range of its level of the late 1990s. Under these conditions, NASA could be authorized to begin preparing for future exploratory voyages.

If space station success were coupled with substantial NASA and private-sector progress in developing second- and third-generation reusable space transportation capabilities that substantially lower costs, there could be a "break out" into space as the cost-benefit calculus for various large-scale space ventures shifts in their favor.[6] If this were to happen, then human travel beyond Earth orbit could well be not just possible but even required. If this happens, then a final forecast by Sir Arthur C. Clarke could become reality: "The exploration—and later exploitation—of the solar system will be the main business of the next Millennium."[7]

NOTES

1. Sir Arthur C. Clarke, "A Thousand Years Hence," *British Heritage* (August–September 1999): 46.
2. See, for example, Timothy Ferris (with illustrations by Robert McCall), "A Space Station? No Big Deal!" *New York Times Magazine,* 28 November 1999, 124–29.
3. Howard McCurdy, *Space and the American Imagination* (Washington, DC: Smithsonian Institution Press, 1997).
4. John M. Logsdon, *The Decision to Go to the Moon: Project Apollo and the U.S. National Interest* (Cambridge: MIT Press, 1970), 109–10, 126; emphasis in original.
5. Clarke, "Thousand Years," 46.
6. Gregg E. Maryniak and Richard Boudreault, "Resources of Free Space vs. Flags and Footprints on Mars," *Space Policy* (May 1996): 103–17.
7. Clarke, "Thousand Years," 46.

9 Commentary
From Vision to Reality

Howard E. McCurdy

P EOPLE who imagined future space policies some fifty years ago
created a wondrous vision. In their minds, individuals assembled
winged rocket ships and flew them to a large rotating space station.
From this orbital platform, astronauts conducted aerial reconnaissance,
lessening the threat of military attacks around the globe. Astronauts assembled flotillas of spacecraft around the space station and launched
them toward the moon and Mars. They constructed lunar bases, established Martian colonies, discovered extraterrestrial life, and revolution-
ized the ability of humans to scrutinize the heavens through large orbiting telescopes.

As is typical when new technologies appear, actual accomplishments
fell short of expectations. Americans traveled to the moon but did not
stay. Elected officials approved the construction of an Earth-orbiting
space station but not on the scale proposed by early pioneers. Politicians funded the development of a winged space shuttle, but it did not
reduce the cost of spaceflight. Military personnel built reconnaissance
platforms, but they did not have people on board. Scientists dispatched
robotic spacecraft to Mars but failed to find extraterrestrial life. Both the
Space Station and the Space Shuttle cost more and delivered less than
early advocates hoped. Martian expeditions revealed a landscape more
lunar than earthly, disappointing a generation of Americans raised on
tales of exotic beasts and water-bearing canals.

The first visionaries believed that humans—not machines—would
dominate the exploration of space. The visionaries assumed that astronauts would occupy orbital spy platforms, retrieve film from space telescopes, explore the moon, and search for life on Mars.[1] These prophets
wholly failed to anticipate the power of remote sensing—the ability of
scientists to construct far-traveling machines capable of collecting and

transmitting detailed information back home. In the 1950 film *Rocket-ship X-M,* actors explain that signals from an outward-bound spacecraft a few thousand miles from Earth would fail to reach home, a suspicion previously advanced by experts no less notable than Robert Goddard and Arthur C. Clarke.[2] Remote sensing, one of the great surprises of the Space Age, led to robotic spy satellites and to spacecraft that could return images from the edge of the solar system and beyond.

Some visionaries imagined that the great discoveries could be accomplished without space policy—that is, by individuals receiving financial support from private sources operating free from government interference. This was a recurring fantasy. In the classic 1950 film *Destination Moon,* American capitalists finance the first expedition to the lunar surface after government attempts to construct workable rockets fail. The capitalists are motivated by the explanation that the first people to establish missile bases on the moon will control the world. For the story line in his 1929 film *Frau im Mond,* director Fritz Lang allows German industrialists to bankroll the mission. They are inspired by the promise of precious metals, which the first explorers obligingly discover.[3]

Real space pioneers abandoned private sources. They requested tax funds to accomplish national goals, an inevitable development, given the sums of money involved. Congress appropriated $25 billion to send Americans to the moon—the equivalent of $170 billion in year 2000 dollars—and approved billions more to develop a national reconnaissance capability. No private entrepreneur possessed such wealth. Space exploration, in the minds of the first pioneers, required public funding and implementation through large government organizations. Congress created the National Aeronautics and Space Administration (NASA) and quietly approved a large but secret national reconnaissance effort. As a consequence, space exploration became synonymous with space policy —elected officials approving missions financed by tax dollars directed through big government organizations. Still, the idea of private entrepreneurs moving quickly to open the space frontier continued to enchant people anxious to develop and explore. This dream may soon come true, reshaping twenty-first-century space policy in significant ways.

Government's Changing Role

Until the last decade of the twentieth century, government spending dominated the final frontier. In the fiscal year ending September 1997, for example, NASA spent $12 billion on various space activities. The

U.S. military spent another $12 billion, primarily on reconnaissance.[4] (Other governments of the world, according to rough estimates, spent about $14 billion more).[5] This money was raised through taxation, allocated by political leaders, funneled through government organizations, and consumed by aerospace firms operating under government control. Traditionally, this is how space policy has been conducted.

In 1997, however, an important shift occurred. For the first time, according to the best estimates, privately funded space activities matched government spending.[6] By 1999, the total size of the worldwide commercial space market had sped past government outlays. The commercial market topped $60 billion, while government expenditures remained in the $40 billion range.[7] Business executives raise funds by attracting investors and selling services through the private sector, mostly within the telecommunications industry. The sum of privately funded space activity does not include monies that aerospace firms receive from government contracts, funded through tax dollars and included in the public share.

In the United States, military expenditures for space are likely to grow. Total civil expenditures will remain flat, although the exploration agenda may expand as officials approve lower-cost but more numerous missions. In the aggregate, forecasters do not believe that total government expenditures for space will grow as rapidly as commercial opportunities, even with the expanding military side. Some analysts expect privately funded activities to surpass $200 billion by 2010.[8]

Public officials are accustomed to traditional forms of space policy supported by tax dollars. Scientists and other space advocates interested in conducting specific missions approach politicians and request public funds. Politicians approve missions, often in an incremental fashion. They authorize space telescopes, orbiting stations, spy satellites, and planetary spacecraft. They pay for them with tax revenues. The money goes to large government organizations like NASA and the National Reconnaissance Office where public servants work with mission advocates and aerospace firms to complete endeavors. Most of the money eventually flows to business firms that produce space products. Government space policy emerges from the cumulative effect of individual spending decisions, often summarized in broadly worded documents.

Government involvement in commercial space activities takes a different form. Private entrepreneurs look to government for incentives such as tax breaks or loan guarantees that help their industries grow.

Entrepreneurs seek relief from government regulations where they are onerous and request the protective umbrella of public law where it reduces the cost of business transactions. Most aerospace firms operate in a multinational regime and thus depend on public officials to draft supporting international agreements.

Public agencies like NASA are not well suited to carry out the activities that promote commercial space activity. In spite of its location on the high-technology frontier, NASA is a traditional command-and-control organization set up to manage large engineering endeavors. Its employees are skilled at managing projects, penetrating contractors, and controlling local practices so that they conform to government plans. Traditional command-and-control efforts are not as relevant for the task of encouraging private investment. Inevitably, old efforts will give way to new perspectives as private markets outrace government activities.

Consider this possibility. Shortly after assembly of the International Space Station ends, NASA and its international partners transfer ownership of the orbital facility to a multinational firm. Participating governments rent space on the station, signing long-term contracts that provide the new owners with a predictable revenue stream. The owners sign a contract with an international hotel and resort company whose executives agree to finance a habitat module attached to the station where it serves as a space hotel. Tourists arrive at the hotel from Earth on a newly developed space shuttle, also owned and operated by a private firm.

Under such conditions, the nature of government space policy would inevitably change. Public officials would be obliged to create a supporting legal framework both to settle property issues in space and to expedite multinational cooperation. They would regulate private traffic to and from the station and support research aimed at creating technological improvements. Based on these changes, pressures to create new government organizations and procedures would appear. Participants from the private sector would not view themselves as contractors for large government arsenals producing and operating space hardware. Civil servants accustomed to dealing with aerospace firms in the old manner would find themselves in unfamiliar settings. They would not be able to direct, command, and control—certainly not in traditional ways.

The pace of changes such as these will be determined by the relative rates at which public and privately funded space activities grow. Commercial activities, Earth monitoring, and space access generate the greatest pressure for reform. Protection of Earth, human exploration of the solar system, and the search for extraterrestrial life tend to follow the traditional form, although incursions by private entrepreneurs are occurring in these areas as well.

Commercial Growth

Space entrepreneurs present an impressive vision of commercial opportunities in space. In their vision of the future, humans working in the micro-gravity environment of space discover and manufacture metal alloys, computer chips, and pharmaceutical products that are indispensable to twenty-first-century life. Private firms sell images from commercially owned satellites. Skilled technicians mine helium 3 from the moon to fuel Earth-based fusion reactors that generate huge quantities of electrical power. Scientists beam solar rays from large satellites to power stations on Earth, helping to eliminate human dependence on fossil fuels. People anywhere on the globe possess instant access to anyone else or any form of information through a wireless network of handheld communicators and fast-moving satellites. Ordinary persons travel as tourists to orbiting hotels and lunar resorts. Mining companies extract water ice from dark craters on the moon and remove metals from asteroids nudged into Earth-circling orbits, providing a profitable source of raw materials for space pioneers. All these events are supported by new forms of rocketry as cheap and safe as twentieth-century jetliners.

This is a fantastic vision. It would create strong pressures for policy change if it occurs. People of previously modest means would get fantastically rich. Like other visions, however, it contains substantial exaggeration.

To date, only space-based telecommunications have proven commercially viable. Space manufacturing, mining, tourism, solar powered satellites, and cheap access to space have not blossomed. Even the relatively rich space telecommunications field is challenged by alternative technologies. Engineers can send information in the form of photons to and from space at relatively low cost. The telecommunication satellites to which those photons travel remain expensive, however, so much so that business firms on the ground gain a marginal cost advantage by burying fiber optic cables in areas of high use and dense population.

Space advocates insist that satellites will prevail over ground-based telecommunications systems—as soon as the cost of space access falls. Advocates are betting that government support for spacecraft technology combined with a growing market for launch services will excite private entrepreneurs to develop a new generation of low-cost launchers. This argument contains two flaws. First, as a proportion of total program cost, launch expenses are already low. Project managers for the $3 billion Cassini mission to Saturn, for example, spent $400 million on launchers—a small proportion of the total program budget. Reducing that by a factor of ten would reduce overall program cost only 12 percent. The largest cost savings lie in other areas, such as spacecraft engineering.

Second, the market for commercial launches remains unexpectedly low. One government study predicts that commercial firms worldwide will need only about fifty launches per year through 2010; a private consulting firm predicts about thirty.[9] Fifty flights is hardly sufficient to sustain the levels of investment needed by private firms anxious to invent cheap access to space. For this reason, private firms tend to stay with spacecraft development projects only so long as those efforts are backed by government subsidies. When the subsidies end, so does private investment.

In imagining the future, space commerce visionaries often seek to recreate the past. The mining, manufacturing, and transportation systems that visionaries wish to place in outer space are activities associated with the industrial revolution. In a post-industrial century, extending the industrial revolution into space at a time when traditional industries are declining on Earth is hardly forward-looking.

No one knows for certain whether space commerce will fulfill the potential predicted for it. Many advocates still wait for the specific event necessary to jump-start the commercial space sector. Perhaps commercial space expenditures will exceed government spending by ratios surpassing five-to-one; perhaps they will not. Should this occur, however, government space policy will change in important ways.

To expedite commercial growth, some advocates want government to get out of the way and allow entrepreneurs to take charge. This attitude misreads the historic government role in promoting new technological frontiers. Such an approach is not likely to occur. Contrary to the vision of unencumbered entrepreneurship, people who promoted old technological ventures like commercial aviation and railroads sought and received government support. Public officials subsidized and regulated these forms of commerce.[10] The ways in which twenty-first-century governments could affect space commercialization are similar to those applied to earlier ventures. Some alternatives follow.

• Government officials can provide incentives that ease the difficulties entrepreneurs face in raising capital. Public officials can provide tax relief that allows successful firms to retain a larger share of any profits their owners make. Alternatively, government executives can use their borrowing power to provide insured or guaranteed loans to space entrepreneurs, an approach used to excite the American housing industry during the first half of the twentieth century. Employing such approaches, public officials help to create markets where ones do not exist.

• Government agencies can draft agreements by which they agree to purchase goods and services from space entrepreneurs for long periods of time. This helps stabilize the market for new technologies and provides entrepreneurs with assured sources of revenue. Government officials used this approach during the first half of the twentieth century to support the fledgling airline industry by allowing commercial airline firms to carry the mail.

• Government leaders can subsidize the research and development costs incurred by commercial space firms. They have done this by financing research in government laboratories as accomplished in the previous century through organizations like the National Advisory Committee for Aeronautics, out of which NASA was formed. Additionally, they can finance industrial development efforts that lead to products like space planes that industrial leaders can later mass produce using private funding.

• Government lawyers can regulate the outer space industry. They can stabilize the market for space goods and services by providing it with a measure of regulatory protection as has been done in the past for commercial airlines and farm products. Additionally, government regulators can control the behavior of people in commercial firms by issuing licenses, conducting inspections, and seeking to maintain minimum standards.

Compared to its capacity for producing space missions, the capacity of the U.S. government for promoting space commerce is weak. The government contains many institutions devoted to spacecraft development and operations but few with a history of promoting commercial space opportunities. In the beginning, the latter may be assigned to existing agencies like NASA and the Federal Aviation Administration. As the commercial space sector develops, however, new policies and institutions will inevitably appear. They will depart from the nature of their predecessors in ways as substantial as those that characterized the first years of spaceflight, in which NASA emerged from an uncoordinated collection of civil and military agencies. As Scott Pace points out in his chapter on space commerce (chapter 2), failure to create such policies could severely retard the development of this commercial sector. Bad policy could sink the potential for commercial growth.

Military Implications of Space Commercialization

During the Serbian conflict in the late 1990s, a Colorado-based firm prepared to launch an Earth-monitoring satellite and sell high-resolution photographs to commercial customers. Potentially, the satellite could have provided photographs of NATO air bases or troop encampments to Serbian military officers. U.S. government officials were understandably distressed. The need for a formal policy limiting the distribution of commercial images was rendered moot when the satellite plunged into the Pacific Ocean during its launch;[11] however, the incident highlighted an important aspect of twenty-first-century space policy. As the number of Earth-monitoring satellites proliferates and human activities on Earth become more transparent, governments will be pressed to regulate space activities that affect national security.

Since the advent of the space age, public officials in the United States have maintained their right to fly space vehicles and satellites over the territory of any other nation. Leaders of the Soviet Union, vigilant in maintaining an iron curtain of secrecy around their empire, inadvertently established this principle by launching *Sputnik 1,* since the satellite flew over the United States. During the Cold War, U.S. officials encountered little resistance to the principle of free overflight. Few nations possessed the capability to disable reconnaissance satellites, and none tried.

During the twentieth century, spacefaring nations constructed an impressive array of Earth-monitoring and other special-purpose satellites. Government satellites provide visual images of military activities and eavesdrop on wireless communications. Infrared satellites identify missile launches, providing the first link in missile defense early warning systems. Satellites under government control provide secure communication channels for military and diplomatic correspondence. Global positioning satellites guide weapons to their targets. Civil satellites monitor long-term environmental effects such as global warming and ozone depletion and pinpoint pollution. The capabilities of these satellites are growing as are the number of nations and institutions that operate them.

During the twenty-first century, military officers in industrialized nations will use space in new and creative ways. A seamless network supporting military activities will stretch from the ground to geostationary orbit. The network may be used to place drones over enemy positions and guide robots into hostile camps. Military officers may place kinetic rods in orbit—inert pieces of metal that when launched toward Earth could destroy bunkers and fortifications with asteroid-like force. Military services may purchase spaceplanes and use them to transport special forces to remote locations in record time. Military space command could achieve co-equal status with land, sea, and air forces.

Military officers worry that hostile groups might attempt to disable the networks upon which this activity depends. The growing importance of space-based assets for intelligence gathering and military operations has already encouraged the development of defensive plans. This has begun with fairly traditional efforts—giving satellites the capability to maneuver or defend themselves and moving toward a capability where the United States could disable satellites under the control of a hostile power. The national security implications of satellite attack and defense certainly will prompt diplomatic negotiations similar to those used to achieve regulation of transit across air and sea.

In the 1997 movie *Contact,* the White House national security adviser contemplates the seizure of the receiving station that obtains the first signals from an extraterrestrial civilization. His attempt to limit access to extraterrestrial information is frustrated by the knowledge that any person in any nation with a good receiver can join in.

Issues of access and protection illuminate a key feature of twenty-first-century space policy—the globalization of space. All major space endeavors now possess global complications, transforming what were once engineering issues into ones with diplomatic repercussions. When President John F. Kennedy decided to race to the moon, he assigned the initiative to a NASA organization that was well insulated from both international concerns and domestic politics. Apollo program officers obtained a degree of technical insulation unusual by any policy standards. Development of the International Space Station, by contrast, has been embroiled in diplomatic considerations. The same features are affecting military space. International involvement will increasingly complicate what were previously engineering issues, requiring diplomatic agreements to resolve technical designs.

Future space activities will look more like the International Space Station and less like Project Apollo. This development is inevitable, given the proliferation of space capabilities among different nations and business firms. As more multinational firms and more governments achieve space capabilities, the need for regulatory frameworks will grow.

Regulators will issue licenses, they will meet to draw up international agreements, and they will resolve issues involving international trade. Such activities typically involve lawyers, diplomats, and economists. Government organizations traditionally involved in space policy are dominated by scientists, engineers, and military officers. As the nature of government space policy shifts, new types of people and organizations will naturally appear. The new order will not resemble the old.

The Old Regimes

Traditional institutions like NASA and the National Reconnaissance Office need not fade away once confronted by commercial and international complications. They may not dominate the new space policy to the degree of the past, but they will not disappear. Initially, old institutions will maintain their preeminence by pursuing those policies most easily implemented through traditional command-and-control operations—reconnaissance, scientific discovery, exploration, and planetary protection. The maintenance of traditional forms will depend on the importance of these policies relative to other space initiatives and the degree to which their advocates continue to draw funding from tax-supported treasuries.

From the Cold War to the Persian Gulf, military communication and reconnaissance satellites played a vital role in twentieth-century warfare. For nonconventional campaigns such as the war on terrorism, ground-based investigations may prove more decisive. Nonetheless, space-based reconnaissance should continue to provide vital information, and the officials that operate such systems are likely to use traditional command-and-control institutions financed by government funds.

While specialists use satellites to search the Earth for security threats, scientists use telescopes to search space for them. Planetary protection could become a major space issue during the next fifty years. Scientists are preparing a catalogue of objects in Earth-crossing orbits; at least one is capable of striking Earth during the next fifty years.[12] An Earth-bound asteroid or comet could do more damage than a nuclear bomb. Scientists stress the statistical fact that an individual human has a much higher chance of being killed by an asteroid or comet impact than dying in an airline crash.[13] Regarding public policy, the meaningful statistic is the likelihood of a sudden impact, not individual risk. Discovery of an object with a moderate probability of striking Earth soon would provide a precipitating event for governmental activity.

The response to such a discovery could be international. Given the obvious organizational complications involved in mounting an international deflection effort, the United States might decline to participate and instead create a single engineering organization. Many space advocates believe that this office would be located in NASA, where scientists have taken the lead in elucidating the threat. A civil response is not assured, however. An asteroid strike could be viewed as a national security issue demanding a military response, giving the Department of Defense equal claim on the implementing policy.

Some visionaries view interplanetary migration as the only sure means for avoiding the consequences of asteroid and comet strikes. In *Pale Blue Dot,* Carl Sagan recommends planetary diversification as the ultimate strategy against civilization-threatening impacts.[14] This is unrealistic for a number of reasons. Migration is not cost effective compared to deflection, and it ignores the obvious interests of taxpayers left on the home planet where the objects land.

Early space pioneers believed that many decades of exploration would be required before humans ventured to other planets. In a 1952–54 *Collier's* magazine series, Wernher von Braun predicted that humans would need "a century or more" to reach Mars.[15] The principle scientific justification for sending humans to Mars—the search for extraterrestrial life—has been weakened by the capability of robotic spacecraft to traverse that planet, conduct biological experiments, and return samples to Earth. The national security justification that launched the race to the moon—the use of space to impress uncommitted nations in a broad global struggle—has mostly disappeared. It is unlikely that humans will colonize or terraform Mars in time to affect twenty-first-century space policy. Given competing budget priorities, humans may not go at all.

An international expedition to Mars, financed by public funds, would dwarf the organizational challenges posed by Project Apollo. It would make the intergovernmental complications of the International Space Station look like minor perturbations. Precautions necessary to reduce risk on a 900-day expedition could prove very expensive. Such obstacles have frustrated previous attempts to induce a tax-funded human expedition. In the future, these impediments could shift government policy in the direction of using tax funds for a more modest objective—establishment of an Antarctic-type research base on the moon.

NASA officials are investigating low-cost methods for getting humans to Mars that could reduce fiscal disruptions. Those "faster, better, cheaper" methods are quite different than the space age management techniques that guided Project Apollo.[16] Some experts believe that a Mars mission could be completed for less than one-third of the inflation-adjusted cost of Project Apollo—about $50 billion. Others cut that estimate in half; Mars advocate Robert Zubrin believes that a privately run expedition could be completed for as little as $6 billion.[17]

At such levels, interesting possibilities emerge. A privately funded venture would reduce the inevitable delays and complications associated with government work. It would revive an old fantasy: space exploration without government interference. Ultimately, one must remember that the money necessary to fund any Mars expedition comes from the same source—the pocketbooks of private individuals. Where mission costs are large, program advocates historically have turned to involuntary taxation as the means of collecting necessary funds. As mission costs decline, the difficulties of fund-raising through voluntary contributions decrease. At a certain point, those difficulties decline to the point that they become less pronounced than the disadvantages inherent in running a high-technology enterprise through a governmental system.

Private funding already supports one branch of space exploration—the search for extraterrestrial life. The U.S. Congress halted direct public support for SETI in 1993; program supporters turned to private sponsors as a consequence. (Supporters also receive public funds indirectly through government grants.)

The search for extraterrestrial life could be a major force driving civil space policy in the twenty-first century. Government activities are focused on three initiatives: robotic and possibly human missions to Mars, robotic missions to Europa and other distant moons, and the development of special telescopes that can capture images of extrasolar planets. From the public perspective, this will surely be one of the most exciting aspects of twenty-first-century space policy. International cooperation is likely, but the endeavor is quite traditional in the manner of its policy and organization. Advocates of traditional space policy gather here.

Nature may conspire to defeat them. The reality of extraterrestrial life differs considerably from popular images of it. According to the original vision, Mars was thought to be a wet, Earth-like world. Venus was thought to harbor primitive vegetation, whereas other solar systems were thought to have produced intelligent beings. Even scientists who doubted these images nonetheless expected to find simple life forms, a hope re-expressed in 1996 when a team of scientists announced the possible discovery of relic biogenic activity in a meteorite that had fallen to Earth from Mars. Many scientists continue to believe that simple life forms like those that dominated Earth for three billion years are quite common throughout the universe. Intelligent or complex life, however, may be extremely rare.[18]

Government efforts to discover extraterrestrial life could be outrun by private initiatives. A race is on to discover extraterrestrial life, and one branch of that effort is privately sponsored—SETI's search for radio signals from alien civilizations. No one knows who will prevail or when. The winning team may be part of a private effort, creating government space policies that are reactive rather than enabling.[19]

In spite of the absence of any confirming evidence, humans continue to believe in a biological universe. Like so many beliefs about space exploration, the vision has been constructed over long periods of time out of the fabric of historical experiences on Earth. Much of the traditional vision pushes space policy toward its traditional form—highly technical, relatively nontransparent endeavors conducted through large government organizations. Commercial efforts and international proliferation push that policy in a different direction, one about which visionaries have also dreamed.

NOTES

1. Wernher von Braun, "Crossing the Last Frontier," *Collier's,* 22 March 1952, 24–29, 72–74.
2. Esther C. Goddard and G. Edward Pendray, eds., *The Papers of Robert Goddard* (New York: McGraw-Hill, 1970), 1:121, 418; Maurice K. Hanson, "The Payload on the Lunar Trip," *Journal of the British Interplanetary Society* (January 1939): 16; H. E. Ross, "The British Interplanetary Society's Astronautical Studies, 1937–39," in *First Steps Toward Space,* ed. Frederick C. Durant and George S. James (Washington, DC: Smithsonian Institution Press, 1974), 209–16.
3. Howard E. McCurdy, *Space and the American Imagination* (Washington, DC: Smithsonian Institution Press, 1997).
4. NASA, "Aeronautics and Space Report of the President, FY 99," 100.
5. Futron Corporation, "Commercial and Government Space Expenditures by Mission (1997)," Bethesda, MD, 28 October 1998.
6. Futron Corporation, "Future Space Commerce Market Growth," Bethesda, MD, 28 October 1998.
7. Space Publications, "State of the Space Industry, 1999," International Space Business Council, n.d., 5.
8. Futron Corporation, "World Commercial Space Revenue Projection," Bethesda, MD, 28 October 1998.
9. Federal Aviation Administration, "1999 Commercial Space Transportation

Forecasts," May 1999, iii; Philip McAlister, "The Global Demand for Launch Services," presentation to STAIF, Futron Corporation, February 12, 2001.

10. Richard White, *"It's Your Misfortune and None of My Own": A History of the American West* (Norman: University of Oklahoma Press, 1991).

11. Richard J. Newman, "The New Space Race," *U.S. News & World Report,* 8 November 1999, 30; Ben Iannotta, "Setting the Rules for Remote Sensing," *Aerospace America* (April 1999): 34–38; Warren Ferster, "U.S. Agencies Grapple with Regulatory Issues," *Space News,* 8 March 1999; "Federal Regulations Could Sack Remote Sensing Programs," *Space Business News,* 6 June 1999.

12. William Harwood, "Speeding Object May Have a Date With Earth," *Washington Post,* 4 November 2000.

13. Clark R. Chapman and David Morrison, "Chicken Little Was Right," *Discover* (May 1991): 40–43.

14. Carl Sagan, *Pale Blue Dot: A Vision of the Human Future in Space* (New York: Random House, 1994), 326–27.

15. Wernher von Braun, "Can We Get to Mars?" *Collier's,* 30 April 1954, 23.

16. Stephen J. Hoffman and David L. Kaplan, eds., *Human Exploration of Mars: The Reference Mission of the NASA Mars Exploration Study Team* (Houston, TX: Lyndon B. Johnson Space Center, July 1997).

17. Theresa Foley, "NASA Team Modifies Mars Direct Mission, *Space News,* 5 February 1995; David L. Chandler, "Mars on $5m a day," *Boston Globe,* 5 August 1996.

18. See Peter D. Ward and Donald Brownlee, *Rare Earth: Why Complex Life Is Uncommon in the Universe* (New York: Copernicus, 2000).

19. SETI, "Declaration of Principles Concerning Activities Following the Detection of Extraterrestrial Intelligence," n.d.

Conclusion

Adapting NASA for the Twenty-First Century

W. Henry Lambright

WHAT IS the role of NASA in space policy in the twenty-first century? Those who gathered in Washington in the spring of 2000 for the symposium, "Space Policy in the 21st Century," were conscious that space policy was undergoing a profound change. It was not just the advent of a new century and millennium. It was the sense that times were really different, starting with the end of the Cold War and extending to some indeterminate future. Some of those present looked ahead and envisioned Mars as a logical destiny, but that bold prospect seemed far away and its realization daunting to most. In the interim, there was a troubled present with Space Station delays and overruns. And after the Space Station, what would NASA do if a viable Mars mission did not materialize to engage human spaceflight? Uncertainty was a dominant theme among those who attended.

In the midst of the uncertainty was NASA. What was its relation to space policy topics considered by the writers: access to space, commercialization, Earth monitoring, asteroid threat, Space Station, Mars, and the search for life in the universe? The answer was unclear, but whatever it was depended on NASA's defining its role in the twenty-first century. Such a task was not new. NASA has continually had to adapt since its birth. That adaptation both reflects and shapes larger space policy.

The last time academics and practitioners focused intensely on space policy was after *Challenger,* surely a crisis for NASA. What *Challenger* revealed in 1986 was that something internal to NASA had gone awry, resulting in flawed decision making. What is different in the current situation is that external changes are predominant. The 1990s were a period of great discontinuity for the agency. It was a decade when the Cold War ceased, when a president declared the end of Big Government, and when Republicans returned to congressional power for the first time in decades. It was also a period when globalization gained salience as a term describing new relationships—dependencies, alliances, rivalries—in the world. In 2001, with the terrorist attacks, came the realization that globalization also brought new kinds of security threats. All the while, NASA's budget hovered at a relatively constant level.

It is in NASA's interest to influence its future lest others define the future for it—and not necessarily for the good of NASA or space policy. The role of NASA in policy decisions will depend on the interplay between the agency and its national and global environments. There is a three-level interaction among forces concerned with space policy.

At the first level of this tripartite structure is NASA. At the second level are national policymakers. Finally, at the third, or global level, are various other nations and institutions. Policy making occurs at each level. However, it is most useful for our purposes to focus on NASA and how it interacts with national and global forces. The future of NASA—and, to a large extent, the civilian U.S. space enterprise—depends on this interaction.

NASA as a Policy Entrepreneur

NASA is the advocacy base from which U.S. policy making in civil space most concretely begins. As a science and technology agency, its work involves the creation and development of new capabilities in space. It can be seen particularly as embodying advanced technology—rockets, spaceships, satellites—and the human beings who develop and (in the case of spaceships) man them. To what policy ends are those technical-human systems directed? Are means themselves ends?

NASA stands at the first level of policy making, designing technical programs, performing research and development (R&D), and marketing programs. This does not mean that all NASA programs are equally worthwhile, and certainly it does not mean that national and global forces accept them as desirable. It does mean that NASA was established to be a focus of technical options concerned with space—to be a place where new ideas can be developed, nurtured, and promoted externally. NASA is thus a governmental interest group, or policy entrepreneur, which designs and advocates the space mission. For NASA to play that role, it must formulate a coherent policy position and then effectively persuade others to come along. It is not the adoption point of policy in a democracy, but it is often at the point of initiation as well as of implementation.

NASA is a large and complex agency with 18,500 employees. The dominant organizational interests within NASA are the Washington headquarters' central managers, the program offices, and various decentralized field centers. The major space programs are those concerned with human spaceflight, space science, and Earth observations. The ten field centers are scattered across the country. Different field centers relate to different programs. For example, the Johnson Space Center in Houston works mainly with the Washington human spaceflight program. The Jet Propulsion Laboratory deals primarily with the Office of Space Science. Each of these centers is a major entity, and each has its own special interests and supporting constituencies. There is always a tendency for program and center directors to pursue their own goals at the expense of the larger organization. NASA administrators, the top political executives who aspire to influence space policy at the national and global levels, must first master their internal rivals and minimize the centrifugal forces.

NASA acted most coherently as an agency in the 1960s when Apollo provided an urgent and clear goal. Since then, the parts have been in competition with the whole, and leaders have had difficulty giving the organization direction and focus. Some NASA leaders have been more successful than others in truly running their organization rather than being run by it.

Brewer has argued that there are certain organizations—public and private—that at least for a while perform so remarkably well that they stand out and may even achieve mythic standing. He writes that they are perceived as "being the best organizations human beings could create to accomplish selected goals. If not the best or perfect, they were nearly so . . . close enough."[1] NASA of the Apollo era was an example of such an exceptional organization.

What made NASA so effective in the Apollo era was a combination of circumstances that have not been repeated at NASA—a clear goal, exceptional talent throughout the agency, high morale, outstanding leadership at the helm, ample political support, and lots of money—all energized by Cold War competition.

By the time of *Challenger,* NASA was a middle-aged organization characterized by "goal displacement" in the sense that the goal of Apollo was displaced by the goal of survival. Programs were designed to keep the organization going. After *Challenger,* writers noted that many of NASA's problems lay in denying the reality of change. NASA officials looked back with nostalgia to the 1960s and avoided adapting to new times. According to Brewer, once-"perfect places" have the hardest task of all organizations to change. He believed it would take "the shock of heavy cannon" to wake up a former perfect place like NASA, although *Challenger* should have been sufficient.[2]

Logsdon, in chapter 8 of this volume, suggests that it took a hard-driving administrator in the 1990s, Dan Goldin, to begin the change process. Echoing Brewer, Logsdon sees NASA as a bureaucracy that was locked into an "Apollo hangover." This was a mental set that not only looked back but also approached virtually all technology programs in an "Apollo-like" way. No doubt there are some programs that require a large-scale approach. However, even if they did not require this big science or big technology mode, this was what NASA as an organization liked to do, considered desirable, and promoted. Unfortunately, it was an approach that became harder to afford, increasingly out of touch with political reality, badly needing adaptation.

Times change. When Goldin came to office in 1992, the centers and programs of NASA were in competition with one another to the detriment of the whole organization. To be sure, the manned programs (Space Shuttle and Space Station) were expensive and problematic. However, equally troubled were the unmanned programs—space science and Earth observations. They were growing in such a way as to rival human spaceflight. The NASA budget, however, was not expanding, and something had to give.

For better or worse, Goldin sought to bring NASA under control from the top down by imposing a new paradigm, at least on the robotic programs, called "faster, better, cheaper." He argued that use of revolutionary microelectronic and other new technology would allow NASA to produce better results while scaling back in cost and size. The new technologies also meant NASA could have results more quickly because smaller, cheaper spacecraft could be launched more often. Even if they failed, the fact that they were less expensive meant that they would cause the agency less political grief than the loss of a $1 billion spacecraft. Hence, the agency could take more risks. Faster, better, cheaper has had its successes (*Mars Global Surveyor* and *Pathfinder* in 1997) and failures (*Mars Climate Orbiter* and *Mars Polar Lander* in 1999). However, faster, better, cheaper was a necessity owing to budget reality, and change had to be imposed.

NASA in the early twenty-first century reflected the policy and administrative reforms of the controversial Goldin. In addition to promoting faster, better, cheaper for virtually all science and Earth observation efforts, Goldin pushed privatization of the Space Shuttle and a "return" to R&D, which means an emphasis on NASA's core mission of discovery and development of new capability. Under this philosophy when a technical system becomes operational (i.e., routine), it should be transferred to industry or another agency.

Goldin's hand in this policy was strengthened (and forced) by political reality. The 1990s were a decade of downsizing government, and he made NASA a poster child. If NASA had fewer employees, it was argued, it could pull back to a core governmental role of R&D and carry that role out more efficiently.

The Goldin years (1992–2001) were a time when a strong administrator pushed a personal agenda. That agenda included an effort to forge a new coherence across programs. It included an informal policy to direct NASA toward Mars. The unmanned Mars program gained priority— in a faster, better, cheaper mode. A new program, Origins, was developed that highlighted the search for life. In his rhetoric and speeches, Goldin talked about Mars as a goal, even though his political masters in the White House and Congress had not approved the objective, at least for human spaceflight.

Goldin also linked NASA's dominant program—the Space Station— to a manned Mars mission. In the 1990s the Space Station's primary purpose came to be to serve as a laboratory to study how human beings could cope with the physical, biological, and psychological challenges of long-duration spaceflight such as an eventual Mars voyage. While other tasks (e.g., space manufacturing) were cited as a rationale for the Space Station, it was the human spaceflight mission that was key. Thus, implicitly, the Space Station and robotic missions to Mars were linked to an overriding strategic purpose that aimed at manned flight to Mars.

Goldin thus gave NASA a new sense of direction, priority, and long-term goal. The dilemma he faced was that this informal policy could not be pushed openly to the external world for legitimation. NASA as entrepreneur had to await the development of new, cost-effective technologies regarding access to space. Successful completion of the Space Station was also required if NASA was to have credibility as an advocate for Mars.

Moreover, it is easier to be an innovator in an agency that is young and getting started than in one that is middle-aged with an accretion of programs on its plate. For the leader of an older organization, there are significant internal resistances to change. Innovation can require removing and changing people in a mature agency that is not expanding. Goldin linked the Space Station with Mars as the goal and was a principal policy advocate behind bringing Russia aboard the Space Station, a move that connected the Space Station with U.S. foreign policy goals. However, he could not make the changes in the Space Station design that he might have liked. The Space Station seemed representative of Apollo's "large-scale approach," not of Goldin's "faster, better, cheaper" paradigm. But it was really a different model of the large-scale approach. The Apollo model was not just organizational and technical—it had a political dimension of external support. The political support was minimal for the Space Station, and thus there were severe budgetary constraints, leading to frequent technical and administrative redesigns. At the time of this writing, the Space Station, with a huge overrun, threatens other NASA programs, current as well as future.

The Space Station must succeed—or at least not appear to fail—for NASA to move forward. There is, for NASA, no choice. NASA's influence as an agency lies in its reputation for technical competence, and that reputation was severely damaged by *Challenger.* Goldin and his associates sought to rebuild NASA's reputation in the 1990s. The major test for the agency in the first decade of the twenty-first century is the Space Station. It is an opportunity to show success. Conversely, it represents a threat of failure.

Today NASA most likely shares Goldin's dream about Mars as its long-run destiny. It is perhaps the only goal sufficiently grand and inclusive to unite leaders, programs, and centers. Most can share in this special quest as their counterparts did in the moon program. However, the route to Mars is through the Space Station—not necessarily because of technology, but because of politics. It is a formidable hurdle. It is the test President Bush's appointee as NASA Administrator, Sean O'Keefe, faces.

NASA and the Nation

What NASA does internally depends on what happens externally, and vice versa. A large-scale approach to space is justifiable when the goal is large, the technical requirements demanding, and the political support present, but not when such conditions do not apply. The reforms of faster, better, cheaper reflected political reality from outside NASA. In return for downsizing, NASA regained some measure of autonomy from political masters in its technical decisions. Realizing any program goal requires NASA's building a certain measure of support. The bigger the goal, the larger must be the political coalition to nurture and fund it.

Coalition building for NASA has always meant gaining the president as a backer for a policy it favored. If there is an Apollo paradigm, then it includes presidential decisions to launch and sustain big programs. This has been the case—at least with respect to program initiation decisions—with Kennedy (Apollo), Nixon (Space Shuttle) and Reagan (Space Station). Presidential endorsement does not always work, as it did not in the case of Bush's decision to launch a Moon-Mars program. There has to be some commitment behind the words. But without presidential endorsement, it seems extremely difficult for NASA to begin a large-scale technological program.

Since Congress provides the funds, and space programs typically extend beyond any one president's term, the need for Congress, or at least a majority of lawmakers, to be part of a space coalition is obvious. The House and Senate space committees and two appropriations subcommittees charged with space affairs are central elements of a NASA coalition if a major program is to survive over time. In winning congressional converts, it is clear that contracts and jobs loom large. There are a few lawmakers who can appreciate visions of the big picture and grand quest to explore the heavens. However, far more lawmakers are interested in how NASA benefits jobs in their state or congressional district.

In the 1990s the shifting politics of Congress seemed not to make that much difference for NASA in partisan terms. Democrats and Republicans implicitly agreed to subordinate space interests to deficit reduction and budget-balancing policy. They concurred in 1993 to sustain the Space Station by a five-year commitment of $2.1 billion a year.[3]

Congress was thus brought into a coalition behind NASA's flagship program and struck a deal not only with NASA but also with the White House. This reflects the success of NASA and a few key legislative leaders in persuading Congress that longer-term stability is critical to the success of major programs. The $2.1 billion figure did not hold the full five years due to NASA's implementation problems, including those with Russia. However, the fact that such an arrangement took place at all is important and shows that a political alliance can be constructed around a particular program, even one large in scale and cost. Such an alliance, in turn, provides a buffer against political interference. Stability is necessary for effective program execution.

Smaller programs also require coalitions, but the coalition is not only less extensive but includes different players than seen in the larger efforts typically associated with human spaceflight. For example, space science involves the scientific community, but who is that? The community is fragmented in its interests when it comes to space. There are those scientists who want to study Mars. Others, like Chyba (chapter 7 in this volume), believe it essential to search for life elsewhere and include Europa or Titan as priorities. Still others want to take advantage of particular launch windows, not necessarily to search for life but to gain knowledge about a particular planet or moon, as in the early twenty-first-century controversy about whether or not to go to Pluto.

Similarly, the Earth observation programs involve NASA with other agencies in coalitions that sometimes work and sometimes do not in terms of bolstering particular programs. One of the longest standing and most successful Earth observation programs has been that of weather satellites. NASA is developer and the National Oceanic and Atmospheric Administration (NOAA) is user. There have been occasional bumps in this relationship, but to a remarkable degree it has held steady since the 1960s. Less successful has been the interagency alliance of the U.S. Global Change Research Program (USGCRP), a vast effort involving many diverse agencies concerned with climate change. NASA provides space observations. Other agencies specialize in land, ocean, or lower atmosphere observations. Everything is supposed to come together in what is sometimes called "Earth Systems Science." Success depends on coordination, but coordination is horrendously difficult to achieve given conflicting agency interests, budgets, and requirements. Furthermore, climate change is politically controversial. There are interest groups and legislators who resent knowledge that strengthens their opponents in the global warming debate.[4]

Still, USGCRP exists because virtually everyone agrees that coordination is needed when national programs are distributed across many agencies. Effectiveness is another matter. There are innumerable other examples involving NASA alliances with other organizations. In the case of the Space Shuttle, NASA and industry have united with privatization a goal. Moreover, NASA is seeking to reestablish ties with the university community toward the end of enticing more top technical students into fields where NASA needs talent in the future. From the huge aggregates necessitated by the Space Station, to the smaller and nascent connections represented by university programs, NASA is a player in national policy. Sometimes it leads, sometimes it follows; sometimes it coordinates, sometimes it does not. Partnerships abound.

In influencing national space policy, NASA has certain advantages through its special relation to the media. The media are not formally in a NASA coalition, but they can be useful to NASA politically. McCurdy notes in chapter 9 that space has always fired the American imagination. Probably more than any other agency, NASA has sought to use television to win public (and thus congressional and presidential) support. Media attention encourages NASA to hype certain ventures as it did the Hubble Space Telescope. However, when Hubble's first images proved blurred, the hype backfired in ridicule. When Hubble was repaired, the images were as impressive as advertised, and the Hubble program drew euphoric praise. The media seem to be a magnifier where space is concerned, causing sharp rises or deep declines in public favor.

In the late 1990s, NASA saw the media as a double-edged sword in connection with its Mars program. In 1997 when *Pathfinder* landed safely on Mars and sent back images, the media were ecstatic. Two years later came twin Mars failures, and the media excoriated the agency. Still NASA is better off being an object of media attention than being ignored.

NASA would like to use the media to get the general public into its coalition, but the public is too amorphous to be captured easily. It can also be fickle. *Pathfinder,* however, showed how fascinated the general public could be with space, especially with Mars. Millions of men, women, and children connected with space personally, exploring the Red Planet via the Internet as the tiny *Sojourner* crawled along the Martian soil. Someday, as Chyba points out, the public will see more sights from robotic craft that fly to Mars and distant planets. If an average citizen can become, vicariously, a space explorer, will that connection redound to NASA's political benefit? NASA hopes so, for it cannot realize its own goals unless those goals are shared by others, including the general public. NASA's influence in national policy ultimately depends on connecting with the American people.

NASA and the Global System

Just as NASA can appeal to public opinion to assist it politically at home, so it can seek to use foreign nations to advantage domestically. They can be part of the NASA coalition. The global system represents a third level of policy into which NASA can tap, just as that system influences NASA. Indeed, this third level of policy is likely to be ever more critical for NASA in the twenty-first century.

NASA has always had to deal with other actors on the global stage, but they have become ever more pervasive of late, and they can be expected to grow in number and importance in the future. With respect to other spacefaring nations, NASA has gone from having one huge competitor in the 1960s to having an expanding group of smaller but still aggressive cooperators or competitors in the early twenty-first century. The International Space Station alone has sixteen nations involved.

A child of the Cold War, NASA was in charge of one front of the protracted conflict between the Soviet Union and the United States. It was the international competition between two superpowers that defined space policy in the 1960s and within which NASA formulated its own policy. In the 1970s, the space enterprise in the United States and USSR continued, both countries pursuing manned programs in near-Earth orbit. Meanwhile, in the United States, the Space Shuttle kept human spaceflight visible, but it caused great budget stress on other programs. NASA reached out to Europe and Canada. While they may have been called partners and provided equipment, the reality was that Europe and Canada were more like contractors than true partners in the Space Shuttle program. It was a U.S. venture with modest allied help. In the 1980s when Ronald Reagan gave new life to the U.S. space enterprise through his Space Station decision, he asked NASA to seek international cooperation. However, the relation with the Soviets then remained one of strong competition.

Europe, Canada, and Japan soon joined the Space Station, this time negotiating more status than was accorded those who assisted on the Space Shuttle. They expected to be treated more equitably as partners in the Space Station program. Such a relationship made sense. Space capability had diffused over the years. The allies had more to offer in the 1980s than in the 1970s, although they were still junior partners in relation to NASA.

Then came the 1990s and upheaval in the USSR. In December 1991 the Soviet Union dissolved, and the United States' chief international competitor in space was no more. Cold War competition vanished, at least where the USSR was concerned. However, Russia was still there and was still a global power in space.

The Clinton administration now used space for its own post–Cold War foreign policy.[5] Bringing Russia into formal partnership on the renamed International Space Station (ISS) made the Space Station a symbol of the new relationship between the old rivals. Simultaneously, Clinton used space (and NASA) to provide funds and technical work to help deflect Russia from transferring state-of-the-art missile technology to other nations. The aim was to make the still-dangerous Russia a peace-oriented space partner—to forge swords into plowshares. For the moment, space was again at the center of world politics, but in a vastly different way than in the Cold War era. Now Russia was linked with international science cooperation and arms control. Apollo had been the embodiment of national interest in space in the 1960s. The ISS became the personification of a global space interest after 1993. Russia, which had far more experience with space stations than the United States had, came into ISS as America's dominant partner. In fact, as Leib discusses in chapter 4, the United States was dependent on Russia for critical components in ways it had not been with other nations.

Globalization is the term used to describe forces shaping the twenty-first century. It includes economic, security, and technological interdependencies pulling nations (and people within them) ever closer on the planet. In an era of globalization, many problems require organized action well beyond the nation-state. Moreover, in the relatively less-complex time of Cold War politics, when the primary adversaries were the United States and the USSR, external threats pulled disparate interests within each country together. It was easier to get domestic policy consensus when there was an identifiable enemy to be faced. Space policy largely followed from this reality. It could be reactive to the Soviet threat, real or perceived.

In globalizing politics, relationships are more tentative and fluid. Borders count for less. Enemies are hard to locate. Globalization pulls various subnational interests together across the boundaries of nation-states. This does not mean that nation-states do not continue to be significant players. It is that there are simply more players overall on the world stage: national, subnational, transnational. As the number of spacefaring nations (and other actors) expands, it will become more difficult to know who are partners and who are competitors in space policy. The national interest will be less clear. The role of government will be more in question. The answers will be decidedly uncertain and the environment turbulent from the standpoint of an agency like NASA seeking to chart a course.

Nevertheless, NASA is going to have to develop a stance vis-à-vis the global political context. It has little choice. One reason is that while space has enlarged as an arena in which many space powers act, none of these nations (or other actors) seems financially willing to extend far into the next frontier on their own. This is even true of the United States. The ISS, with all its problems, is one model of a future cooperative space enterprise. NASA's role in such a model becomes more and more that of a grand coalition builder: getting a joint enterprise underway, keeping it going, and realizing its potential.

Rivalry among space powers will continue but in ways different from the Cold War period. Much of it will be among allies as they search for advantage within alliance projects. Moreover, there are "wild cards" on the horizon of space policy, such as China. With China moving rapidly to build a manned space capability, it is obvious that space is still one way nations can demonstrate and seek to achieve great power status. Would China develop a human space capability strictly for peaceful purposes? Maybe yes, maybe no. The uncertainty about motives is part of the new global politics of space with which NASA must deal.

If NASA vanished tomorrow, the space enterprise would continue, led by other nations. Within the United States, other agencies, particularly the Department of Defense, would continue to move into near-Earth space. The private sector would maintain its pursuit of space-based markets. What would be missing would be a civilian R&D agency pressing beyond Earth orbit to the next frontier of discovery.

Conclusion

As the focal point of civil space policy in the world's foremost space-faring nation, NASA has potential leverage in the global system. However, much has changed since NASA was born in 1958. It once dominated the realm of civil space policy and had little need for international partners. That realm of policy has grown and diffused, globalized and commercialized; and NASA has shrunk from its Apollo-era prominence. There are now many more actors in space policy. Even private individuals, if they are wealthy enough, can influence the policy agenda, as space tourists or in some other capacity. The future of NASA lies not in control (an impossible feat) but in a more subtle style of leadership than was the case in the time of the Cold War. While Russia has shifted from foe to partner, it is by no means docile, nor are other nations. Within models of cooperation, there is much room for disagreement and jockeying for advantage. Leadership lies with persuasion.[6]

As we move further into the twenty-first century, the glory of Apollo recedes more and more into the mists of history. Most readers of this book know of Apollo only through the written word and have not had the experience a few of the authors in this book have had, witnessing a mighty *Saturn V* rocket blast off to the moon. The Apollo experience, exhilarating as it was, is gone. But it is still possible to have dreams and visions that lift humanity beyond the planet's confines. Making such visions happen is what NASA is about—if it can be up to the task.

The space policy process, from the NASA standpoint, occurs today and in the future at three levels—agency, national, and global. However, the global level is destined to become increasingly salient in agency decision making. As the gyre of space policy widens and the number of players grows, there is a danger of a future of fragmentation and chaos, and an inability to accomplish extensive and complex projects with urgent deadlines. There is thus a continuing need for leadership that creates relationships and catalyzes action around big challenges and opportunities. NASA is well positioned to play a leadership role if it concentrates its energies at the frontier of space and fashions coalitions that embrace many nations and the business and university communities.

Forging global coalitions and maintaining them over years will be difficult and contentious. It requires short-term victories that sustain the longer quests. Perhaps the greatest contribution the ISS can make lies in its being a learning laboratory (with both positive and negative lessons) for global cooperation around large multinational spacefaring projects. The emphasis on faster, better, cheaper is desirable as a general approach for unmanned ventures; however, when men and women go into space, the larger-scale multinational approach is more applicable. The issue is to adapt and refine that coalitional approach—to make it work more effectively in a new era. The twenty-first century is an era when interdependence among organizations and nations becomes an overriding reality and when domestic and international politics blend. The events of September 11, 2001, and its consequences for global action surely make that interdependence clear.

Assuming the United States continues to be the world's leading spacefaring nation, NASA will be critical in catalyzing transnational and public-private hybrids as means to accomplish significant ventures. The niche it can fill lies primarily at the frontier of space, in the coordination of high-risk missions in science, technology, and exploration. NASA can be vigorous as long as it conceives of itself as a pioneering agency and evolves with changing times. The frontier of space is not only a challenge to science and technology, but it is also a challenge to public policy and management. NASA cannot play its pioneering role unless its political masters invent ways that more operational functions can be spun off to other public and private organizations. NASA cannot go to Mars if it is indefinitely running the Space Station.

Space is a daunting, unending test for individuals, institutions, and nations in every way. That is why the politics of space presents NASA with an opportunity and requirement for continual renewal. To the extent that humanity has a destiny beyond Earth and will someday return to the moon and on to Mars, it will need a NASA to mobilize the forces to take it there. This will not be the NASA of Apollo or of the Space Station, but a different NASA, honed for global leadership, an organization of the future.

NOTES

1. Garry Brewer, "Perfect Places: NASA as an Idealized Institution," in *Space Policy Reconsidered,* ed. Radford Byerly Jr. (Boulder, CO: Westview, 1989), 158.
2. Ibid., 159.
3. W. Henry Lambright, *Transforming Government: Dan Goldin and the Remaking of NASA* (Washington, DC: PricewaterhouseCoopers, 2001), 18.
4. W. Henry Lambright, "The Rise and Fall of Interagency Cooperation," *Public Administration Review* 57, no. 1 (January/February 1997): 36–44.
5. J. M. Logsdon and J. R. Millar, "U.S.-Russian Cooperation in Human Spaceflight: Assessing the Impacts," *Space Policy* (August 2001): 171–78.
6. See Robert Keohane and Joseph Nye, *Power and Interdependence,* 2d ed. (Glenview, IL: Scott, Foresman, 1989).

Contributors

Christopher F. Chyba received his Ph.D. from Cornell University. He currently holds the Carl Sagan Chair for the Study of Life in the Universe at the SETI Institute and is codirector of the Center for International Security and Cooperation at Stanford University and an Associate Professor (Research) in the Department of Geological and Environmental Sciences at Stanford University. Dr. Chyba's research includes the origin of life and the search for life in the solar system as well as topics related to biological terrorism and nuclear proliferation. A MacArthur Fellow, he chaired the Science Definition Team for NASA's Europa Orbiter mission and is a past chair of NASA's Space Science Advisory Committee's Solar System Exploration Subcommittee.

Ronald J. Deibert received his Ph.D. from the University of British Columbia and is Associate Professor of Political Science at the University of Toronto. He has been a consultant to the Canadian Department of Foreign Affairs and International Trade on projects relating to Internet security, information and communications policies, and satellite reconnaissance. He is working on a book on the politics of Internet security. His writings include *Parchment, Printing and Hypermedia: Communication in World Order Transformation;* and "From Deep Black to Green? De-Mystifying Military Monitoring of the Environment," *Environmental Change and Security Report.*

Daniel H. Deudney received his Ph.D. from Princeton University and is Assistant Professor of Political Science at the Johns Hopkins University. His areas of research include international relations theory, political theory, and global issues (particularly environmental politics and space policy). He has published extensively on international relations theory, nuclear weapons, geopolitics, environmental politics, and space policy.

His writings include *Contested Grounds: Conflict and Security in the New Environmental Politics;* and "Ground Identity: Nature, Place and Space in American and Earth Nationalism," in Yosef Lapid and Friedrich Kratochwil, ed., *Nationalism and Identity in International Theory.*

W. Henry Lambright received his Ph.D. from Columbia University and is Professor of Political Science and Public Administration at the Maxwell School, Syracuse University, and Director of the Maxwell School's Center for Environmental Policy and Administration. He has written or edited six books, and approximately 250 other publications and papers in the field of science, technology, and public policy, including a biography, *Powering Apollo: James E. Webb of NASA.*

Roger D. Launius received his Ph.D. from Louisiana State University. Formerly Chief Historian of NASA, he is Chairman, Division of Space History, Smithsonian Institution. He has written several books and articles on aerospace history, including *Imagining Space: Achievements, Predictions, Possibilities, 1950–2050; NASA and the Exploration of Space;* and *Frontiers of Space Exploration.*

Karl A. Leib is a recent Ph.D. in Political Science from the Maxwell School, Syracuse University. He is Assistant Professor of Political Science, Wabash College. His primary research concern is the role of science and technology in world politics. His doctoral dissertation examined the role of foreign policy in the development of the International Space Station. His publications include "International Competition and Ideology in U.S. Space Policy" and "Facing the Technology Gap: European Cooperation in Science and Technology."

John M. Logsdon received his Ph.D. from New York University and is Professor of Political Science and International Affairs at George Washington University and Director of the Space Policy Institute, Elliott School of International Affairs. He has longstanding expertise in space policy and history. He is the author of *The Decision to Go to the Moon: Project Apollo and the National Interest* and the General Editor of a planned eight-volume series, *Exploring the Unknown: Selected Documents in the History of the U.S. Civil Space Program.*

Howard E. McCurdy received his Ph.D. from Cornell University and is Professor of Public Administration at American University. He is the author of *Space and the American Imagination* and co-editor of *Space Flight and the Myth of Presidential Leadership.* He is often interviewed by the media on public policy issues and has appeared on the *MacNeil-Lehrer Report, Firing Line,* and CNN's *Newsmaker Saturday.*

Scott N. Pace received his Ph.D. from RAND Graduate Institute. He is Deputy Chief of Staff, NASA. Dr. Pace's contribution to this book was written while he was at RAND, where his work focused on space policy issues involving interaction of national security and economic interests in emerging technologies and space commerce. He was formerly the Deputy Director of the Office of Space Commerce at the U.S. Department of Commerce.

Debora L. VanNijnatten received her Ph.D. from Queen's University and is Assistant Professor of Political Science at Wilfrid Laurier University in Waterloo, Canada. Her research, publications, and consulting have focused generally on policymaking processes in the United States and Canada, mainly, though not exclusively, in the area of environmental protection. She is interested in citizen participation in space policy. She is co-editor of *Canadian Environmental Policy: Context and Cases.*

Index

Developing nations: and asteroidal
governance, 165; concerns about
earth monitoring, 10, 94; and information inequality, 94, 106;
natural-resource issues, 94–96, 103
Direct Audio Broadcast (DAB), 67
Direct Broadcast Satellites (DBS), 67
"Dual-use" technology, 56, 78

Earth monitoring from space: and
concerns of developing nations, 10,
94; consequences of increased privatization, 105–6; consolidation of
military and environmental activities, 106; and end of Cold War, 96;
environmental monitoring, 96–98;
expansion of sources, 99–100, 101;
and global governance, 105, 109–10;
and global politics, 89, 90; military-
intelligence constraints on, 91–94;
modes of governance for, 105, 106–
7; and multilateral security regimes,
106–8; need for unfettered observation, 90–91; possible reversal of
constraints, 101–5; and possible
weaponization of space, 108; practical applications, 89–90, 96–99; and
relaxation of security restraints, 10;
sovereignty and national resource
issues, 94–96, 109; technological
advances, 100–101; unraveling
constraints, 96–101; U.S. "shutter
controls," 102–3. See also Remote
sensing
Earth Observation International Coordination Working Group (EO-
ICWG), 107
Earth Observing System (EOS): and
global climate change, 5, 97; and
ozone hole, 5; reduced ambitions
for, 238; transnational nature of,
107
Earth Science Enterprise, 97
"Earth Systems Science," 263
ELV. See Expendable launch vehicles
Endeavour, 124
Environmental satellites, 56, 97

EOS. See Earth Observing System
ERS-1, 100
ESA. See European Space Agency
Europa: envisioned lander mission,
207–11; and liquid water, 198, 200,
202–3, 207, 218; planetary protection for, 214–15; radiation environment of, 208–9; search for life on,
203
European Space Agency (ESA): creation of, 47–48n.26; industrial
policy of, 50n.53; and the Space
Station, 120, 143n.39; supports
Arianespace, 64
Exobiology: vs. astrobiology, 221n.1;
definition of, 221n.1; rebirth of,
199–201
Expendable launch vehicles (ELVs),
23; and commercial launches, 26;
launch reliability rate, 40; new rules
for, 26; program reinvigorated, 26;
relative costs of, 40–41; vs. RLVs,
38–42
Extraterrestrial life, the search for,
11–12, 198–231; astrobiology in this
century, 201–5; beyond the solar
system, 216–18; Europa, 207–11;
human spaceflight and Mars sample
return, 207; issues of cross- contamination, 12, 191, 198–99, 207,
213; organic molecules in space,
200; and origins of life, 201, 203;
planetary protection, 212–16; plans
for Mars infrastructure, 202, 206–7;
policy conclusions, 218–19; rebirth
of exobiology, 199–201; robotic
exploration of Mars, 205–7; Titan,
Callisto, Ganymede, 211–12
Extra-Vehicular Activities (EVAs),
116, 136

Federation of American Scientists
(FAS), watch-dog use of imagery,
102–3
Florini, Ann, 106
Freedom, 115, 117, 120, 237. See also
Space Station